Mediating Knowledges

Mediating Knowledges

Origins of a Zuni Tribal Museum

Gwyneira Isaac

With a Foreword by Jim Enote

The University of Arizona Press   Tucson

The University of Arizona Press
© 2007 The Arizona Board of Regents
All rights reserved

Library of Congress Cataloging-in-Publication Data

Isaac, Gwyneira, 1966—
Mediating knowledges : origins of a Zuni tribal museum /
Gwyneira Isaac ; with a foreword by Jim Enote.
p. cm.
Includes bibliographical references and index.
ISBN 978-0-8165-2623-9 (hardcover : alk. paper)
1. A:shiwi A:wan Museum and Heritage Center (Zuni, N.M.)
—History. 2. Zuni Indians—Museums. 3. Zuni Indians—
Research. 4. Information policy—New Mexico—Zuni. I. Title.
E99.Z9I82 2007
978.9004'97994—dc22   2007015087

Publication of this book is made possible in part by the proceeds of
a permanent endowment created with the assistance of a Challenge
Grant from the National Endowment for the Humanities, a federal
agency.

Manufactured in the United States of America on acid-free,
archival-quality paper containing a minimum of 50%
postconsumer waste and processed chlorine free.

12   11   10   09   08   07   6   5   4   3   2   1

For my parents

Contents

Figures

All photographs are by the author.

Foreword

A:shiwi A:wan Museum and Heritage Center . . . if we had not been so enthusiastic at the time, we might not have chosen such an ambitious name. However, the ideas we were exploring for creating a museum were larger than exhibited storage. Museums in a conventional sense are old-fashioned—at least *we* thought so. But we also understood the basic idea of a museum is to inform, and we needed to do that in a way that is relevant primarily to our community's interests. As we proceeded, our forming intention went along rather uneven lines, and even today the path is not always a straight one.

This book is the first thorough accounting that I know of devoted to the evolution of a tribal ecomuseum. It presents the vision of a Zuni ecomuseum that was among the first in the Native American heritage movement to emerge beyond the conventional "come learn who we are" model. The founding A:shiwi Museum board members, as exponents of ecomuseums, encouraged creating what had never been done before. The spirit of that effort extends now to current activities at the A:shiwi Museum, where the message is still pertinent to our contemporary community.

This book also takes an investigative and critical look at what we have been calling an ecomuseum—the term we learned to use that represented our idea of a community-based museum. Consequently, it is more than an interpretive survey of the museum effort at Zuni; it is a revelation of how we individually and collectively developed our position and behavior as tribal museum workers and museum users. Although the informants in this book are of different generations and their interests represent diverse styles of expression, a common element among them can be detected: the sense that the museum is *A:shiwi a:wan* . . . it belongs to the A:shiwi people.

The people who steered the A:shiwi Museum have contributed to innovative methods of outreach and programming that surpass the boundaries of established museum agendas. The A:shiwi A:wan Museum does not exist solely under the roof of the institution. It exists in the schools, households, and government of the Zuni community.

As we take the first steps beyond the threshold of the twenty-first century, the world of tribal museums today is rapidly changing and becoming more and more diverse. This book, therefore, is very timely. It offers a view of recent native perspectives and shows the passion of revisionists who have sought to break through the margins of museum and heritage work.

Friend and scholar Dr. Gwyneira Isaac wrote this provocative book while visiting Zuni many times since 1997. Under the auspices of the A:shiwi A:wan Museum, she conducted her research at Zuni and has presented her findings here. She has, in the best fashion, stirred critical thinking about what tribal museums are doing and what they can be doing.

—Jim Enote
Executive Director
A:shiwi A:wan Museum and Heritage Center

Acknowledgments

Although this book has my name on it, it, like its subject, the mediation of knowledges, has been born through a process of discussion, negotiation, and collaboration. The rewards have been the friendships formed and the remarkable generosity shown to me as a visitor to the Pueblo of Zuni. In particular, I thank Wendy Fontenelle, Shalie Gasper, Gordon Quam, Brenda Othole, Alex Seowtewa, Pablo Padilla, Susie Pablito, and their families for sharing their homes and their hospitality. My deepest appreciation also goes to the staff and board members of the A:shiwi A:wan Museum and Heritage Center for making this project not only possible, but also extremely gratifying. They include Malcolm Bowekaty, Jessica Chimoni, Rita Edaakie, Georgia Epaloose, Tom Kennedy, Vernon Quam, and Ronnie Cachini. I also thank Jim Enote and Roger Anyon for their unfailing enthusiasm as "on-site" supervisors while I was in Zuni. Without their willingness to share their knowledge, this book would not have materialized.

This research is also the product of a fruitful collaboration with Howard Morphy and Elizabeth Edwards, which was generously funded by the Economic and Social Research Council of the United Kingdom. As a graduate student at the Institute of Social and Cultural Anthropology at Oxford University, I received invaluable criticism from Chris Gosden, Laura Peers, Jeremy Coote, Alison Petch, Chantal Knowles, and Joshua Bell. During my research visits to the Smithsonian, I was attentively assisted by Nancy Fuller, Paula Fleming, Robert Leopold, Candace Greene, William Sturtevant, Thomas Killion, and JoAllyn Archambault.

In preparing the book, I benefited enormously from the advice of T. J. Ferguson, Nigel Holman, Wilfred Eriacho, Rhys Isaac, Rosemary Joyce, Rubie Watson, Martin Sullivan, and Seline Szkupinski-Quiroga; at the University of Arizona Press, Allyson Carter and Harrison Shaffer; and copyeditor Annie Barva. Friends including Hamish Shorto, Criana Connal, Betsy Schneider, Nat Stone, and Sean Walsh have also contributed their expertise to this work. Most of all, I thank Ceri Isaac, Christian Widmer, and especially my mother, Barbara Isaac, who shared her expert knowledge and gave her untiring support.

Mediating Knowledges

1
Introduction
October 1997

You enter the museum through a walled courtyard, with a large cotton-wood tree at the center. To one side is a cluster of waffle gardens molded from red earth, the labors of a joint project between the museum and the Zuni Farmers Co-operative. Here, in the summer, squash and beans are grown and tended to by elder Rita Edaakie and high school interns who work at the museum. The main door from the courtyard opens directly onto the public gallery and an exhibition of nineteenth-century and contemporary photographs of the Pueblo. Alongside these images are printed narratives by Zuni elders discussing the changes that have taken place in the Pueblo over the past century. At the far end of the gallery, an area with an adobe fireplace and large carved wooden benches has been constructed to replicate *wowo*'s house, grandmother's house. Woven textiles hang from the walls alongside brightly embroidered ceremonial kilts. This space also hosts a series of colorful board games designed by museum staff to instruct children about the cultural landscape and place-names linked with Zuni historical events. To the left of the gallery is the office that forms the nucleus of museum activities. Here, Edaakie, the "Tradition Bearer," translates into English the interviews she has conducted with Zuni elders at the Senior Center. The community programs coordinator and museum technician, Vernon Quam, uses the adjoining space to organize and construct exhibits. Along the far wall is a series of desks and computers for the director, Tom Kennedy, and the museum administrator, Jessica Chimoni. In the middle of the office is a large desk, where tribal archivist Wendy Fontenelle and I work on the tribal records and photographic collections.

Although the gallery space is relatively quiet, the offices are a hive of activity. The museum takes shape in these back rooms: staff meetings, research, the construction of exhibits, and the meeting of deadlines. With the staff inhabiting one room, all tasks are shared and ideas are communicated here. This room is also the area where community members come to seek help with their inquiries. Although the gallery may be

Elder Rita Edaakie in *wowo*'s House, A:shiwi A:wan Museum and Heritage Center, 1997.

the manifestation of Zuni history and culture, the museum staff members are the creative source of and, for me, the inspiration behind my research. The A:shiwi A:wan Museum and Heritage Center is not only a space designated for the exhibition of Pueblo cultural life, but also a site of imagining where the processes involved in the transmission of knowledge and the linking of generations take place. Exploring these processes and how people engage with their history has become the focus of my research.

The origins of this book can also be attributed to the Zunis' desires to explore the museums of North America. In the same way that anthropologists of the late nineteenth and early twentieth centuries had seen the Pueblo of Zuni as a resource for cultural knowledge, members of the Zuni tribe in the 1980s came to view museums not just as resources for historical knowledge, but also as sites for interrogating the past practices of Anglo-American scientists. It is this growing critique of museums and the shifts in the movement of knowledge that captured my imagination and shaped the foundations of this research.

In 1995, while researching one of the first anthropologists to work in Zuni, Matilda Coxe Stevenson, I developed an interest in the nature of the two distinct contemporary settings for her photographs: the National Anthropological Archives (NAA) at the Smithsonian Institution and the A:shiwi A:wan Museum and Heritage Center in Zuni. The photographic collection was represented in a national repository for anthropological data, and, at the same time, a duplicate collection was sent from the Smithsonian in 1991 and housed within its local context and location of origin. Of greater significance was the recent history of these photographic collections. Once the images arrived at the Zuni museum, they were assimilated into the Zuni system for the control of knowledge. The collection was divided into two parts, and the images revealing sensitive or esoteric imagery were moved to the Zuni Heritage and Historic Preservation Office (ZHHPO) in 1994, where access was granted only to initiated members of the religious societies (Holman 1996a). The contrast between the public nature of the NAA collection and the restrictions applied to the images in Zuni represented an opportunity to look at the two different approaches to and expectations about the transmission and control of knowledge in each institutional context. In 1996, in collaboration with Howard Morphy and Elizabeth Edwards at Oxford University, I received a grant from the Economic and Social Research Council of the United Kingdom to develop a comparative case study of the

Middle Village, with the Nuestra Señora de Guadalupe Mission and the sacred mesa Dowa Yalanne in the background, Pueblo of Zuni, 1997.

NAA and the A:shiwi A:wan Museum and Heritage Center. I initially identified repatriation as a process that actively renegotiated not only the role of museums as guardians of cultural property but also the use of and access to related knowledge. This point was important because the ownership of knowledge is an issue that cuts to the core of community and curatorial authority when defining the role of a public space or resource, such as a museum. Yet the individuals in Zuni who were specifically involved (i.e., religious leaders) were not free to discuss the knowledge connected to repatriation claims, so the majority of the community was not part of the discussions or decision-making processes. The decision-making role was given to members of the Zuni Cultural

Resources Advisory Team (ZCRAT)—a select group of religious leaders who are the official representatives for the Pueblo of Zuni in matters concerning cultural property and repatriation.

The topic of repatriation in Zuni was off-limits to me, but the designation of what was public and what was private knowledge became equally intriguing and soon became the focus of my research. The museum, as an active participant in the narration of Zuni history and culture, was located at the center of these issues. I began to ask, What kind of museum could work in Zuni? Why was there a distinction made between public and private knowledge? What forms of knowledge could be shared with non-Zunis? These questions were also at the forefront of staff members' minds, and I soon learned that the museum was developing ways to negotiate differences between Zuni and Anglo-American systems of knowledge. Answering these questions also required investigating responses to different cultural approaches to knowledge transmission and examining specific principles that informed the process of mediation between knowledge systems.

By focusing on people's expectations about how their system of knowledge operates, I was able to examine the museum's negotiation of conflicting cultural meanings, including the elements of museum practice that had originated in Anglo-American museums. Identifying the principles by which Zunis negotiate or control knowledge also resulted in the recognition of Zunis' instrumental role in these processes and therefore their agency. I also chose to move beyond the walls of the museum and to contextualize the museum within the wider cultural and political arena in which it was situated. I chose to use documentation methods that would allow the information from the museum and the community to be accorded equal weight, so I incorporated the local community's responses to the museum as well as the museum's responses to local hierarchies and to the external interests that have affected the Pueblo of Zuni. What emerged was a case study designed to address a gap in the ethnography of museums: how local and culturally specific hierarchies and knowledge systems influence the narration of cultural histories.

In effect, this ethnography of the A:shiwi A:wan Museum is centered on the relationships people have created with their history and how these relationships are both negotiated during the development of a public institution and continually renegotiated through its day-to-day operations. As a result, I argue here that the A:shiwi A:wan Museum and

Heritage Center has actively developed specific strategies to move between Zuni and Anglo-American approaches to knowledge.[1] The museum negotiates the use and maintenance of cultural knowledge both within its own constituency and across cultures, and it consequently takes on the role of mediator between internal and external expectations about Zuni history. This book is the story of the Zunis' struggles not only to define their museum but also to come to terms with different cultural approaches to the transmission of knowledge and therefore with the ways in which they would retain and pass down their history for future generations.

Aside from the issues that determined my fieldwork topics, however, another story must be conveyed about factors that profoundly affected this inquiry. This particular story is about the way in which Zuni systems of knowledge control affected the nature of my research. The Pueblos of the Southwest have earned a formidable reputation as being closed to anthropologists, and this book explores some of the historical events in Zuni that have led to this closure. Beginning with contact in the nineteenth century, citizens of the Pueblos objected to anthropologists' collecting of esoteric knowledge, and by the 1970s and 1980s tribal councils' growing confidence and tribes' awareness of the vast number of scientific and anthropological publications about them acted as catalysts in formalizing restrictions regarding research on the reservations. The American Anthropological Association also adopted its codes of ethics in 1971, forcing anthropologists to recognize the need for informed consent in the communities in which they worked. The initiation of the Institutional Review Board required both university and tribal committees to evaluate research proposals and set requirements about the appropriate treatment of the subjects as well as resulting data. Although it is often rumored that anthropologists can no longer work in the Pueblos, because of land claims, land disputes, and the process of repatriation, Pueblos have actively contracted anthropologists to conduct research in their communities. As a result, particular areas of anthropological research still take place. Proposals, however, are based commonly on community-directed topics, and projects are screened by tribal councils or cultural preservation officers. In addition, the knowledge produced and published largely falls under Puebloan systems of control.

Because it was clear from my proposal that I did not wish to look at ritual knowledge, I was given an unpaid position as visiting researcher at the museum and as an adviser for an Institute of Museums and Libraries

Services grant to renovate and reorganize the Zuni tribal archives. I was subject to rigorous control mechanisms that determined the areas in which I could or could not work. The most obvious of these restrictions is the request that researchers not attempt to learn the Zuni language. Clearly, Zunis' familiarity with the products of anthropology now contribute to the way in which the tribe has successfully challenged the mechanisms that control the terms under which fieldwork takes place. My interviews and all of my conversations in the Pueblo were conducted in English, which clearly determined the nature of the narratives presented in this study. Yet as a case study of the Zuni museum and analysis of the expectations about the transmission of Zuni knowledge, this research is expected to reflect the specific processes that control knowledge within the Pueblo. Although not learning the Zuni language did prevent me from an intimate understanding of Zuni religion, it did not close off entirely an exploration of Zuni philosophy and public institutions such as the museum. Moreover, being subject to the mechanisms that control knowledge was one way to experience firsthand how the system operated. Consequently, this book not only is a product of this system of control but is also representative of the relationship between the discipline of anthropology and Zunis' negotiation of the external influences that affect the Pueblo.

When I first arrived in Zuni in December 1996, I was invited to write an article for *Cultural Survival Quarterly* on the A:shiwi A:wan Museum as part of an edition devoted specifically to indigenous museums. In January 1997, I collaborated with the tribal archivist, Wendy Fontenelle, to organize a series of interviews with individuals involved with the Zuni museum. These individuals included two board members, Georgia Epaloose and Malcolm Bowekaty; an elder, Rita Edaakie; and two community members, Noreen Simplicio and Alex Seowtewa, who were connected to the museum through their interest in Zuni material culture and history. The interviews resulted in the article "A:shiwi A:wan: 'Belonging to the Zuni People': Interviews from the A:shiwi A:wan Museum and Heritage Center in Zuni, NM" (Isaac, Fontenelle, and Kennedy 1997). By experiencing firsthand how anthropological inquiries and the subsequent products were used in a publication, people became more amenable to participating in the fieldwork for my main project; they now knew where and how their words and views were going to be used.

At an unexpected yet fundamental level, these interviews informed the methodology for the remaining portion of the project. They provided an opportunity for the museum staff to participate in my research by providing feedback on the interviews. In this way, my questions were scrutinized and my research was opened up to those persons immediately affected by it. The responses from staff members and participants highlighted the need for documentation methods that would encourage the recording of Zuni perspectives on the museum. These responses led me to concentrate on interviewing those individuals who agreed to have their names included with their transcripts because this approach emphasized the idea of narratives emerging from specific authors. In designing a methodology for interviews, I provided each interviewee with a copy of the questions before I interviewed him or her. Some researchers might object that this approach prevents immediate and candid responses to questions, yet because of it people shared thoughtful and in-depth perspectives on the issues discussed. All interviews were taped and then transcribed verbatim in order to underline the individual style and performative aspects of each interview, thereby asserting that the interviews were authored, narrative accounts on the history and current functions of the Zuni museum.

It is also critical to point out that my research methods were influenced by the active role I was given within the Zuni museum and the Zuni Tribal Archives Project. I was immersed in a wide range of the processes that were an integral part of running a museum: I participated in staff meetings, held workshops with other tribal departments, and attended tribal council and museum staff meetings. I was at the museum every weekday, and I suppose I eventually became a regular fixture. I leaned more toward participation than observation, but each of these roles was as important as the other in developing my relationship with museum staff and, more significantly, in helping to establish their relationship with my research. This immersion in museum activities provided insight into the issues that most mattered to the staff and the community.[2]

If the reader were to assume that restrictions I encountered regarding the collection and circulation of knowledge were represented only by the Zuni systems of control, he or she would be profoundly wrong. The academic community has a similarly complex hierarchy of "elders" who are given the responsibility of screening scholarship and determining its acceptability for public dissemination. I was surprised to find that my ethnographic research concerning Anglo-American anthropological structures of knowledge turned out to operate under restrictions that were equally as challenging as those at Zuni. In addition, anthropologists repeatedly told me that my research on the boundaries set by tribes for the dissemination of research and on the control of knowledge would not be funded or encouraged by the anthropological community because of current fears that it would work as a catalyst for developing stricter controls by the Pueblos and ultimately might reduce anthropological academic freedom. Certainly, I found that interviews with anthropologists were often almost impossible to obtain. Some people were extremely helpful and interested in the project, but many seemed fearful about joining in the discussion about the changing landscape of the control of knowledge for anthropologists and Pueblo communities. Ironically, when I first developed the project, one anthropologist told me that I should forget about doing research in Zuni because the Pueblos were off-limits to anthropologists and that I should conduct my research at a national museum such as the Smithsonian. At the end of the two years of research, I looked back in surprise at how both communities defied their stereotypes—the Zunis by being more open and the academy by being more restricted than expected. Most anthropologists are, of course, acutely aware of the politics of knowledge and of the shifts that can take place in the power structure when there is a redistribution of knowledge. This awareness has made many of us extremely difficult subjects of study.

Mediating Knowledges

No one in the Pueblo of Zuni simply assumed a museum should be there. The very existence and purpose of a museum has constantly been questioned, and, as a result, the museum's development presented a multitude of challenges to the leaders and community members involved. Did the difficulties arise because the concept of a museum was considered Anglo-American? Or because the means by which Zunis retain their history through oral traditions are antithetical to institutional repositories such as museums?

To situate the A:shiwi A:wan Museum's negotiation of different knowledges and ultimately dissimilar political systems in a broader context, we must consider the role ascribed to tribal museums in contemporary Native American societies. Native Americans have traditionally handed down their heritage through oral traditions and ritual practices, but complex demographic shifts and a growing gap between younger and elder generations have profoundly inhibited these practices today. Fuller and Fabricius attribute the development of tribal museums to the "rapid erosion of tribal knowledge" and to an increased sense of self-determination. Consequently, "the need for a new forum to transmit cultural knowledge has melded with the needs for autonomy and self-sufficiency," resulting in the development of "a plethora of museums and cultural centers managed by and for Native Americans" (1993:224). Similarly, Erikson sees tribal museums as a response to Anglo-American colonialism, external control, and the problems of being defined by others. By adopting "a media that is globally respected as a knowledge making institution," tribes have come to see museums as a viable means to represent their own identity (2002:17). The argument that tribal museums provide a necessary means for self-representation is also linked to political self-determination. As Oxendine points out, "Until recently, the Indian image and other cultural interpretations have been controlled by external sources rather than from within the cultural group itself. . . . One of the ways Indian tribes have chosen to address these issues is by developing and establishing tribally owned and operated museums where total control of all aspects of museum operation, from collecting to curating, lie within tribal jurisdiction" (1992:177–78).

The establishment of tribal museums as vehicles for empowerment and governmental autonomy has also been linked to the civil rights movement that gained momentum in the United States during the 1960s and 1970s (Simpson 1996). During this era, the number of tribal museums also rapidly expanded as a result of federal funding programs that promoted economic self-sufficiency on American Indian reservations (Fuller and Fabricius 1993; Archambault 1994).

If tribal museums are vehicles for self-empowerment, however, we need to know the following: Who develops and directs them? What facets of culture and history do they emphasize? Which individuals do they seek to recognize as tribal historians, and who receives this knowledge? In short, who empowers whom within the community? Until now these particular questions have largely been ignored, yet there is considerable need to look at how people experience these institutions and, more important, to address the political relationships that affect how these institutions empower particular people or groups.

Each Native community must evaluate and adjudicate disparity in a number of complex arenas, both within itself as well as between itself and other tribes or Anglo-Americans. Yet existing accounts of tribal museums to date have shied away from discussing the politics of differ- ✓ ence in Native communities. The literature has presented these museums as a panacea for the inequities created by the Anglo-American represen- tations of Native cultures that resulted in an overly Western-centric iden- tification of the "other," a continual ideological preoccupation of the discipline of anthropology. The ideologies in the literature have added to the critique of the colonizers' cultures, but not to an understanding of Native cultures or, more important in this inquiry, to the relationships between the two. The discussion of these processes has largely focused on a reading of the legal arenas in which these negotiations take place. These topics often do affect the political arenas that academics quite rightly avoid, but by hiding behind an academic smokescreen of "issues of representation," researchers belie the real and heartbreaking challenges faced by Native Americans, in this case by the Zunis, when they are working to develop an institution that will benefit the needs of their community and at the same time will receive support and recognition from outside cultures.

To understand these localized relationships between knowledge and control, I have chosen not to focus solely on judicial or theocratic realms of power, but to emphasize what I have classified as the "vernacular" approaches to the control of knowledge. The term *vernacular* implies both formal and informal approaches through which people borrow and discard practices outside the official decision-making processes. The for- mal structures of power in Zuni have been well documented (Pandey 1967). Outsiders do not, however, fully understand the informal and ini- tial stages through which different contradictory cultural systems and ideologies are negotiated in Zuni. The Zuni museum was made up largely of people not represented in the executive offices of government or in positions of religious leadership. During my fieldwork, it became apparent that the museum was finding innovative, colloquial, and every- day solutions to problems not addressed by central or recognized struc- tures for the transmission and control of knowledge in the community. This is not to say that I ignore judicial, theocratic, and governmental controls in my analysis; I treat them as foundations for expectations about knowledge systems. A distinction must be made, however, be- tween the negotiation processes located within official offices and those located alongside and external to these offices, such as in the museum.

Prevailing models have located tribal museums according to postmodern or postcolonial theories, or both, investigating issues of representation and the redistribution of power. Before addressing the limitations of these theoretical approaches, however, I want to discuss how they have shaped current museum ideologies and practices. Without oversimplifying the complex landscape made up of critiques of so-called empirical objectivity, it is possible to argue that postmodernist perspectives have raised issues about subjectivity in the interpretation and exhibition of cultures and have questioned Anglo-American assumptions about the supposed "neutral" space of the museum (Karp and Lavine 1991). When applied to ethnographic museums, postmodernist methods have been used to reexamine past expectations about the objective nature of the museum space and to uncover the multiple narratives silenced by Anglo-American constructs of history and culture. An important turning point in this ideological shift took place at the conference "The Poetics and Politics of Representation" held at the Smithsonian Institution in 1988, where the collection of papers from participants was published as *Exhibiting Cultures: The Poetics and Politics of Museum Display* (Karp and Lavine 1991). In reflecting on the outcome of the conference, the book's editors suggested that the "objective" display of culture was impossible because "every museum exhibition, whatever its overt subject, inevitably draws on the cultural assumptions and resources of the people who make it" and that we need to recognize how "decisions are made to emphasize one element and to downplay others, to assert some truths and to ignore others" (1991:1).

In the same tradition of the postmodernist deconstructions of European and Anglo-American knowledge systems, postcolonialist theories have sought to interrogate the cultural ideologies that created asymmetrical relationships under colonial rule and to expose the inequities that are the legacy of colonialism. Ethnographic museums are largely attributed to colonial origins, so they are imagined to embody the historic functions and structures of colonialism: "museums of anthropology were born out of a need or desire to create order out of the material debris of cultural contact swept into Europe from the far corners of the earth in the Age of Discovery" (Steiner 1995:4). In his exploration of colonialism in the Americas, King privileges museums and argues that "while the emergence and significance of these cultural patterns in the contemporary United States could be isolated within any number of contexts, exhibitionary spaces afford uniquely powerful sites in which to interrogate the colonial contours of American culture" (1998:8).

If museums are indeed manifestations of their cultures of origin, we need to initiate a new framework for understanding tribal museums, one that is also sensitive to internal tribal politics and to tribes' mechanisms for the control of knowledge. At a fundamental level, postmodernist and postcolonialist approaches share the same paradigmatic basis—that is, they are critiques of European or Anglo-American culture and ideology, and therefore employ methods not easily adapted to an examination of alternative tribal histories. As postmortems of "Western" culture, however, these theories have often resulted in the transposition of essentialized and reified ideas of colonialism onto non-Western societies, thus themselves becoming authoritative voices that silence the very people they originally sought to empower.

The need for new frameworks is therefore especially pertinent when looking at tribal museums. When postcolonial and postmodernist perspectives are applied as a combined method, with the only rationale given for the development of a tribal museum being that it is a response to colonialism, they do not allow for the nation or community developing a museum to be seen as an agent in its own interpretation of its history. Although the postcolonial critique may help highlight the changes that have occurred as a result of the deconstruction of colonialist viewpoints, it is capable of illuminating only half of the total equation of analysis: it simply acknowledges that tribal museums have been developed in order to promote self-representation within a postcolonial world. Kaeppler asks in her study of the museums in the Pacific, "[D]o Pacific Islanders want museums, or are museums a colonial hangover whose purpose is to assuage the collective conscience of a colonial administration that has destroyed the traditions that they now seek to enshrine?" (1994:19). Undoubtedly, we need to find methods that provide room for the exploration of internal perceptions or agendas in addition to those that have arisen out of the nation or community's relationship with the colonizers.

Although these interrogative stances are problematic in their often well-concealed concentration on Anglo-American ideologies, it can be suggested that in recognizing the subjectivity of museums and the complex influences of colonization, they are an inevitable part of our exploration of the Zuni museum. They clearly influence aspects of the investigative framework, but additional facets must be introduced to interpret, in their own right, the values and driving forces that structure the Zuni knowledge system. For the purpose of my research, therefore, it became crucial to understand what exactly were the assumptions in Zuni about the transmission of knowledge and how these assumptions were reflected in the way in which the A:shiwi A:wan Museum operated.

It has also become clear that we should not impose Anglo-American expectations about the immediacy or accessibility of local knowledge or history onto tribal institutions. In my examination of the literature on museums, I gave special attention to the work carried out on tribal museums (Clifford 1991; Fuller 1992; Oxendine 1992; Fuller and Fabricius 1993; Archambault 1994; Erikson 1994, 2002; Simpson 1996; Lee 1998; Rosoff 1998; Clements 2000; Tweedie 2002; Wedll 2002). The majority of studies make the assertion that a *local* museum is *representative* of the community. Not only was I faced with having to expose the reification of local history, but also the reification of the concept of community. Although numerous studies have looked at locally operated museums, few have incorporated the local population's reactions to their museum. An exception can be found in *Performing the Past: A Study of Israeli Settlement Museums* (1997), in which Katriel looks at the presentation of the Zionist settlers' history through museum guide narratives. Her framework acknowledges the various ways in which the Israeli settlement museums hold assumptions about regional histories and explores how different sections of the local population have different reactions to the museums. Katriel also points out how these small and locally operated museums are affected by and actively participate in regional politics:

> As culturally sanctioned sites for telling and retelling the pioneering story, settlement museums are under ideological pressure to stabilize a privileged, once-hegemonic version of a particular past that is now under siege. What is at stake here is not just a matter of nostalgia. The discourse of settlement and its ramifications go to the very heart of Israel's most divisive political debates over control of the land and attachment to place. It is a debate that will eventually determine the future shape of the country and the possibility of peace in the region. It is therefore no wonder that settlement museums promote a version of the past that is cherished by those who have sponsored them. They are a part of the cultural politics of contemporary Israel. (1997:159)

If the literature does not consider regional politics, it often depicts locally operated museums as presenting an unmediated and unprejudiced history somehow free of the politics and biases found in the national museums. To counteract these notions of neutrality, Katriel reveals how the settlement museums have not incorporated the history of the neighboring Arab farmers and demonstrates the need for a framework that does not limit or reify our assumptions about "community" or "local history."

Although tribal museums are recognized as forums that affirm tribal identity and as institutions that have sought to reestablish traditional practices, few studies have explored in any detail how these concepts operate on the ground. We need to move beyond issues of representation and consider ways to understand vernacular approaches to the control of knowledge. My research involves identifying both preexisting and current Zuni expectations about the narration of history, the transmission of knowledge, and the interpretation of Zuni agency in distinguishing the principles that help mediate between external and internal perspectives.

Developing a framework that recognizes the dynamics of mediation calls for an examination of methodologies based on the political, social, and ideological interactions between different cultures, such as the methodologies presented by White (1991), Pratt (1992), Bhabha (1993), and Clifford (1997). In a history of Algonquian and European relations in the Great Lakes region, White overturns reductionist notions of colonial political control and explores the idea of "the middle ground" as "the place in between cultures, people, and in between empires and the non-state world of villages" (1991:x). He portrays a world in which the Algonquian were active agents in creating the economic territory through which their relationships with Europeans were negotiated:

> The middle ground grew according to the need of people to find a means, other than force, to gain co-operation or consent of foreigners. To succeed, those who operated on the middle ground had, of necessity, to attempt to understand the world and the reasoning of others and to assimilate enough of that reasoning to put it to their own purposes. Particularly in diplomatic councils, the middle ground was a realm of constant invention, which was just as constantly presented as convention. Under the new conventions, new purposes arose, and so the cycle continued. (1991:52)

This approach contributes significantly to reassessing colonial history and the negotiation of power through cultural representations, but it focuses more keenly on diplomatic interactions within formal political arenas rather than on vernacular settings, providing partial insight into Algonquian experimentation with the processes that controlled meaning and the circulation of knowledge outside its original context.

The theories used to analyze relationships that have developed between cultures have often explored these interactions through the reexamination of archival sources or literature (i.e., the "products" of cross-cultural exchanges). For example, the term *hybridity* has been applied to highlight the split identities created by colonial culture in India (Bhabha 1993). However, as Thomas argues, the shortcomings of Bhabha's analysis are that "the allowance made for subversion on the part of the colonized is distinctly gestural, and that this style of theorizing reifies a general structure of colonial dominance in a manner that is curiously at odds with its pluralizing and disarticulating intentions" (1994:40). Thomas implies that there is a discrepancy in how the encoding of history by the colonizer, on the one hand, and by the colonized, on the other, has been analyzed—and thus a failure to recognize the "heterogeniety in colonial modes of recognition" (40). We need to be reminded of the dangers of transposing top-down approaches, those based solely on the archives and textual records of the dominant society. These models often reduce our ability to perceive local idioms or, as Thomas suggests, the "subversion" used by the colonized to reengage with preexisting systems of knowledge and power (40).

Through the process of identifying intercultural spaces, the concept of "contact zones" has become extremely popular in the analysis of museums (Clifford 1997; Erikson 2002). Pratt first introduced this concept in 1992 to look at transculturation in travel writing and at how "subordinated or marginal groups select and invent from materials transmitted to them by a dominant or metropolitan culture" (1992:6). According to Pratt, a contact zone is "the space of colonial encounters, the space in which peoples geographically and historically separated come into contact with each other and establish ongoing relations, usually involving conditions of coercion, radical inequality, and intractable conflict" (6). The most well-known example of the use of contact zones in museum anthropology comes from Clifford's highlighting of how museums operate as contested sites that reveal not only the "past histories of dominance," but also the ongoing "power-charged set of exchanges" (1997:192–93).

The methodologies behind the theories of the "middle ground," "hybridity," and "contact zones," however, are centered largely on textual analyses. As a result, they downplay the distinct dynamics of oral tradition and alternative methods for the transmission, negotiation, and control of knowledge. In addition, these theories are designed to look at the intersections of cultures and therefore observe the products resulting from the merging of ideas, so that they often downplay the vernacular modes for selecting, discarding, and retaining ideology and practices. By focusing on museums as spaces of cross-cultural interaction, or "contact zones," scholars have successfully recognized the blending and conflicting of ideologies. However, they have often presented discrete cultural approaches to knowledge as convergent, such as in the concept of hybridity. If the focus is on the hybrid product or contact zone, the dynamic practices that determine what is retained, marginalized, or forged together become obscured.

The principles of mediation I observed within Zuni philosophy provided a more appropriate framework through which to explore the processes that have negotiated or controlled the use of knowledge within the A:shiwi A:wan Museum. Although it is not possible to suggest that the term *mediation* refers to the same set of practices in all cultures, I would argue that the act of mediation, however conceived, occurs regularly in many societies. To understand fully the Zuni perspective on mediation, however, we must also recognize that Zunis have observed and learned culturally specific negotiation methods from Anglo-American legal and governmental arenas. This is not to say that Zunis' ideas about mediation can be seen only as a hybrid product of Zuni and Anglo-American practices, but that according to the context of dispute, Zunis may use different tactics. We can agree, therefore, that the term *mediator* carries a number of meanings that are often culturally determined. At a fundamental level, I would argue that a mediator is an intermediary agent that, through the negotiation or control of disparate meanings, promotes an accordant relationship between different elements or perspectives. I do not suggest, however, that the mediator is neutral or that the processes involved are free from political, economic, or cultural biases. The idea is that mediation involves the negotiation and reconciliation of differences, even if the end result biases or manifests only one set of values. The central concern here is to define the A:shiwi A:wan Museum as an agent within a wider network of social processes. As a result, a framework premised on mediation allows specific elements to be separated out and analyzed. It also aids an examination of how these elements work in tandem with other elements: that is, by viewing the museum as an intermediary between elements A and B, such as between (A) esoteric knowledge and (B) public knowledge. This approach also helps reveal which elements or principles define the Zuni museum's ability to negotiate between and question Zuni and Anglo-American ideologies. Thus, the museum staff have been agents in the reconciliation of internal inquiries regarding the tensions between the past and present or regarding the esoteric and public spheres of knowledge, and the museum has been a space that privileges the process of mediating between *internal* and *external* viewpoints on Zuni history and culture.

Thus, what can we learn from how Zuni philosophy places an emphasis on the values of mediation and from the ongoing processes through which opposing forces or paradoxes are negotiated and balanced? *Philosophy* here denotes a culturally specific system of principles and concepts informed through religious beliefs and modes for framing and interpreting behavior and social ethics. In Zuni, religious ceremonies not only restore equilibrium to the world but also affirm people's instrumental role as agents within this ongoing process of negotiation. The origin and migration stories portray how Zunis traveled great distances and suffered hardships in order to find Halona:wa Idiwana'a, or the Middle Place, the area where the Pueblo of Zuni is now located. The migration is symbolic of the relationship between clans, the knowledge of the ancestors, and therefore the principles that assist individuals in finding the Middle Place. Zunis' focus on the ongoing processes by which individuals seek parity in the natural world accepts all people as agents in determining the nature or outcome of these processes. In order to maintain even the primary resources of life such as rain, individuals must avoid confrontation and disputes and must encourage harmonious interactions between the people around them and the members of their family and clan (Wyaco 1998). Specific positions or social institutions in Zuni are also understood to act as mediators. The Bow Priests are charged with the power to protect and maintain peace, and the Zuni tribal council and governor are understood to be intermediaries between religious leaders, the community, and the U.S. government. In this manner, Zuni has a well-documented history of diplomacy with Spain and later with the United States. I would also add here that Zuni political vehicles have been extremely successful in negotiating with the U.S. government in recent years, but this success should not be seen as a case in which the people of Zuni have simply adapted their institutions to work more effectively alongside Anglo-American institutions; it should also be understood as coming from an inherently Zuni approach and a sophisticated mastery of the art of mediation.

Museums are integral to broader ideas about the reconciliation of different value systems. The idea of museums as negotiation sites for disparate ideologies has been presented previously, although it has largely served to illustrate the complex political climate in which national museums operate (Karp and Lavine 1991; Henderson and Kaeppler 1997; Gieryn 1998). Katriel (1997), for example, argues that settlement museums in Israel are "cultural sites" through which various political tensions are "articulated and negotiated." In addition, in a recent review of the different approaches to museums that have evolved out of regional interests in Melanesia, Bolton points out that these museums must negotiate not only national politics but also the European ideology that has accompanied them:

> Founded by colonial governments, all the Melanesian museums were established both to preserve and document traditional practices and to assert the common identity of groups of people united by geographical contiguity and the accidents of history. Today, however, the staff of Melanesian museums struggle to make sense of their institutions in the double context of international museum practice, and the variety of local formulations of "culture." Most such staff have been exposed through training courses of one kind or another to the principles of museum practice promulgated by organizations such as UNESCO [United Nations Education, Science, and Culture Organization] and the International Council of Museums. Such courses usually privilege objects, emphasizing cataloguing, materials conservation and display techniques. (1997:29)

Bolton's perception of the "double context" in which these museums operate acknowledges the relationship between internal and external perceptions of history and culture—as well as the methods used to examine or transmit these perceptions through the museum. Similarly, Erikson recognizes how local museums in Mexico work as interfaces between the national and regional agendas in Mexico and that "there is a tendency for external concepts and techniques to be brought into the pueblo and naturalized in the community via the museum" (1994:44). In the same way, Fuller and Fabricius use the term *mediate* to describe the negotiations that have taken place between the Colorado Indian Tribes

Museum and federal agencies over archaeological sites, and how "the museum functions as a broker or mediator between the tribal community and non-tribal groups" (1993:231). In an exploration of the developmental history of the Ak-Chin Him-Dak Eco-Museum in Arizona, Fuller specifically identifies the museum as an agent in renegotiating relationships of power and argues that "the museum functions as a mediator in the transition from control of a community by those who are not members of the community to control by those who are" (1992:361).

Although the concept of mediation as a function of museums has been identified, no studies have used it as an analytical perspective. In employing it as the key concept in building a framework to elucidate how a community conceptualizes local and national arenas of contest and power, I can portray specific negotiations over the cross-cultural transmission and control of knowledge. Because Zuni philosophy also places an emphasis on finding and maintaining equilibrium between the past and the present as well as between convergent perspectives on Zuni culture, I am able to explore and compare Zuni and Anglo-American ideas about mediation. Mediation holds a central place in the Zuni value system, so my approach is also grounded in the social context in which the museum is located, thereby recognizing the culturally specific modes for controlling the meanings of things, both in the community and within the institutional context of the museum.

The Pueblo of Zuni

A natural successor to the tour of the museum and the description of the origins of this research is an introduction to the Pueblo of Zuni and the community through which this project was shaped. Zuni is the largest of the twenty Indian Pueblos in New Mexico and Arizona. Located in the northwest central portion of the state of New Mexico, the Zuni Reservation spans some 420,926 acres and covers a diverse ecological territory on the southeastern rim of the Colorado Plateau. The Pueblo itself lies in a river valley at an elevation of 6,283 feet, nestled between a complex of mesas and canyons. The sacred mesa Dowa Yalanne in the southeast and the Twin Buttes in the northwest surround the Pueblo and embrace and protect what is referred to by the people of Zuni as Halona:wa Idiwana'a, the Middle Place. The Pueblo is also surrounded by springs at Nutria, Pescado, and Ojo Caliente, each of which is the location of a farming village. The springs support limited riparian woodlands of cottonwood and willow and provide water for domesticated crops. The majority of the region is semiarid grassland with a scattering of sage shrubs, rabbit brush, and juniper trees. At higher elevations, the Zuni Mountains are crowned with ponderosa pine and piñon trees. Annual precipitation in the region is extremely variable, ranging between five and sixteen inches per annum in the valley where the Pueblo of Zuni lies, the majority of which falls in August and September (Ferguson and Hart 1985:13). At lower altitudes, the valley supports grassland; however, the majority of land within the Zuni Reservation is fragile and prone to erosion—an environmental factor that has increasingly determined the growth rate of ranching interests and farming practices.

Halona:wa is the oldest part of the Pueblo and rests upon the ancient tell of houses and gardens.[3] Generations of Zunis have continued to build layers of interconnected home upon home, thus creating an ever-increasing mound that rises above the Zuni River floodplain. With the rapid growth of the population following World War II and the move of residents from farming villages to the central Pueblo, the construction of buildings has steadily expanded out from the village. In the 1970s, the tribal council introduced a development project to build individual family homes, and these homes now thread together an expansive community of more than six thousand residents.[4] Most of what can be seen in Zuni today is this outward growth of the central village—subdivisions, family homes, trailers, schools, grocery and gas stores, and tribal government buildings. No single house is the result of a particular period of Zuni architecture. All family dwellings in Zuni have expanded and changed with each generation's needs and resources.

Similarly, the name *Zuni* itself does not describe a small, homogenous, or easily defined group of people. At the beginning of the twenty-first century, the Pueblo of Zuni comprises a growing and diverse population with varied interests and ideas. Within the group that call themselves Shiwi, or People, there are those families who still farm at Ojo Caliente, Nutria, and Pescado. Some people invest heavily in livestock rather than in crops and view the gullies and canyons as an expansive food source for livestock. Some still see a number of resident families as Mexican rather than Zuni because of their introduction into the Pueblo only one to two hundred years ago. And some families have produced professional politicians who have governed at intervals over almost half a century.

Many Zunis are self-employed and earn their income through the sale of arts and crafts. A strong tradition of apprenticeship in the creation of fine silver jewelry, pottery, and carved fetishes encourages the young to follow on in the same line of work as the older family members. These arts are sold to tourists in Zuni and exported nationally and internationally. The average income derived from the sale of arts is low, however, largely due to a dramatic difference between a high and low season in sales. In the U.S. Bureau of the Census report for 2000, the average Zuni per capita income was $6,908, with the median joint household income being $22,559, illustrating how resources are united in order to support families. In addition, unemployment figures are high. In 2000, approximately 10 percent of the population was unemployed, with an overall figure of 49 percent of the population not in the workforce, largely due to the high number of school-age children within the community (U.S. Bureau of the Census 2000). Zunis explain that a high percentage of people choose to earn a living through the production of arts because self-employment enables them to carry out their religious observances without conflicts arising from competition between employer's demands and religious duties.

The complex makeup of Zuni society and leadership is the result of an intricate and multilayered hierarchy upon which secondary and external systems of governance have been imposed. Since the sixteenth century, the people of Zuni have experienced and found ways of coexisting with three colonial regimes: the Spanish (1540–1821), the Mexican (1821–48), and the U.S. (1848–present). In attempting to uncover the nature of Zuni leadership prior to Spanish colonization, archaeologists and anthropologists have commonly projected their interpretations of the historic religious leadership and transposed them onto the prehistoric era. Zuni tribal educator Wilfred Eriacho, in his study of the history of the Zuni government, states that "the absence of any documented information describing the Zuni Government structure and procedures prior to 1540 has made it impossible to describe the Zuni Government with any degree of certainty."[5] In order to build on what is known, however, Eriacho uses Spanish descriptions of the Pueblo, the oral history found in the Chimik'yanak'yapkya stories (origin stories), anthropological literature, and "conversations with those people who have served as leaders of the Zuni."[6] He suggests that prior to the Spanish, the welfare of the Zuni community was considered the responsibility of the religious leaders, who had the knowledge and influence to maintain the natural forces and elements that make up the Zuni world. From a contemporary Zuni

perspective, therefore, the religious structure that is still recognized today was, in some form, in existence prior to Spanish colonization.[7]

Eriacho explains that the Zuni religious hierarchy consists of four
levels. On the first level, the A:shiwani (Rain Priests) are responsible for
the "welfare of the total Zuni world" and thus are capable of influencing
not only the people of Zuni but the elements of the universe, such as
rain, wind, and all life forms.[8] The second level of leadership is reserved
for the Kodikyanne (Kokko [Kachina] Leaders), who are responsible for
maintaining connections with the ancestral spirits and therefore for the
welfare of Zuni through the overseeing of ritual observances. On the
third level, the A:biła:shiwani (Bow Priests) are in charge of the laws that
maintain civil obedience within Zuni, including the defense of Zuni
from external forces and invaders. The fourth level is made up of the
Dikya:we (Medicine Orders), which are responsible for administering
medicine and for healing.

The arrival of the Spaniards in the sixteenth century brought new
demands and changes to Zuni religious leadership. In 1539, Esteban, a
former slave and Moor who had survived the wreck of the *Panfilo de
Narvaez* off the coast of the Gulf of Mexico, joined with Friar Marcos de
Niza to explore the New World in the hopes of finding the riches of the
fabled Seven Cities of Cibola. Esteban had adorned himself with feathers
and bells and carried a gourd rattle, "all in an effort to impress any natives
with whom he came into contact" (Ferguson and Hart 1985:29). Although his appearance may have made a favorable impression on the
tribes he had already encountered, his behavior in Zuni aroused immediate suspicion when, according to Zuni accounts, he made demands for
women and riches. He was held hostage and eventually executed. The
leaders of Zuni sent a message to the surrounding tribes that the new
invaders were a threat and that they were also mortal and should be killed
(Ferguson and Hart 1985:20). Friar Marcos de Niza, however, managed to
escape, and he returned to Mexico laden only with the stories of his
travels, rather than with the riches he had set out to find. He chose to
elaborate his accounts so that they included his discovery of the wealth of
the Seven Cities of Cibola. Enticed by Marcos de Niza's alluring stories,
Francisco Vasquez Coronado organized in 1540 a force of armed men and
set out to conquer and plunder the wealth of the Pueblos. At the village of
Hawikku, Coronado succeeded in subduing the Zuni forces. Yet after he
returned to Mexico and for the next sixty years, the Zunis successfully
resisted any further incursion of Spanish missionaries and explorers.

In 1598, however, Juan de Oñate received permission from the Spanish king to colonize the Pueblos, thus opening the area for permanent settlements. His delegation intervened in Zuni affairs and eventually forced the people of Zuni to agree to the Act of Obedience and Vassalage and to become subjects of New Spain. After Oñate's arrival, the Spanish enforced upon the Pueblos a secondary mode of leadership that called for a governor, lieutenant governor, and deputies (or *tenientes*), thus creating a branch of authority through which the Spanish could gain further influence over Pueblo affairs (Hart 1983).[9] Although the Zuni religious leaders were forced to accept this system, they chose to use the governor only as the liaison for external affairs and therefore continued to maintain the central theocratic form of government within the Pueblo. Under the Spanish system, the people of Zuni agreed that the Rain Priests had the power to appoint and remove a governor at their discretion, which reasserted the priests' status as leaders within the Pueblo.

In the nineteenth century, with the arrival of troops and eventual assumption of control by the U.S. government, the theocratic system of leadership in Zuni was increasingly challenged. The intensification of raids by Navajo and Apache bands also encouraged the people of Zuni to form alliances with the United States. Shifts in power appeared with these new alliances, and the governor and the Bow Priests gained prominence and visibility within Pueblo affairs. Because of important strategic negotiations with the U.S. military in the late 1800s, the governor of Zuni, Pedro Pino, assumed more and more control over internal affairs in Zuni. Continual demands by troops and U.S. representatives for hospitality placed Zuni civil government in a more strategic position in political dealings (Crampton 1977).

By the 1880s, the railroad had reached Gallup, New Mexico, just forty miles north of the Pueblo. Missionaries, traders, and school staff brought new ideas to Zuni and expectations of how it should be administered and governed. In 1902, U.S. government administrators set up the Blackrock Indian Agency, which "functioned under the jurisdiction of the United Pueblos Agency, Albuquerque," as well as under a Bureau of Indian Affairs (BIA) division, thus adding an additional administrative authority to the already complex and overlapping system of government in Zuni (Pandey 1967:69).[10] Factions that had developed alongside competing Zuni and colonial leaders had proven difficult to dissolve, and in 1934 the BIA agent installed a new system so that candidates for governor would be determined through a nominated selection committee (Pandey 1967:69).

The missionaries, schools, and BIA agency not only challenged the religious leaders' authority but also attempted to discredit belief in Zuni religious philosophy. Aggressive attempts to assimilate Native Americans into the Western mode of thought were supported by the U.S. government, especially in the case of designing policies to place children in boarding schools. In *The Kachina and the White Man* (1985), Dockstader explores the history of Anglo-American influences on Pueblo religion. He argues that "youngsters in Indian schools were forbidden to use their native tongue, and all other evidences of tradition were suppressed as much as possible." Within the Anglo-American system of education, the children were exposed to "ridicule, censure, and criticism" (90–91). Many Zuni youngsters were sent to institutions where speaking English was compulsory and where they were often prevented from participating in their religious ceremonies. By 1911, the BIA agent had assumed the authority to determine whether Zuni children at the boarding school in Blackrock could attend the yearly Sha'lak'o ceremony, which, from a Zuni perspective, was a crucial part of a youngster's religious education.[11] The Blackrock school was situated only five miles from the Pueblo.

During a time of rapid social change in the 1960s, President Johnson introduced federal programs designed to fight a "war against poverty" and initiated what became known as programs for a New Society in the United States. The growth of these government organizations in Zuni required the Zuni community's increased involvement in civil affairs. In Johnson's plan, the emphasis was placed on providing funds for the development of infrastructure within urban and rural communities that had previously been ignored by federal and state funding agencies. The goal was to use federal funds to train the local population to develop and manage organizations that would encourage economic development. As a result, Zuni inherited a network of federally funded programs, such as Headstart for preschool education and Women, Infants, and Children for prenatal care, child care, and nutrition. Economic initiatives were also developed for employment training, which now are known as the Junior Training Program Association (JTPA); the Training, Employment, and Recruitment Office; and the Home Improvement Program.

This period, marked by the transformation of the federal infrastructure, was also concurrent with the development of a new form of Zuni government headed by Robert E. Lewis, who dominated the political arena in Zuni from the mid-1960s up until the 1990s.[12] Lewis actively sought federal funding for development projects in Zuni in the hope of creating economic growth within the Pueblo. In 1969, at a launch of the five-year comprehensive development plan, he explained the need for more federal involvement in economic affairs in Zuni: "We live in accord with the Zuni Pueblo concepts and, in the past, have asked little of those not of our pueblo. Now we want to achieve a level of living such as other Americans enjoy. We have a long way to go in a short period of time" (quoted in Sando 1998:135).

In an attempt to resolve internal conflicts that had arisen from the different and competing spheres of influence in the Pueblo, Lewis also sought to redefine the Zuni system of government. To encourage a higher degree of self-determination in Zuni governance, a survey was completed that would help define the tribal council's responsibilities and its relationship with various branches of government. Following consultation with the community and BIA advisors, the Lewis administration developed the Zuni Constitution, which outlined twenty-one articles to guide the electoral process through a series of mandated protocols. When the constitution was ratified in 1970, it set up executive and judicial branches of government and determined protocol for legislation, amendments, and tribal membership and rights.

In 1997, when I was conducting fieldwork, the Zuni governmental structure was dominated by administrative services that managed the seventy-three tribal programs, which were subsidiaries of six departments: Youth and Education; Manpower and Training; Health; Human Services; Natural Resources; and Public Safety. Although the size of these programs fluctuates in accordance with funding initiatives from Washington, the Zuni employment rolls of 1997 showed that tribal programs had the highest number of people on their payrolls and employed more than any other organization within the Pueblo. With the increase of federal funds for the administration of social services in Zuni, more and more jobs are created within Zuni tribal programs.[13] Many of these organizations must enforce federal and state government guidelines, thus continually testing the relationship between theocratic and democratic authority.

Outsiders have often misinterpreted the changing nature of the division between religious leaders and tribal government. From an external perspective, the constitution was seen as a move to separate church and state, and its development was seen to mirror the evolution of the European tradition of government. Crampton suggests in his account of the history of the Zuni Constitution that "by this action the priests were removed from direct political authority; secularization had been achieved, thanks in large part to those who sought to bring the Zunis' external affairs into closer harmony with the American system at large" (1977:157). He also agrees, however, that the transition has not been fully determined and that "people still take sides on the form of government the Zunis should have" (1977:157). Similarly, the diversity and differences in approaches to authority in Zuni are often explained in terms of a divide between "progressive" and "traditionalist" factions (Pandey 1967).

In the ongoing debate in Zuni over the relationship between secular and religious leadership, rather than focusing on which of these parties is more influential, it is more apposite to discern that the community views governance as an ever-evolving process that demands advice and guidance from the religious leaders. The frequent appearance of factions divided along the lines of religious societies and clans suggests that the core of Zuni society is still determined along the traditional social system of stratification. Although government officials are elected by a majority vote, their constituency will always be smaller than the number of people who are in a relationship of obligation with the priests. Regarding the decision-making process at Zuni, if one includes the entire network of social obligations that link people to their clan members and religious leaders, it is clear that priests or religious leaders hold a form of authority that wields considerable influence over the community *and* elected officials.

From a Zuni perspective, it is difficult to divide sacred and secular affairs. This distinction would require a division in the Zuni world that simply does not exist. All subjects have a place within the sacred form of the world. *Secular* is an Anglo-American term that misconstrues how Zuni government actually operates. Consequently, the people of Zuni maintain a system of governance in which officials are elected, and the majority of these officials seek advice from the priests.

In the past decade, significant shifts have occurred in how government operates in Zuni. The recent increased recognition of self-determination in tribal government has been paralleled by an increased development of arenas in which religious leaders are asked to make decisions regarding issues of government. This development has placed religious leadership, from an external perspective, at a more *visible* level in Zuni governance and decision making. In the 1980s, the Zuni tribal council hired lawyers and expert witnesses to pursue two court cases on behalf of the Zuni tribe. In these cases, *Zuni I* and *Zuni II*, the Pueblo of Zuni sued the U.S.

government and won damages for land taken without compensation and for mismanagement of land administered by the BIA (Hart 1995). These cases required vast amounts of information on traditional land use, sacred sites, and religious pilgrimages. Religious knowledge was used to determine the Zuni habitation of land prior to intervention by the United States and the development of the Zuni Reservation. By request from the tribal council and legal consultants, religious leaders gave testimony in court that would assert cultural affiliation to this land. The partnership between religious leaders and councilmen that developed in this public area further encouraged the establishment of cultural resource–management programs for Zuni and the protection of sacred sites located in the Four Corners region (Utah, Colorado, Arizona, and New Mexico).[14] This partnership is most apparent in the development of ZCRAT, which consists of religious leaders who advise the council and external agents in their relations with the Pueblo and on land use. Zuni officials have worked toward developing a system that promotes self-government, but a constant negotiation is required between the tribal government and the religious leaders. External interests in Zuni have also continually challenged theocratic control and the traditional style of Zuni government. These dynamics have forced Zunis to develop specific approaches to the U.S. government and recurrently to redefine their relationship with the outside world.

2
The Familial and the Privileged
Zuni Approaches to Knowledge

On returning from a long journey, each Zuni pauses at the perimeter that defines the start of Zuni lands and offers a prayer to express thanks for his or her safe return home. This prayer prepares travelers for their final steps toward their family and confirms their place within Halona:wa Idiwana'a, the Middle Place. The prayer is a personal orientation within a cultural landscape that defines Zuni's placement in the center of the world. Orientation within the Middle Place is determinate, and one greets and gives prayer to the rising sun in the east and sleeps facing the west. Each niche or curve in the landscape is a sentient metaphor for current lives maintained alongside the ancestral creations and beings within Halona:wa Idiwana'a.

Religious ceremonies such as Sha'lak'o, the winter solstice, recount the creation and emergence of the Zuni people and the ancestral migrations to find the center of the world. During their journey, the ancestors learned invaluable lessons from the hardships they endured and from the alliances they forged with the immortal gods who led them to safety. The ancestral migrations led to the creation of the Zuni clans and the sacred societies as well as to an understanding of the medicinal benefits of the plants they encountered along their route. The oral accounts performed during religious ceremonies not only re-create these journeys and pass down lessons from the ancestors that orient individuals in their pursuit of a balanced existence within the Middle Place, but also animate the ancestors and their knowledge within the present day.

This chapter serves as an exploration of the intellectual and geographic landscape of Zuni, both as a physical location and as a philosophical approach to a place and its history. It must start with uncovering a series of misconceptions about Pueblo social structures and systems of knowledge that until recently have determined how these societies have been viewed. The first fallacy that needs reexamination is the depiction of the Pueblos as egalitarian societies, largely founded upon the perception that there were not marked distinctions in wealth,

Bread ovens in the Middle Village, Pueblo of Zuni, 1997.

material possessions, and behavior between leaders and nonleaders. Eggan's (1950) application of British structural functionalism with its emphasis on kinship and social structure led to his identification of the equality of descent groups and, as Brandt points out, a "universal Pueblo type marked by the presence of the matrilineal clan, lineage, and household complex, which he [Eggan] called the Western Pueblo" (1994:11). Any differences among the Pueblos Eggan explained by degeneration from west to east. This model was questioned by Fox (1967), who argued there was not one single universal type of social structure but three subdivisions, represented by the individual systems found in the western, central, and eastern Pueblos. Ortiz (1969) also disproved the single-type theory by showing that there were multilayered authority systems in the Tewa communities.

Moreover, if we view knowledge as the most valuable resource and service within these social structures, then the argument that Pueblos were egalitarian societies is quickly dismantled. The critique of the egalitarian view originates from Elizabeth Brandt's significant revision of the ethnography and archaeology of the Pueblos, in which she argues that "as long as ritual knowledge, information, possession of songs, chants, prayers, oratory, and ritual paraphernalia was [*sic*] not considered property of significance by anthropologists, or if [their] possession did not 'count' in the same way that possession of material goods did, then a view of egalitarianism could be maintained" (1985:2). In recognizing the heterogeneity and complexity of the distribution and control of knowledge, we can reach a closer understanding of how the Pueblos were and are nonegalitarian and hierarchical communities "with multiple layers of decision making" and, in particular, that there are "inequalities maintained by a well-developed system of information control managed through secrecy, surveillance, and privacy" (Brandt 1994:14).

If it is argued that the locus of value and logic underpinning these systems resides in the transformative power attributed to knowledge, the result is a perception of Pueblo society that is closer to its participants' view of it. Discussing both the constraints of and the privileges provided by the knowledge system is a major preoccupation for Zunis who are either still learning the protocol required for their level of responsibility or for those individuals who feel excluded from religious societies. Although the knowledge itself is never discussed in public, the taboos and restrictions associated with it are very much a part of daily conversation. Brandt argues that Puebloan society is highly stratified and that "a major consequence of internal secrecy is the establishment of hierarchies based on access to knowledge" (1980:130). The social structures common to the Pueblos are made up of multiple and overlapping layers of secular and religious leadership, resulting from highly specialized roles and membership within religious and ceremonial organizations. The level of access to knowledge also mirrors an individual's access to resources, so that those with a high degree of rights to use knowledge form an elite class that manages trade, manufacturing, and land distribution. In Zuni, this high degree of control in the reproduction of power through the transmission of knowledge results in the view that those without religious or esoteric knowledge or access to ceremonial property are "poor" (Parsons 1939:112). Religious societies are also ranked. Both Elsie Clews Parsons and Peter Whiteley have identified the Kachina Society—or, as is specific to Zuni, the Kokko Society—as a form of commoner religion and have suggested that membership in elite religious societies and the holding of religious office in particular are associated with differences in the possession of property, such as masks, costumes, songs, and prayers (Brandt 1985:12).[1] In Zuni, individuals may hope to achieve higher status for themselves and their families by acquiring certain types of property: "A poor man, one without ceremonial connections, is especially desirous of having his own mask in order 'to save his life, to make him valuable'" (Bunzel 1932b:849).

The second misconception about Puebloan social structures involves the limited role ascribed to secrecy as a device used to control the transmission of knowledge to outsiders. Since the late nineteenth century, the Pueblos of the Southwest have been identified as cultural groups that exemplify an extremely restrictive approach to knowledge. Anthropologists attributed the emphasis on secrecy in Puebloan communities to the history of oppression and forced Christianization by Spanish colonizers. According to this line of argument, secrecy became more important as people were forced to carry out their religious practices underground (Dozier 1961; Spicer 1962). This argument was also carried through to the comparative ethnography of the wider Rimrock region (Vogt and Albert 1967) and of the relationships between Zuni, Navajo, and incoming settlers: "the close proximity of Spanish settlements following after intermittent Spanish attempts to stamp out the native religion certainly played an important part in augmenting the importance of secrecy in [Zuni] ritual" (Bellah 1967:258). In an analysis of the nature of secrecy in Taos Pueblo, however, Brandt suggests that "[this] classical explanation ascribes only one function to secrecy, the maintenance of traditional religion in a hostile context. It also implies that secrecy is a phenomenon practiced only against outsiders, which is definitely not the case" (1980:125).

Secrecy actually serves a variety of functions in the Pueblo systems of knowledge. In conventional anthropological perspectives, it is argued that knowledge is powerful because it is secret. Within the intellectual architecture that determines how knowledge is viewed and transmitted in Zuni, however, knowledge is secret because it is powerful. More important, in order for it to remain powerful, it requires a specific burden of responsibility in using it appropriately. In this system, knowledge is considered to lose its power when it is diluted—that is, if it is shared with too many people or used unnecessarily and therefore irresponsibly. Anthropologists have largely placed an emphasis on secrecy as the agent that maintains knowledge as power (Fardon 1985), so that "knowledge is seen as powerful because it is restricted and because some people are denied access to it" (Morphy 1991:77). However, if we explain knowledge only in terms of social control, we lose sight of Puebloan perceptions about the transformative potential of knowledge. Morphy argues that the conventional view of secrecy denies the varying levels of knowledge that may exist in these restrictive systems and the fact that knowledge is cumulative; "in many respects the layering of knowledge can be thought of as a pedagogical technique," "one that emphasizes the variability in understanding that exists at a given moment among different members of the society" (1991:77). According to Morphy's analysis of the Yolngu system in northern Arnhem Land, "secrecy often marks the division between inside and outside knowledge," so that it "is a system of revelatory knowledge, and secrecy helps structure the process of revelation" (1991:77). The social patterns described by Morphy show how secrecy may operate as a pedagogical device that encourages the receiver to acknowledge each level of knowledge as a new revelation, creating reflective pauses as he or she traverses to the next hierarchical layer. The advantage to Morphy's analysis is that it explores secrecy via the participants' perspective, thereby providing the motivational structure and elements that maintain and reproduce the system.

Understanding the Zuni system of knowledge is greatly enhanced by viewing secrecy as not just exclusionary but also as a pedagogical device. This perspective allows restrictions to be seen not only as mechanisms that prevent people from accessing knowledge but also as mechanisms that teach an individual his or her responsibility toward knowledge acquired. The system encourages students to master each level and the specific duties and responsibilities attached to it before they move on to the next level. Jim Enote, the former director of the Zuni Conservation Program and a member of the museum board in 1997, explained that "there is a lot of prerequisite information that you need [in order] to understand some of these things," so the order and the way in which youngsters are given knowledge are crucial.[2] The restrictions do in fact limit who receives knowledge and as such are devices for social control. However, they must also be recognized as steps within an individual's education about the structuring of the cosmos and the rationale behind the use of powerful knowledge. For Zunis, obtaining and using knowledge is directly correlated with an individual's ability to affect weather, injure people, or bring fertility. People with knowledge are viewed as having power, with consequences for their instrumental capacity to do good or harm.

Any study of the Zuni knowledge system must also take into account how oral communication is used as a highly effective control mechanism. As Brandt points out, when secrecy and reliance on the oral tradition coexist, people can restrict the specific context in which knowledge is divulged, so that access "requires a social relationship for transmission of information" (1981:190). Outsiders cannot fully understand the need to control access or oral communication of knowledge without recognizing the Pueblo belief in thought and speech as an extension of the soul. From a Zuni perspective, oral tradition is the primary mode for the transfer of knowledge, and this view forms a fundamental foundation upon which a philosophical architecture is constructed that highly values thought and speech for giving life to experience and wisdom. Language and speech are viewed as animate and "carried outward on moist breath," thus giving weight to the idea that "the creative power of thought is typically actualized through speech in chants and songs" (Brandt 1981:186). Although anthropologists often recognized this theme previously, they had not articulated its full significance to the system of knowledge until Brandt's analysis. There are examples, however, where early ethnographers noted the importance of breath in the Zunis' philosophical framework. Stevenson, in her ethnography, wrote that "every Zuni is taught that in inhaling the sacred breath from his fetishes or in breathing upon the plumes he offers to the gods he is receiving from A'wonawi'lona [the supreme life-giving power] the breath of life or is wafting [by] his own breath prayers to the gods" (1904:24).[3] Bunzel also wrote that "breath is the symbol of life," "the means by which spiritual substances communicate and the seat of power or mana" (1932a:481).

The idea that thought and language create the world is prevalent among the Pueblos. Unlike Christian traditions with beliefs based on a single creation, Pueblo cosmogonies include the concept of ongoing creation through present-day actions. In Zuni, the world is still evolving through thought and human actions, and the creation of life, the universe, and the Zuni people is ongoing. Ancestral creations are reminders of the power and presence of the gods and their constant interaction with the world. Knowledge, language, and landscape are three integral agents within an animate, malleable cosmos. But because "thought and speech create the world, both must be under close control, or improper and undesirable outcomes will result" (Brandt 1981:190). The transformative powers of esoteric knowledge and language that can alter this world make them potentially extremely dangerous and their guardians greatly feared.

Responsibilities toward Knowledge

Two realms of responsibilities determine the manner in which knowledge is circulated in Zuni: the familial realm, where knowledge is needed for everyday transactions, family roles, and subsistence; and the differentially privileged realm, where knowledge is restricted according to membership in religious societies. The familial is defined by knowledge that connotes belonging to a particular family, clan, and cultural landscape, and it includes practices required for paying respect to the ancestors and maintaining a balanced way of life. It is the basis of one's responsibility for one's self, one's family, and the world around one. Privileged knowledge, in contrast, is associated not just with one's immediate family, but with the responsibilities of caring for and protecting the Zuni people as a whole—their world, the larger cosmos, and the natural elements. This global and celestial realm is controlled largely by the priesthoods with their direct communication with the ancestors and the gods according to a subscribed calendar of tributes, prayers, and offerings. Moreover, responsibility toward knowledge structures the categories of knowledge as well as the social hierarchies.

In the familial realm, knowledge is taught on a need-to-know basis during day-to-day activities, which are also influenced by gender and age affiliation. I encountered a number of perspectives that dealt specifically with the significance of the context in which knowledge is transferred: first, how an individual's specific roles are viewed; second, how people develop apprenticeships or relationships in which expert knowledge is transmitted and controlled; and third, how people gain an understanding of their religious philosophy through engagement with storytelling and the landscape.

Community members use the term *role* to describe how an individual fulfills knowingly his or her particular position or positions within Zuni society.[4] History and cultural practices are passed down to younger generations while they are being trained to understand and perform their specific roles. At a basic level, women and men have particular gender roles that encourage responsibility toward their family and ancestors. An individual's role is also further defined by his or her clan membership, position within a family, and membership in medicine lodges or religious societies. The elder advisor for the A:shiwi A:wan Museum, Rita Edaakie, explained how learning is determined by an individual's role: "As we are growing up, as girls, they would teach us the ways of how to go about doing things. A lady is given a role. When a child is born in a family, there are ways for a lady to go about doing that. For our nieces, if he or she is having an initiation or anything like that, that is also a role, where we have to look among our elders to find out how to go about carrying out a lady's role."[5] An emphasis is placed on the individual's gender and position, and on the relationship that he or she develops with his or her mentor, as well as the transfer and use of knowledge that should exist within this determined relationship. One must be seen to have a role to play in order to receive and interpret appropriately the knowledge bestowed by teachers. From this perspective, familial knowledge is shared on a need-to-know basis.

Those who are considered carefully observant and therefore mindful of the responsibilities that come with knowledge are more likely to be encouraged to participate in activities, to form relationships, and thus to develop a multitude of roles. These relationships then allow for youngsters to ask the appropriate questions. Malcolm Bowekaty, a former director of the museum board, emphasized this view of observation as part of the relationship between tutor and pupil.[6] Here, again, the younger generations are seen to inherit particular skills according to their roles:

> In the old days, the way kids learned was to observe what the elderly people were doing. If they were building a house, kids would learn how the elderly men were stone quarrying, how they did the masonry. If they were curious enough, they would ask questions. The same thing when they were using the adobe, they would tell you about the texture of the mud, the reason why you added certain things. If you were lucky enough to go farming with them, they would talk about different things as you went along with them. If you were into sheep herding they would give you a lot of that information.[7]

The term *apprenticeship* can also be applied to the style of teaching in Zuni. A ZHHPO staff member suggested that "the common task of knowledge is something that happens on the day-to-day basis" and that these interactions involve the transfer of specific skills: "A lot of it comes down to a skilled area. They learn by example and learn, for instance, by making masks from a craftsperson demonstrating how you would do a certain task or a certain piece of art or jewelry. . . . The learner sees certain methods that are included in the development of a jewelry piece. You would see that [and gain] hands-on experience."[8] The context or relationship will determine the type of knowledge given. Although this description appears to argue for the existence of a rigid system that allows little flexibility for individuals to determine what they learn, the lines between what should be taught and when are neither visible nor fixed. The system relies largely on individuals' discretion, which would also explain why the teaching of responsibility is emphasized so heavily. Specific taboos regulate boundaries for the specific treatment of certain knowledges; however, Zunis are expected to show sensitivity when interpreting the differences between the social responsibilities linked to using knowledge.

Although there are divisions between familial and privileged knowledge, no boundary separates the sacred from the secular elements of life. Many community members express awe for areas that are associated with mystery and the ambiguous or unknown—an individual cannot know everything in his or her role because the role is always changing and evolving. The undefined and often ambiguous areas are as important to acknowledge as those apprehended with clarity and definition. All knowledge is at some level sacred, so the distinction between apprenticeships that involve practical knowledge and those that involve esoteric knowledge are considered extremely subtle, with both involving the teaching of responsibility. All tasks absorb from and provide strength to the universe. Through instruction, practical tasks and skills gain meaning within the Zuni cosmos. A symbol painted upon pottery may link to the complex core of the religious world, like a tendril that grows out from a live root, and these day-to-day uses of knowledge are seen as affirmations of the spiritual well-being of the world.

The landscape also provides stories that teach new generations about the lives and events that have molded the Zuni people. In the same way that all objects and tasks are fed with a spiritual life, so too is the landscape. As one member of the Zuni community expressed this notion, "the landscape is our church, a cathedral. It is a sacred building to us" (quoted in Ferguson and Hart 1985:51). Teaching younger generations about their history is not just about explaining the events and their

Jim Enote and his niece planting corn at Ojo Caliente, 1998.

meaning; it is also about transmitting the significance of these events within the landscape. In describing this link between history and the landscape, a Zuni elder stated that

> Zunis maintain their knowledge through storytelling, a lot of the history, the place-names, and the landmarks, significant dates, the locations have already been told through the oral storytelling—but also in terms of stories affiliated with landmarks and names, locations, plants. They call all the landmarks with a particular event or incident happening, and that is where the name occurs, and that is the storytelling portion around that. The gist of the information is retained in the storytelling method . . . they pick a select landmark, and a story is built around that . . . to highlight the actual location, but also the significant events surrounding that location. In that sense, people know that the story belongs to a certain place or location.[9]

When youngsters participate in key subsistence activities, such as farming, wood collecting, ranching, and sheep herding, the stories they learn create a spiritual and geographic map. The Zuni elder and artist Alex Seowtewa pointed out to me that he was taught about ancestral interactions with this landscape. He described the petroglyphs, the drawings on the rock faces around Zuni, and how they engaged him with his ancestors:

> The earliest art that you can probably still witness or view are the petroglyphs: pictographs from the earth's pigment. Our ancestors were pretty sophisticated people. . . . They had all this wisdom because it has been handed down from generation to generation of who we are, where we came from. When I was still growing up, I always assisted my father during lambing time, because he had sheep as well as cattle, horses, ranching. At times he took me to the nearest drawings where his customary lands were in the northeastern corner of the reservation—which is in the Nutria area. He took me in those hills and explained certain symbols. I shared, passed on, what my father taught me, how to remember these symbols, to recognize them.[10]

I found that Zunis were exceptionally nostalgic about the role storytelling played in their formative years, and they saw it as the most cherished way in which younger generations learn about their culture and heritage within the family or social settings. The accounts I was given were often accompanied by the regret that storytelling was no longer a focal point for family life within the Pueblo. Vernon Quam, the museum technician and coordinator for community programming during the time of my fieldwork, talked about what he saw as the way in which people had traditionally learned their history in the past: "After supper everybody would sit around the fireplace, and the elders would start sharing their knowledge, the history or important events, or anything which related to the history of the Zuni tribe; they would explain that to you."[11] In another interview, Georgia Epaloose explained her view of the group discussions that she considered "instructional conversations":

> My grandparents, they were very social. They had groups of people come into their homes all the time. Grandma knew how to make really good sweet stuff, so they always had a crowd. The purpose wasn't just to socialize; they would all dialogue with each other and have these instructional conversations when they didn't understand something, and they would try and predict the outcome. They highlighted some of the problems, and they looked at things in a hypothetical manner. They made time to do that, now we don't. They had conversations that were more for our sake, to instruct us on how to be Zuni, or what does it mean to be Zuni?[12]

Oral tradition is considered not just long-term memory, but memory held within a person who is able to engage the past at particular moments in current life. Quam gave an account of this aspect of storytelling wherein

> Grandfathers used to talk about various occurrences that, at this point in time, we are approaching. It scares some people when I tell them, for example, the coming of this comet and even some of the conflicts that have happened recently—the world wars—those were predicted a long time ago. They were handed down orally. I know a lot of prophesies were involved in Zuni oral history. You get talking to a person that knows a lot of that—you will get a sense of an idea of where we are now.[13]

The calendrical context in which storytelling is performed is also a key topic of discussion in Zuni. A Zuni elder commented on the appropriateness of the context of storytelling and how it is determined by the religious calendar; he suggested that "stories are interpreted for entertainment—at the same time they carry moral values, and those [stories] are done during the winter only. There is a time and place that is appropriate for that interaction." Moreover, "the more sensitive types of knowledge only occur in certain settings, like, for instance, the stories that are passed down of certain events like the migration, or other stories that cover certain morals and values, upbringing. These are done in a situation where it is an appropriate time and place."[14]

Membership in the religious societies becomes a central issue when examining the level of knowledge available to the younger generations. With membership comes the learning of the specific use of knowledge and therefore the associated responsibilities for its care. One of the Zuni elders I interviewed suggested that younger men who want to learn about Zuni history and culture are most likely to find tutorship within religious societies: "there is also that avenue for those kids that are very inquisitive, but also want to be responsible. There are avenues where they can go and be involved with the esoteric fraternities, the societies, the medicine societies."[15] It is within this complex hierarchy of religious societies and medicine lodges—the privileged realm of knowledge—that individuals are taught the values and responsibilities that extend beyond the family to the welfare of society and the Zuni cosmos.

As noted previously, the religious hierarchy consists of four levels, each one with specific duties: the A:shiwani (Rain Priests) are responsible for the well-being of the entire Zuni cosmos; the Kodikyanne (Kokko Leaders) maintain connections with the ancestral spirits and oversee ritual observances; the A:biła:shiwani (Bow Priests) oversee civil obedience and the defense of Zuni from external forces; and the Dikya:we (Medicine Orders) are responsible for administering medicine and for healing. At a fundamental level, membership in these societies is determined by gender, age, and family position within the religious leadership of Zuni. According to Bellah, "the twelve rain priesthoods are composed of from two to six members each and are mostly hereditary in the matrilineal line" (1967:256–57). Bunzel also wrote that if a young man is "connected with a sacerdotal household he may be called upon to join one of the priesthoods" (1932a:476). These positions are seen as the most exclusive within the community. The most inclusive religious society is the Kokko (Kachina) Society, made up of six ceremonial groups, "to which all Zuni males and a very few women belong" (Bellah 1967:256–57). Initial initiation takes place between the ages of eight and twelve, but the more formal initiation takes place at puberty: "the final ceremony at which knowledge is revealed takes place anywhere between the ages of 10 and 20, depending on the interference of schooling" (Bunzel 1932a:541). Membership in the twelve medicine societies is open to men and women and is largely by conscription, usually being the result of a cure by that society (Bellah 1967:256–57). Entrance to the Bow Priests is limited to men who have killed an enemy or "taken a scalp" (Bunzel 1932a:476).

Within the privileged realm, there is a distinct division between knowledge acquired voluntarily and knowledge received through recruitment. Bunzel's vivid descriptions of how medicine society members acquire knowledge highlight the competitive aspect of this system and illustrate the differences created between social responsibilities toward and individual rights in knowledge: "If [an individual] has sufficient intellectual curiosity to pay high for esoteric knowledge he may, by accumulating knowledge and the supernatural power which knowledge gives him, advance to a position of influence in his society. For a successful career as a medicine man, intelligence and ambition seem more important than piety and virtue" (1932a:542).

Similarly, men can advance within the Kokko Society through experience and aptitude, and "as their knowledge of dance forms increases they may advance to formal office in one of the six dance societies" (Bunzel 1932a:542). Moreover, "those who display an aptitude in memorizing long prayers, if of exemplary conduct, may be appointed to impersonate one of the gods" (Bunzel 1932a:542). In this manner, individuals can acquire more knowledge according to their willingness to learn and ability to perform the responsibilities accorded to their role within these societies. Bunzel's observations therefore support the argument of a layering of responsibilities that increase with the power attributed to the knowledge.

The potent and potentially dangerous knowledge associated with the Rain Priests is the most highly restricted. This knowledge is used not just for the welfare of the tribe, but for the whole cosmos and therefore comes with an immense burden of responsibility:

Membership in priesthoods is even less a matter of free choice than curing societies. Priesthoods are hereditary in maternal families, and to fill a vacancy the members select the least quarrelsome rather than the most intelligent of the eligible young men. The priesthoods are the branch of religious service that carries the greatest prestige and heaviest responsibilities. Because of the heavy responsibilities the of-

> fice is avoided rather than sought, and considerable difficulty is expe-
> rienced in recruiting the priesthoods. As one informant said "They
> have to catch the men young to make them priests. For if they are old
> enough to realize all that is required of them, they will refuse." She
> was not thinking of the taboos and restraints of the priestly life, but of
> the sense of responsibility for the welfare of the tribe which lies so
> heavily on the shoulders of the priests. (Bunzel 1932a:542)

Young men occasionally admit their fear of being "kidnapped" by religious leaders who are known to handpick successors surreptitiously for
these positions. Membership in these societies starts as an apprenticeship in which knowledge is taught, and, subsequently, it is this mentor/
mentee relationship that controls and determines the context in which
knowledge is absorbed and used.

No individual is expected to know or be responsible for the entire
religious cosmology, and the oral accounts of the history of the Zuni
people are compartmentalized among different religious groups, societies, and clans. Bowekaty related that "we need to know that a lot of that
oral information was a repository in each of those people that were like
storytellers, the religious leaders, those people that participated in those
particular roles of the religious activities."[16] Pandey also argues that
the religious societies exist expressly for the maintenance of knowledge:
"There are many kinds of groups in Zuni society. One of the responsibilities that all these groups had was to have knowledge of their ecology,
to have knowledge about themselves, to have knowledge about others,
and to preserve that knowledge for the sake of their children and de-
scendents. . . . The Zunis stored a vast knowledge of their past in the
heads of various specialists. These were the people who were the cus-
todians of oral tradition" (1995:18). In an interview, a non-Zuni high
school teacher commented about this fragmented aspect of knowledge
in Zuni:

> The knowledge of the religion is very fragmented, and there is a very
> strong feeling that things are told on a need-to-know basis. There are
> things people would rather take with them to the grave than tell
> someone who is not supposed to know. Different kiva groups have
> different information about the history of the Zuni people. There are
> very few people who have a comprehensive view of the Zuni religion.
> There is a really strong belief about secrecy. If someone is too curious
> in wanting to know about what is going on with another kiva group,

or another aspect of religion, that is very dangerous and is met with a great deal of suspicion. As with most groups, the idea of seeking knowledge that rightfully shouldn't be yours is an attempt to acquire some power which rightfully shouldn't be yours.[17]

A Zuni museum board member equated this closed system with issues of hierarchy and control and declared that younger generations are sometimes perplexed by the strict regulation of knowledge by the religious leaders: "When the [kids] go to the religious leaders . . . there is a sort of hesitancy. Consequently kids get frustrated because they say 'the elders don't want to tell us anything—they say it is prohibited.' I think it is more [the] control of information. Power is the control of information."[18]

Caretakers of knowledge are taught to guard and control it and to fear its abuse by those inappropriately seeking power. Within the privileged realm, an individual is highly regarded if he or she is humble about his or her status within the religious hierarchy. In order to be privileged with knowledge, a youth needs to show respect for the social architecture and the values that restrict the inappropriate circulation of knowledge. Suspicion arises in Zuni when someone is too pushy in asking for knowledge, and knowledge is rarely offered or advertised. The process by which pupils are tutored within the privileged realm is both selective and discriminate.

Understanding the development of a relationship that controls the context of learning and the transfer of responsibility is central to understanding the Zuni perspective on the oral tradition. When asked if they wanted to see their history written down, many younger members of the community responded by saying they would prefer to learn directly from family members: "I would rather have someone tell me . . . I would rather have my grandmother, or my mother or father pass it down to me orally than to have to see it written."[19] The emphasis, again, is placed on the relationship because it allows for the explanation of areas that may not be openly apparent: according to Seowtewa, "If it is written down and you don't understand some of the things, you need someone to tell you, to point things out."[20] Seowtewa emphasized the importance of a mentor, or someone who can accompany a youngster to the religious events and help explain their meaning: "My mother died when I was only four and a half [or] five years of age, but my mentor, who happens to be my maternal grandfather, was a Rain Priest. He didn't speak a word of English, but most of the time I was under his care. He was a wise man because he taught me a lot of basic things—how to listen in about my history or culture-related events, and before the event occurred, he could explain the meaning, the importance of the event."[21]

According to Bowekaty, when an individual is trained within the societies, "their caretakers will translate orally their role."[22] Discussing esoteric information outside its original context is taboo. Similarly, writing it down or recording it is met with the same response: "There are a lot of religious prayers and other activities that can only be handed down orally," Quam told me. "They cannot be written down; those type of things are something at a different level, because if you start writing it down or recording it, it could come against a taboo. Especially some of the very sacred prayers—they are not supposed to be recorded."[23]

Bunzel wrote that "revelation of the secrets of the katcina [sic] cult to the uninitiated is a crime against the gods and is punishable by death and decapitation" (1932a:479). Similarly, Matilda Coxe Stevenson stated that "the Ko'mosona inform the boys that if they divulge the initiatory secrets, especially those associated with the masks, their heads will be cut off with a stone knife" (1904:104).[24] As illustrated previously, oral communication allows for the strict control of the flow of knowledge. Each individual teacher, storyteller, or religious leader can determine whether a situation is an appropriate one for information to be shared, and many community members consider oral tradition the most effective process for obstructing the inappropriate transfer of knowledge. One Zuni High School student argued that reliance on oral tradition prevented non-Zunis from learning knowledge that should not be shared with them: "I think oral is fine because we know it, and if they ask for it, then it is our own word. If they have it written down, then people who come in [outsiders] might ask for it and get it. With oral, we all know it, and some of us would not want to tell someone who comes into our community."[25]

Chim'on A:ho'i: My Generation

Many people in Zuni remark on the rapid changes that the Pueblo has experienced over the past century, most of which are seen to have come from Anglo-American influences. Although there is a shared view that religious practices have held the culture intact, people reflect on the different approaches to Zuni culture expressed by the different generations. The effects of change in Zuni are commonly discussed within conversations about the way in which change has defined the differences between the elders and the younger generations. In an interview, Wendy Fontenelle, the tribal archivist, used the term *chim'on a:ho'i* to describe how elders see the younger generation. According to her definition, this term is a way in which a distinction can be made between older and younger generations and in how the different groups see things: "I myself was very fortunate to grow up with my grandparents, who taught me values of life, told me stories of how Zuni used to be. I sometimes try to compare their way of life and my way of life. It is difficult to do a comparison. 'Shiwi'ma de'chi' tse'me:n iyhap deni,' meaning, 'it is hard to think of in my terms.' It is hard to think way back then, how life used to be, because we are so oriented in today's life and today's society and with all the influences Zuni has encountered."[26]

There is growing concern that youngsters may not be learning as much about their traditional culture and history as earlier generations. This problem is attributed to the fact that wage-earning jobs and schools have brought about changes that have widened the generation gap. The growth in the Zuni population following the Second World War is another factor, and the age pyramid in Zuni now reveals a vast increase in those tribal members who are younger than thirty-four. Figures quoted in a Lila Wallace Project Proposal in 1993 suggested that approximately 50 percent of the population was thirty-five years of age or younger.[27] The census in 2000 revealed that the number within this group had increased substantially and that 60 percent of the population was at that time under the age of thirty-five, with a mere 6 percent of the population older than sixty-five (U.S. Bureau of the Census 2000).

One of the major changes to the structure of family life in Zuni is the shift away from the practice of an extended family living in the same house. Jim Enote commented on the need to have a broad network of family members present in order to ensure that a comprehensive history is learned by the younger generation:

The tradition of sharing history and knowledge orally has changed because of the family structure. Parents are going off to work, and children are going to school. When I was young, my grandparents, great-grandparents, were essentially in the same household. If an older person was unable to answer your questions, others were available to answer your questions. This has changed because of people having their own houses built and people in work and kids going to school. It is not as easy to get the information.[28]

A teacher at Zuni High School also emphasized how much school took away from time spent with family: "The generation gap grows because of school. Kids spend so much time in school . . . links are broken."[29] Some community members also attributed the introduction of television as one of the factors that has changed the way in which families interact and share information.[30] Television has not only discouraged storytelling and the use of the Zuni language but influenced how members of the younger generation see themselves. Another high school teacher commented on how older generations are not comfortable with these changes. They are, as a consequence, fearful of the younger generation as it absorbs these external values: "There is a change taking place, and they see change reflected in their children, and some of it is very frightening to them."[31]

The loss of privileged knowledge due to the death of an elder who has not handed on his or her information is also attributed to the aggressive nature of the younger generation and the intimidation of the older generation. Some argue that, through fear, elders have formed barriers that distance them from younger generations. Elders have also voiced their concern that although the youth want the knowledge, they are too indolent to learn it: "a lot of [people] within their lineage don't really want to participate because it's a big, big requirement."[32] Many young men have attempted to record prayers with the hopes that this will make them easier to learn, but, according to the elders, in doing so they have attempted to assume the power of their teachers, thus alienating them.

The Zuni secondary schools (Twin Buttes High and Zuni High) have introduced a number of courses that encourage students to learn about Zuni history. At Zuni High School, a course was taught on Zuni oral history that used the traditional stories as a way to teach students the Zuni value system and to reflect on their possible application to current issues. The instructor suggested that he taught traditional stories as a way to get students to think about their relevance today. He hoped this approach would encourage students to take an interest in the meanings of things within Zuni philosophy and to apply these ideas to a wider experience. Because many in the community were concerned that this knowledge should not be available to a non-Zuni audience, the course was taught only in the Zuni language. This instructor's approach to teaching traditional Zuni history within the schools raised questions about what was an appropriate context in which this knowledge could be shared. The coursework had removed the knowledge from the traditional "need-to-know basis" for learning and placed it outside of an apprenticeship-master relationship and into a public institution.

Although these types of changes may have put pressure on the traditional system, they have also clarified for Zunis certain expectations regarding how their cultural practices operate. Membership within religious societies is still the most effective way for a young person to learn history and esoteric or privileged knowledge. A Zuni museum board member talked about his experience: "A lot of people that were in very prominent religious positions, I always asked them a lot of questions. They were . . . very reluctant because they felt as though they were divulging information that only comes from partaking a membership in those different areas."[33] Many people still have expectations about the development of relationships that encourage the teaching of responsibility toward knowledge.

Sha'lak'o and the Politics of Knowledge

External influences and the role of non-Zunis in Pueblo life have also brought changes to how people view the religious ceremonies and access to esoteric knowledge. The contemporary debates over whether Sha'lak'o should be open to non-Zunis reveal how community members see these ceremonies as vital educational experiences for younger generations. The commercialization of religious ceremonies has also become a controversial issue due to fears of the circulation of privileged knowledge outside its original context.

I had been in the Pueblo for only a few weeks when the Sha'lak'o ceremonies commenced. I initially heard, although indirectly, that the council had instituted a ban that prevented non-Zunis from attending the ceremonies. In the past decade, this issue over whether non-Zunis or non-Indians could attend the Sha'lak'o house blessings that had previously been open to the public had caused heated debates in the Pueblo. At the time I was in Zuni, members of the Zuni School District circulated a memo stating that some of the Sha'lak'o houses were open to non-Zunis. The memo was accompanied by a map illustrating the location of these Sha'lak'o houses. In the subsequent days, however, I was told that during the Sha'lak'o festivities, tribal police appeared to be enforcing the ban on non-Zunis. From the discussions that ensued, it remained unclear as to whether there had been a ban and to what level it had been enforced.

The debates over who can attend the Sha'lak'o ceremonies are extremely important windows into Zuni politics and the ways in which religious leadership affects decision making in the Pueblo. Sha'lak'o is at the center of the Zuni religious calendar because the annual ceremonial cycle starts and ends with winter solstice. Its purpose is to send out the old year and lay the right conditions for a fertile year ahead (Bunzel 1932a). The process of preparing for the new year is significant for all the religious societies, medicine lodges, and families, thus requiring the energies of the entire Pueblo in order for the purging and blessings to be successful. Once the Bekwinne, or Sun Priest, announces the start of the winter solstice, twenty days of ritual observances begin in which men plant prayer sticks and carve and place the Ahayu:da, or War Gods, in shrines near the Pueblo (Bunzel 1932a, 1932b).[34] All religious societies go into retreat during the preparation for the turning of the new year. Essential substances needed for life—water, fire, breath, corn, and so on—are brought together not just symbolically but in real terms as people are taught the importance of these elements. This lesson is achieved through Deshkwi, or fasting, and a taboo on the use of fire, followed by feasting and the rekindling of fires.

Many of the ceremonies take place in the kivas or within private family ceremonies, but the large public ceremony takes place during the blessing of the Sha'lak'o houses—houses that are built to host the Sha'lak'o gods. The host families volunteer a year in advance, as described by Bunzel following her research in Zuni in the 1920s: "The great public ceremony is held in the houses of prominent citizens who volunteer to provide this service. There should be eight houses, but in recent years the expense involved has become so great that not enough men volunteer. . . . The house is newly built or renovated for the occasion and the visit of the gods" (1932a:523).

For the past century, the Zuni Sha'lak'o ceremonies have attracted a large number of visitors to the Pueblo. And from 1970 to 1990 especially, the numbers observing the ceremonies grew rapidly. By the 1980s, tour guides were bringing coachloads of visitors, many of whom knew little or nothing about Zuni culture or the etiquette that surrounded the ceremonies. Zunis complained bitterly that the religious importance of the event had been taken over by a circuslike atmosphere in which visitors continually attempted to take photographs of the *kokkos*, or ancestral gods. With the entrances and windows to the houses blocked by tourists, community members were prevented from observing and paying respect to the kokkos.

As a result of the collaboration between a number of religious leaders and politicians, a memorandum announcing the restrictions was issued by the Eriacho tribal administration in August 1995. Particular areas of the Pueblo were marked off-limits to non-Indians, so that they were barred from the Sha'lak'o houses and from viewing the entrance and departure of the Sha'lak'o gods to the Pueblo. A year-long restriction was established in which Sha'lak'o and other rituals could be practiced in a peaceful atmosphere, unhindered by tourists' unpredictable behavior. The placement of restrictions on non-Indians, however, caused widespread debates both inside and outside the Pueblo, as illustrated in local and statewide newspaper coverage. The negotiations that accompanied this debate revealed how the people of Zuni sought to control knowledge and imagery, as well as the processes by which these types of decisions are made within the Pueblo. I use accounts and statements published by the tribal council and community members in the local newspapers to discuss Zuni perspectives on the role of contextually controlled knowledge. In turn, journalists outside Zuni shared their opinions regarding Zuni beliefs and the policies designed to prevent the extraction of Zuni religious knowledge by outsiders—thus adding Anglo-American reactions to the debate on access to religious ceremonies and highlighting the difference between internal and external viewpoints.

Before the 1990s even, two factions had arisen in the Pueblo, divided over the issue of whether non-Indians should or should not be restricted from viewing the ceremonies. Those in opposition voiced disagreement not only with the ban, but also with the manner in which it was installed. This group argued that such decisions should be determined with more input from community members and therefore should be a part of a democratic process. Those in agreement with the ban affirmed that a working relationship still continued between the Zuni government and Zuni religious leaders. Kiva leaders who supported the ban on tourists voiced their concern that the ceremony was being commercialized and that its sacred message was under threat: "The religious fathers strongly believe that it is now time to begin the process of regaining control over what has been lost during years of tolerance for inappropriate behavior and for allowing religious practices to become spectacles and tourist attractions for non-residents, foreigners and non-Indians" (quoted in Brenner 1995b).

The Sha'lak'o ceremony is centered around prayers that invoke the creation of the clans and their migration to Zuni, so it is viewed as an educational rite for the younger generations of Zuni. Not only do the kokkos bless the house and family, but they bring with them the knowledge and history of the ancestors to bestow on these families. In a letter written to the *Gallup Independent*, Loren Panteah, a member of ZHHPO, openly compared Sha'lak'o to a history lesson for Zunis. In this example, he chided a Zuni tour guide who hoped to bring visitors to the ceremonies. He suggested that attendance at the ceremony is the same as receiving instruction on Zuni esoteric knowledge.

> It is now time for our religious leaders who hold high authority in their respective religious groups to do something about the negative doings within our religious realm. . . . If the final outcome is in favor of allowing non-Indians to continue viewing our religious ceremonies, the tribal member who made a comment to the *Independent* about running bus loads of tourists . . . should be the one to take charge and present a mini Sha'lak'o ceremony and school for non-Zunis. Then, this same person can present diplomas to them when they graduate from his school. All Zunis in favor hands up. (L. Panteah 1995b)

The manifestation of all these issues on the ground, however, was much less clear. Although those who supported the ban were united by the desire to return the ceremonies to the people of Zuni, those who opposed the ban represented a wider range of interests, not all of which were in accordance with each other. Some felt that the busy economic climate of Sha'lak'o depended on outside visitors and that the economy would suffer if tourists were prevented from attending the ceremonies. Some community members against the ban held the view that Sha'lak'o ceremonies were about the sharing of good fortune and wealth with outsiders, and therefore restrictions were an inappropriate interpretation of the open and communal nature of the religious ceremony. In addition, some religious leaders said that closing ceremonies to the public was a diminution of the ceremony's spiritual essence and power. Community members also shared the concern over democratic process, as mentioned earlier; they felt that the decision to restrict visitors had been determined only by religious leaders, not by the community, and therefore threatened the process of consultation central to the political system within Zuni.

The various stances that surround the debate provide insights into the different approaches to Zuni religion and government, and therefore to the discrete applications of Zuni religious philosophy. The responses to photography and the duplication of religious imagery also reveal the shared values that help define the communality of Zuni religion and philosophy. As discussed previously, the majority of families in Zuni rely for income on the sale of jewelry. Many were concerned about losing the income that came from sales to tourists during Sha'lak'o. The number of tourists had reached into the thousands, so a large number of Zunis were benefiting from the sale of jewelry during the days that surrounded the ceremonies. Although some tribal officials hoped to prevent the "carnival"-like atmosphere, those dependent on the sale of jewelry had seen this atmosphere as a positive aspect of the ceremonies (Eriacho 1995). Similar bans had been tried in earlier years and had met with the same response from those who felt that their valuable income was threatened. In 1990, Dorothy Walema stated that "the decision means bad news for the Zuni economy" because "that's when a lot of people sell their jewelry . . . and some people put up vending booths for bread and tacos" (quoted in Dubin 1990).

Over the years, Malcolm Brenner, a journalist for the *Gallup Independent*, clearly took the side of those who hoped to maintain an open event that welcomed tourists. In an article on Sha'lak'o in November 1995, he took a stance against the ban and stated, "[N]inety-five percent of Zunis are self-employed, they'll feel the brunt of this" (1995a). In response to Brenner, Loren Panteah wrote an editorial that stated, "Zuni Philosophy is against selling our religion, such as making and selling Kachina figures or in the form of jewelry, paintings etc." He was also concerned about the divisive nature of external influences on Zuni religion: "I am sad and appalled that the majority of Zunis (especially religious leaders) would look at the dollars and not try to give support on the sacredness of our dances and religion." He declared what he saw as the priorities: "I know that the majority of us Zunis are self employed and that we all depend on our jewelry sales as income to pay our bills. . . . But I would rather try to safeguard our cultural traditions and religion than look at the dollars" (1995b). Another group of community members argued that the purpose of Sha'lak'o was to provide hospitality to others to ensure good fortune and to teach people how to appreciate what they had been given in life. In December 1989, Leatrice Pinto, a member of the Zuni community, stated that "Zuni has always been pretty open . . . but my grandmother told me it's open because it's to share good things—that's in our prayers, too. She really made it clear to me" (quoted in Schlanger 1989b).

Over the past century, the tribal council and religious leaders have demonstrated varied levels of cooperation in overseeing the governance of the Pueblo. Between 1985 and 1995, the number of religious leaders who wanted to regain control of the ceremonies had grown, and they looked continually to the community civil leaders to enforce their requests. In 1988, Councilman Virgil Wyaco commented that the religious leaders had come "to the council chambers and requested not to have Anglos visit the Sha'lak'o ceremony." Wyaco also argued that the intrusion of outsiders was a threat to Zuni religious observances because the outsiders did "not show any respect when the Sha'lak'os are praying and ask questions that cannot be answered because of the secret Sha'lak'o ceremony" (quoted in Del Valle 1988a). The council did not grant the religious leaders their request to ban tourists in 1988. Its members viewed the request as understandable, but they saw it as a perspective held by a minority of community members. By 1995, however, it became clear that although there was a division between those who supported the ban and those who did not, those in support of the ban had grown, and now a collaboration of religious leaders and tribal administrators assisted in its implementation.

In the 1995 memorandum issued by the tribal council, the control of religious information was declared the crucial reason for restrictions on non-Indians attending ceremonies. The council's eventual support of the restrictions revealed that a group of politicians and priests was, in this particular case, working together. The ban placed the majority of control within the kivas. In his letter to the *Gallup Independent*, Loren Panteah affirmed that the decision to ban non-Indians was the result, in his view, of the traditional and appropriate process for resolution within the tribe: "the meeting that was held on August 29, at Zuni by the tribal council and religious leaders were mainly of the kiva group leaders because they are the PROPER AUTHORITIES who make the decisions where religious dances are concerned" (1995a, original emphasis). Panteah chastised the community members who had vocally branched away from the traditional system of authority. He suggested that "the religious leaders and most community members know full well how the religious authority system is set up and the proper channels in restoring religious order. But yet it seems they do not intend to abide by that setup and so step on higher religious leaders' orders of authority."

Twenty years prior to these debates, with help from the U.S. government and the BIA, the Zuni tribe had established the Zuni Constitution. The BIA rejected the first draft of this constitution submitted by the tribe because it was concerned that too much authority was placed with the religious leaders. The constitution that was introduced in August 1975 under the governorship of Robert Lewis did not allow for involvement of the religious leaders in the process of government. It merely stated that elected officials could not prevent the practice of religion. The processes by which officials are sworn into office, however, are administered by the head priest, or *cacique*. From the perspective of a Zuni religious practitioner, the religious leaders have installed the governor and therefore hold a position of higher authority. An example of how this configuration has played out in recent years is illustrated by the development of a second and competing council in the mid-1980s, set up by religious leaders and members of the community who had grown dissatisfied with the administration of the elected tribal council. The Rain Priest of the North exercised what he saw as his authority and confiscated the canes of office from the elected governor and tribal council. He subsequently invited Robert Lewis to act as the nonelected governor. The two councils met separately: the first elected council had the support of the BIA, but not of the religious leaders; the second "shadow" council was not recognized by the BIA, yet met regularly with the support of the cacique. Ironically, the governor installed by the religious leaders in violation of the constitution was in fact the individual responsible for creating the constitution. Some members of the Zuni tribal council were also religious leaders, and, as a result, the two leadership domains overlapped. It is also worth pointing out that this controversy over dual councils was resolved by the electoral process in the subsequent election, and Zuni has been governed by a single council since then.

Non-Zunis continually present the disputes as a conflict between those who believe in theocratic governance and those who believe in democratic governance. Journalist Nancy Plevin suggested that some community members "believe that the root of the dispute lies in confusion over whether the traditional rule of the religious elders or modern constitutional law is paramount" (1995). From this perspective, one system should have ascendancy over the other. Plevin quoted an anonymous source who stated that "we're supposed to be democratic, but they're running things as a theocracy. . . . There's nothing wrong with running a theocracy, but it is not the system." The Donald Eriacho administration, which instituted restrictions in 1995, responded to these claims by stating it was the tribal council's role to "protect" the religious well-being of the community: "This closure [to outsiders] is fully within the right of the tribe under its status as a sovereign Indian nation to protect, safeguard and maintain spiritual and cultural practices unique to this tribe and people" (Eriacho 1995). The tribal council saw that maintaining the religion was a joint duty shared by the council and the religious leaders.[35]

The debate over the ascendancy of religious or government authority led to the development of two interest groups in the mid-1990s: the Zuni Cultural and Religious Advisory Team (not to be confused with ZCRAT, linked to ZHHPO), which supported the joint decision of the council and the religious leaders, and the Zuni Religious Advocacy Committee, which represented the community members who felt the council had overstepped its position of authority. Martin Panteah from the Zuni Religious Advocacy Committee asked for a recall of the tribal council, arguing that its decision to ban non-Indians was illegal and broke with the Zuni Constitution. He suggested that the council had not followed Article VI, Section 1, Part 1, requiring an ordination to be adopted with the approval of the U.S. secretary of the interior (M. Panteah 1995). It is also worth noting that Loren Panteah took issue with the opposing group's use of the term *religious* within its title, arguing that "[t]he name Zuni Religious Advocacy Committee is misleading . . . because they are not really advocating the true intent of what they call their committee. . . . At present, they are advocating for dollars. So as to their own statement, the committee is null and void" (1995a).

A more nuanced account of the nature of the disputes that also helps to explain the range of perspectives in Zuni was provided by journalist Ted Rushton, who argued that the council consistently relied on the religious elders when facing decisions that concern the religious well-being of the community. He provided an account of an earlier situation where a new business was proposed by outsiders, and council members chose to consult with the religious leaders:

Council members listened to the first explanation, then reported back to their respective kiva societies where the proposal was debated in detail. Various kiva members had questions which were relayed to the company executives at the next Council meeting. Additional questions came up, which resulted in subsequent exchanges between the Council and the kivas. Finally, when the kiva members were satisfied and gave their approval, the Council members relayed the approval to the company executives. (1995)

Rushton also explained that the people of Zuni continually used the council as an interface between the U.S. government and the religious leaders. He suggested that many Zunis believed that this was the way the council had always been administered and the way in which religious leaders' authority was kept intact. From an interview he carried out in Zuni, he provided the view of one community member confirming this perspective: "We Zunis have been running Zuni pretty successfully for a few thousand years, and we know how to make decisions that reflect and uphold the interests of the Zuni people. But if the White Man wants us to have a tribal council, we're glad to oblige. There's no need to upset people. We reach our decisions in the traditional Zuni manner, the White man is told about them in the traditional White Man's manner, and everyone is happy" (1995).

Although the divisions between theocratic and executive authority are often fluid and ambiguous, Zunis are nevertheless brought together over their shared desire to prevent the use of religious knowledge outside of Zuni. Regardless of their division over the restrictions, all Zunis were united by their opposition to visitors' photographing the ceremonies. They differed on the interpretation of authority over ceremonies and therefore on the definition of public and private interests in the ceremonies, but the majority of the community shared the fear of outsiders' duplicating or extracting knowledge. In 1990, Dorothy Walema commented on the restrictions introduced to prevent non-Zunis from attending the ceremonies and suggested that although the news made her feel mixed emotions, "[I]t's good because we can keep our religion sacred now. We knew someone took a picture last year because we saw the flash" (quoted in Dubin 1990).

There are divisions over who should determine the level of restrictions for non-Zunis, but the majority of people in the Pueblo view photographs taken by visitors as a clear sign that knowledge has leaked from the finely structured and partitioned system of control. Even though the visitors who try and take photographs at ceremonies may not understand the religious symbolism they have recorded, it appears to many Zuni that the visitors' intent is to remove or "steal" knowledge. During interviews in Zuni, I asked questions about this particular reading of the photograph as a cross-cultural vehicle for transmitting knowledge. The majority of people were ambiguous about the criteria by which photographs can or cannot be interpreted, but clarified that it was the *act* of duplication that needed to be controlled. Several decades ago Ruth Benedict similarly wrote that the materialized forms of esoteric knowledge required attention to detail and accuracy:

> Zuni religious practices are believed to be supernaturally powerful in their own right. At every step of the way, if the procedure is correct, the costume of the masked god traditional to the last detail, the offerings unimpeachable, the word of the hours-long prayers letter perfect, the effect will follow according to man's desires. One has only, in the phrase they have always on their tongues, to "know how." According to all tenets of their religion, it is a major matter if one of the eagle feathers of a mask has been taken from the shoulder of the bird instead of from the breast. Every detail has magical efficacy. (1934:244)

As introduced earlier, the emphasis on breath as a living animation of thought means that oral communication and knowledge as performance (oral tradition and ceremony) are seen as easier to control than materialized forms of knowledge, such as photographs, which can circulate outside of their original contexts. Repetition is also highly valued, so duplication also carries even deeper meaning: "In Zuni ritual poetry, in songs, in the worship of the Kachinas, in advice given by ceremonial fathers to their sons at initiations and other occasions, the same images are evoked, and the same words are repeated. Thus the repetition of endless orderly rituals multiplied by the concentrated participation of the Zuni people combines with religious and cosmic penetration to work together to instill harmony, balance and peace in Zuni life" (Pandey 1995:16).

The range of perspectives behind the restrictions at Sha'lak'o stems from the tensions in Zuni between an elite portion of the community, made up of the leaders from high-ranking religious societies and their families, and the larger populace, which feels excluded from decisions that ultimately affect the economic and social structure of the community.

There are key examples of how the religious leadership consistently adapts different ways of reasserting control over ritual knowledge that has been removed from its purview. A vast amount of anthropological data in the form of photographs, literature, and collections of material culture have resulted from research on Zuni religion. In order to screen information available to Zunis and non-Zunis, one of ZCRAT's duties is to assist in the handling of traditional and esoteric knowledge in areas outside of direct control by religious societies, such as museum collections, consultation for repatriation, and the identification of sacred sites. In addition, the protection and appropriate care of significant shrines and pilgrimage routes throughout the Southwest has also required ZCRAT's attention. The development of ZCRAT appears to be a joint and collective response by the tribal council, anthropologists, and religious leaders to codify in Anglo-American terms the control of knowledge in contexts affected by external influences.

Both Zunis and anthropologists have given religious and esoteric knowledge an ascendant value, whether for its sacred powers or its importance in the study of Zuni culture. Many Zunis, however, identify anthropology as a contributing factor in the inappropriate use and circulation of esoteric knowledge. The history of the intersection between these two approaches to knowledge is best explored through an examination of anthropological and archaeological research in Zuni. This particular contact history reveals the extensive investments made by Anglo-Americans in the chronicle of Zuni history and the legacy found in Zuni today in the current responses toward outsiders' gaining access to religious knowledge.

3
Anthropology at Zuni
Collecting and the Art of Duplication

The European and American scientific community in the nineteenth century subscribed to the idea of animating the Enlightenment philosophies through empirical methods, eventually organizing all knowledge into an all-inclusive, coherent whole. The idea of comprehensive knowledge indicated that "knowledge was singular and not plural, complete and not partial, global and not local, that all knowledges would ultimately turn out to be concordant in one great system of knowledge" (Richards 1993:7). Scientific methods could be applied in the field to produce transportable facts to be collected, organized, and filed within a central archive and kept intact so as to be retrievable in the future. These underlying assumptions about the possibility of the organization and collectivity of all knowledge dominated the early years of anthropology and helped propel the development of the grand organizing theories of the nineteenth century, such as social evolution and cultural diffusion.

Accompanying these grand classificatory schemas was the idea that consumable, mobile forms of data such as photographs, models, and replicas would further facilitate the organization and collectivity of all knowledge. These materialized forms of knowledge are best understood by linking together nineteenth-century ideas about industry, mass production, and the circulation of commodities with preexisting ideas on the authentication of knowledge through the process of production and mastery of technology. For the Victorians, replicas, duplicates, and originals could coexist within museums, scientific institutions, and the marketplace, their individual importance somewhat equalized by their value as mobile units of knowledge. These collections would eventually reveal, however, the entanglement of ideas on authenticity, connoisseurship, dissemination, and accessibility to knowledge.

This chapter considers the impact of the scientific community's belief in and exploration of comprehensive knowledge on the anthropology of Zuni, as well as the effects this approach had on the community of Zuni itself. Entwined within this history is the Anglo-American view of the anthropological value of Puebloan religious knowledge in aiding the progress of science, and I explore this view alongside the faith placed in the mastering and embodying of knowledge through the creation of replicas and the facilitated circulation of knowledge through its reproduction in objects such as photographs. Although the recent trend has been to focus on how anthropologists and Anglo-Americans have represented, consumed, and co-opted Puebloan culture (Berkhofer 1978; Hinsley 1990, 1992; Dilworth 1996; Whiteley 1998), we have overlooked the underlying motives of the American scientific community in moving toward the desired unification of all knowledges in the nineteenth and early twentieth centuries and have failed to make the crucial recognition that this desire was one of the central forces behind early ethnologists' aggressive collecting policies. The Pueblos play a central role in this history because of their appeal to anthropologists, who were attracted to their complex and colorful religion, viewing it as the cornerstone of life and as the adhesive binding together Pueblo society (Parezo 1993). More important, however, religion was viewed as a storehouse of ancient knowledge—a sanctuary and repository of prehistoric lore and practices.[1] By comparing examples drawn from the ethnography and correspondence of Frank Hamilton Cushing, Matilda Coxe Stevenson, Frederick Webb Hodge, and Ruth Bunzel, I explore Anglo-Americans' expectations and rationale concerning not only the collection of knowledge, but also the duplication and circulation of knowledge within a comprehensive system. Here, the history of anthropological research at Zuni affords insight not only into the inscription and consumption of culture, but also into the multiple performances of Zuni knowledge by Zunis *and* Anglo-Americans, resulting in a complex cross-cultural layering of perspectives on the different utilities of Zuni knowledge.

In the final analysis in this chapter, I look at Zuni responses to the anthropological study of their community. Anthropologists of this period assumed, with a confidence in the communicational transparency of knowledge largely inherited from the Victorian positivists, that the cross-cultural transmission of knowledge was unproblematic. However, the values ascribed by Anglo-Americans to secrecy, access, duplication, and the loss of knowledge were culturally structured in markedly different ways to the values cherished by the Zunis. This problem has been continuous. Over the past hundred years, scholars have endeavored to uncover previously unknown systems of knowledge and to add them to the growing body of science—a process that has forced Puebloan communities to contemplate and respond to Anglo-Americans' attitudes toward the treatment not only of the knowledge they have collected but of the system that has maintained it. This history has also helped shape Zunis' perspectives on museums as defined broadly and on the founding of their own museum.

For more than a century, the Pueblo communities and Pueblo ruins have been regarded as extremely important fields of study in the history of the North American continent. Zuni became, in many ways, a fertile training ground that provided sustained intellectual stimulus and therefore sustenance for the research that contributed to the development of American cultural anthropology and field archaeology. Pandey introduces the list of researchers who have worked in the Pueblos as a distinguished "roll call" of "gifted observers and professional anthropologists" (1972:321), and Peter Whiteley refers to this list as "a metonymic who's who of earlier disciplinary history within the United States" (1998:7). In *The Zunis of Cibola*, Gregory Crampton views Zuni as "a powerful lodestone" for researchers (1977:145). In a parallel account, Nigel Holman suggests that "Zuni culture and history has been analyzed from a wide variety of historical and archaeological, anthropological, linguistic, philosophical, jurisprudential and psychological perspectives."[2]

The first ethnographers to visit Zuni, Col. James Stevenson, Matilda Coxe Stevenson, and Frank Hamilton Cushing, were sent by the nascent Bureau of American Ethnology (BAE) in 1879, thus making Zuni one of the first communities to play a role in the birth of professional anthropology in the United States. Zuni also captured the interest of one the founding British ethnographers, Edward Burnett Tylor, who was invited to visit the Pueblo during the Stevenson Expedition (Parezo 1993) and who later used Zuni pottery designs in his formation of theories on the diffusion of cultural traits (Isaac 1995). The sequence of pioneering women ethnographers who worked in Zuni, such as Elsie Clews Parsons, Ruth Benedict, and Ruth Bunzel is also noteworthy. The physical anthropologist Aleš Hrdlička included Zuni in his survey of the southwestern tribes, as did Beatrice Blackwood (Peers 2003). Significant contributions to southwestern archaeology and to the development of methodology for the discipline as a whole have been made by an extensive list of recognized scholars who have worked in Zuni: Frederick Webb Hodge, Frank H. H. Roberts, Floyd O'Neil, Watson Smith, and more recently Natalie Woodbury, Richard Woodbury, Willard Walker, John Roberts,

Keith Kintigh, John Rick, Nan Rothschild, Barbara Mills, Margaret Hardin, and Richard Ford. Significant contributions have also been made by T. J. Ferguson, Jonathon Damp, and Roger Anyon via tribally sponsored research and through the collaborative design of models for the management of cultural heritage in Zuni.

With the establishment of anthropology as a university discipline in the 1920s, such noted scholars as Franz Boas, Alfred Louis Kroeber, and their students conducted fieldwork in Zuni to investigate how the laws of kinship and ceremony determined the structure of Zuni society (Kroeber 1917; Bunzel 1932a, 1932b; Benedict 1934; Boas 1938). Regional studies and a focus on cultural adaptation and the political organization of the Pueblos were brought to the discipline by Fred Eggan, Leslie Spier, Evon Vogt, John Adair, Dorothea Leighton, Triloki Nath Pandey, and historian Richard Hart. The research on Zuni language and poetry by Dennis Tedlock and Barbara Tedlock and insight into art presented by Margaret Hardin has also kept Zuni on the anthropological map. In recent years, through the work of Roger Anyon, T. J. Ferguson, and Jonathon Damp, the archaeological program at the Pueblo of Zuni contributed to some of the ground-breaking repatriation cases that preceded the passing of the Native American Graves Protection and Repatriation Act in 1990 and that continue to influence national policies on repatriation (Biolsi and Zimmerman 1997; Anyon, Ferguson, and Welch 2000).

The density of photographic activity at Zuni can also account, in part, for the Pueblo's visibility. From the travel journals and the collections of photographs that were designed either to assist ethnographic research or to satisfy a growing interest in the new territories of the West, another list of observers can be drawn: John K. Hillers of the BAE; Matilda Coxe Stevenson, supporting her ethnographic studies with more than nine hundred images of Zuni; Edward Curtis; G. Wharton James; Charles Fletcher Lummis; Sylvester Baxter; H. R. Voth; R. B. Townsend; Sumner Matteson; as well as George Pepper and Jesse L. Nussbaum, who photographed for the Hendrick-Hodge Expedition and the Museum of the American Indian in New York. Owen Cattel made films of Zuni technology during the Hodge Expedition, such as "adobe making, pottery construction, and bread baking," as well as films of the Sha'lak'o ceremony (Parezo 1992). These images circulated, whether in private sales or publications, and were instrumental in constructing and sustaining the Western exoticization of Zuni as a remote and ancient civilization untouched by modernity.

When this extensive list of anthropologists and photographers who worked in Zuni is viewed, the question arises, Why was Zuni such a lodestone for research and exploration in the nineteenth and early twentieth centuries? The strong desire to explain the origins of the earth was paralleled by an imperialist race to chart and claim new territories, and these ideals motivated nineteenth-century scientists to transform the mysteries of the world around them into collectable forms of knowledge. The historical development of human institutions had previously been traced and classified into stages and epochs, but during the nineteenth century scientists sought to uncover "the very laws of progress itself" (Berkhofer 1978:49). Charles Lyell's uniformitarian notions of geological processes soon took apart biblical views of the earth's age and laid the groundwork for Darwin's radical restructuring of natural history. The publication of Darwin's *On the Origin of Species* in 1859 also challenged the scientific community to consider the possibilities of natural variation created from incremental change over long time periods, thereby providing systematic ways to chart these developmental trajectories. The search began for the essential ordering code of human history. In 1877, Lewis Henry Morgan introduced in *Ancient Society* his theories on the "ratio of human progress." Using technological innovations as a primary factor to determine a society's development, he proposed seven "ethnical periods" in the history of culture: Lower, Middle, and Upper Savagery; Lower, Middle, and Upper Barbarism; and Civilization. Anthropologists subsequently sought out "ancient" societies that might provide clues to spell out this code.

The origins of anthropology at Zuni can be traced back to when the Pueblo first caught the attention of the scientific community after the Powell and Hayden Survey visited in 1874 and when the Wheeler Expedition traveled to Zuni in 1879 (Hinsley 1981). In August 1879, the same year as the inception of the BAE, John Wesley Powell assigned Col. James Stevenson to lead an expedition to the Southwest to visit the Pueblos and to survey the archaeological sites within the area around Zuni. Accompanying Col. Stevenson were his wife, Matilda Coxe Stevenson, and John K. Hillers, who had already started his career as a photographer for the U.S. Geological Survey (Fowler 1989). The youngest member of the expedition was Frank Hamilton Cushing, the ethnologist who remained in Zuni after the others had returned to Washington, D.C., and who, following his decision to move in with the governor's family in the Zuni Pueblo, would later be considered the first anthropologist to explore participant observation techniques.

Societies such as Zuni were seen as extremely attractive opportunities to unearth what were perceived to be sanctuaries of ancient knowledge. The lengths to which the Zuni went to prevent access to the religious societies were understood to be proof that this knowledge had not been meddled with by other cultures and was highly valuable for its stability and antiquity. Zuni knowledge was also imagined to have remained intact through Spanish and Anglo-American colonialism in the Southwest. The Pueblos evoked romantic notions about the ancient mysteries of a preindustrial communal way of life that had preserved ancient traditions. The theory was that Pueblo religion had stayed intact during Spanish colonization and would therefore yield data on Pueblo culture in its purest form—ancient knowledge that could be examined alongside that of civilized societies. Matilda Coxe Stevenson and her contemporary Frank Hamilton Cushing came to see the Pueblos as "store houses of knowledge" that had been little altered with the course of time and would therefore yield answers as to the origins of the indigenous inhabitants of North America.[3] Cushing stated that "especially in religious culture, the Zuni is almost as strictly archaic as in the days ere his land was discovered" (1979:184). He argued that the religion had remained unchanged because the people of Zuni had not allowed outsiders to gain entrance to the esoteric realms of religious practices: "The Zuni faith [after] more than three hundred and fifty years of Spanish intercourse, is as a drop of oil in water, surrounded and touched at every point, yet in no place penetrated or changed inwardly by the flood of alien belief that descended upon it" (1979:184). In a parallel analysis, Stevenson also implied that the introduction of the Spanish missions had not altered Zuni religion: "So far as the writer has been able to discover, the religious and social institutions of the Zunis have been but slightly affected by the teachings of the Spanish priesthood, and their mode of thought is practically what it was before the arrival of Coronado more than 350 years ago" (Stevenson 1904:289).

With the rapid westward expansion of railroads and prospectors in the late nineteenth century, there were fears that the people of the Pueblos would be diminished "under the onslaught of civilization" and their history lost if not properly recorded (Ahlstrom and Parezo 1987:267). The railroad came to represent both the unification of the nation and the destructiveness of rapid and unsettling change. Many ethnologists used these changes as mandates to open up esoteric areas to study and initiated the practice of what later became known as "salvage ethnology" (Gruber 1970). Anthropologists such as Stevenson and later on Ruth

Bunzel began to see their mission as rescuing a culture they believed would no longer survive. By making sure this knowledge was recorded in permanent, stable forms, it would be given a place within the more durable and indissoluble scientific body of knowledge.

No one believed more in the totalizing and unifying powers of science and in the ideal of the synthesis of knowledge into a collective whole than Matilda Coxe Stevenson. She believed that by studying Pueblo religion she could uncover the inner workings of its esoteric societies and that by following scientific methods she could sustain these beliefs as invariable facts (Isaac 2005b). Unusual for a woman of her time, Stevenson had received an intensive scientific training from Dr. Mew of the Army Medical School in Washington, D.C., where she studied geology, mineralogy, and chemistry. After the death of her husband in 1888, she was committed to finishing the work she had started in Zuni in 1879, and she pursued and was granted a paid staff position within the BAE to put her husband's papers in order (Parezo 1993). Like Stevenson, Powell desired to build a collection of data of the first Americans and to develop comparative models of indigenous languages and technology, so he eventually sent her back to Zuni to continue fieldwork. With remarkable diligence, she subsequently returned to Zuni in 1890, 1900, 1904, 1906, and 1907 (Isaac 1995). In all, she remained devoted to working in the southwestern Pueblos for more than twenty-five years and is recognized as having compiled the most comprehensive ethnography of Zuni religious practices.[4]

Although many anthropologists have been critical of Stevenson's exaggerated attention to detail and her apparent lack of interest in theory, she can be fully understood only in light of her concern with comprehensive knowledge and her belief that facts were raw knowledge that, following collection, could be organized by others. In a letter to Powell, Stevenson wrote, "I want to do a comparatively complete and connected history of an aboriginal people whose thoughts are not our thoughts, weaving all the threads into an intelligent and satisfactory whole for the civilized student. . . . I feel I can do the most for science in this way."[5] To obtain these facts, or, as she also referred to it, "the anthropological truth," she employed the technique of cross-referencing data from different informants. She wrote in a letter to the BAE: "I never record anything until I have had it from at least three Indians neither one knowing they have spoken with me. Thus was Mr. Stevenson's plan as it has always been mine."[6]

Much of the ethnography of the late nineteenth and early twentieth centuries is fraught with growing tensions between coexisting ideologies of stasis and change (Isaac 1995, 2005b; Hinsley and Wilcox 1996). The contrast between rapid technological change taking place in the cities and peaceful agricultural villages of the Southwest created a duality that attracted many easterners wanting to escape the cities and explore the historic origins of the Americas. Underneath the process of change lay continuity and "knowledge untouched by the ravages and distractions of industrial time" (Hinsley and Wilcox 1996:30). The idea that Pueblo societies were unlikely to survive the age of industry was paradoxically linked to a fascination with how the Pueblos, against great adversity, had maintained their religious practices during Spanish rule and the introduction of the Catholic missions. Hinsley suggests that the lure of the Southwest for ethnologists was also a reflection on their wish to leave behind the crowded and industrial life. A romantic picture of the desert and its "gentle" dwellers appealed to many who were in search of "an invigorating climate; sedentary populations of artisans in weaving, pottery and silver; mysterious, bird like cliff dwellings of the remote past [with] possible links between the high civilizations of Central America and the North America aborigines" (Hinsley 1981:92).

The idea of the Southwest as the old New World developed, which American anthropologists hoped would answer their questions about the history of human life on the North American continent. In Frank Hamilton Cushing's accounts of Zuni in 1879, the desert canyons and valleys of what would become New Mexico and Arizona came to represent the cradle of civilization that would reveal to him the history of the tribes of this continent. In *My Adventures in Zuni*, he recalled one of his first impressions of the Pueblo, women drawing water from a well: "[A]s I watched the women coming and going to and from the well, 'How strangely parallel' I thought, 'have been the lines of development in this curious civilization of an American desert with those of Eastern nations and deserts'" (1979:54). He described the scene as reminiscent of the "Pools of Palestine" (1979:54), and in so doing he placed Zuni at the heart of a comparison between the origin of European cultures and the origin of North American cultures. He initiated a quest to unravel the mysteries of the indigenous civilizations of the New World with the same fervor and expectations that held his contemporaries in Europe, who were hoping to apply scientific methods to the excavation of the history of the Old World.

With the contours of the body of scientific knowledge becoming refined and mapped in more detail, a separation between experiential knowledge and empirical authority developed. Divides also appeared because of the growing territoriality between Americans and Europeans over archaeological and anthropological sites. By the turn of the twentieth century, the newly professionalized anthropologists voiced their concerns that the growing interest in history and artifacts had led to amateur looting and that "foreign emissaries" had already started to pillage the ruins of the Southwest without regard for method or science. Special-interest groups of scientists and citizens lobbied to develop laws that would transform these sites into national landmarks preserved for science. Unsurprisingly, we find that Stevenson played a role in the rising nationalistic identification with American history in her call for the stabilization and protection of ruins. In a letter to General Van Stone, she outlined the purpose of passing an antiquities act to protect ethnologists' interests in the Southwest:

> The purpose of the bill is two fold: it is not only for the protection from vandalism of the remains of the past civilization but the bill as I understand, provides that these remains shall be properly excavated by expert students recommended by the scientific departments of the government, or universities, such students to make careful photographs and reports upon their work, and that the lares and penates of the long since departed peoples, brought to light through these excavations shall be so classified and preserved as to make them an open book for study for generations to come.[7]

Assumptions concerning the permanency of scientific institutions allowed ethnologists and archaeologists to amass large collections that were to be kept for future generations. Opening the Pueblo "store houses of knowledge," as Stevenson had put it, also included the transformation of the related materials into government property to be transferred to the growing storehouses of the Smithsonian Institution. Following the Civil War, a genuine need was felt to find a prehistory that would forge and unify the new nation by providing national treasures and creating a belief that "the ancients earthly ruins would serve as a medium of lineage from American fathers to sons" (Hinsley and Wilcox 1996:185).

Cushing's view of the role of science in anthropology is a stark contrast to Stevenson's obsessions with empirical methodology. Throughout his career, Cushing depicted himself as the hero of a romantic novel—an

adventurer who strove to unearth the secrets of the early inhabitants of
North America—with Zuni as his picturesque and mysterious backdrop.
In a letter to the BAE, he wrote, "[M]y disappointment would be almost
irreparable, were I unable to study for a period almost as great, from the
inside, the life of the Zunis, as I have from the outside" (quoted in
Hinsley 1983:58, original emphasis). He was given this opportunity during the 1879 expedition to Zuni when, with encouragement from Powell,
he decided to stay behind while the rest of the expedition moved on to
survey the Hopi villages. He viewed his self-imposed decision to detach
himself from the rest of the party as a way to develop trust and confidence with the people of Zuni (Cushing 1979:68).

Cushing was so persistent that, according to his own records, he was
eventually initiated into a religious society, the Priesthood of the Bow, a
position that he used to obtain the esoteric religious knowledge he so
fervently desired. In a review of Cushing's ethnography, Pandey emphasizes Cushing's awareness of the benefits of initiation into the priesthood;
he knew "that as a Bow Priest he would have access to both sacred and
secular organizations of the tribe" (1972:323). His interest was in obtaining the broadest scope of religious knowledge and issues of governance.
In a letter to the BAE, Cushing wrote:

> Being now a *Pithlun shiwani* or Priest of the Bow, I am secured the
> privileges of this strictly exotic society, as well as entrance into any
> meeting of, though not for the present membership in, all the other
> secret, medicine, or sacred orders of the Tribe. I bent all my energies
> toward this supreme order of the Zunis, for more than a year, and my
> success in gaining admission to it, is the greatest of all achievements of
> my life perhaps; for it breaks down the last shadow of objection to my
> gaining knowledge of the sacred rites, not only of this, but of the
> Maqui [Hopi] tribes, and others as well. (quoted in Pandey 1972:323)

Cushing's drive to obtain privileged knowledge dictated his ethnographic
methods and directed his view of the nature of anthropology. In a letter to
his niece, he wrote, "I have to have knowledge of savage life, and it matters
less to me where I find it, than it does in what measure I find it. Zuni . . . is
attractive to me because of the satisfaction it gives to my craving after
knowledge of savage lore and life" (quoted in Hinsley 1983:56). He also
justified his intrusions into the esoteric facets of Zuni life as a way of
discovering their early origins, something that he saw as crucial to understanding the prehistory of the continent.

According to Nigel Holman, it is worth questioning whether Cushing was in fact "initiated" into the priesthood. He may have "stretched the truth to tell a story to his readers," and there was probably disagreement among the Zunis with whom he was interacting as to whether he was really initiated.[8] Nonetheless, both Cushing's version and the later versions of this story are good examples of the high degree of ambiguity found in Zuni concerning the interpretation of religious or governmental powers and how these spheres of influence govern the circulation of knowledge.

To Cushing and his contemporaries, "the revelation of secret knowledge" was "nothing less than epiphenal, the most sought after and highly prized of southwestern experiences" (Hinsley and Wilcox 1996:31). As Hinsley and Wilcox have pointed out, visitors to the Southwest made intriguing comparisons between Pueblo and Anglo-American cultures: Sylvester Baxter, whose father had been a member of the Masonic Order, found similarities between it and the geographically and culturally diverse secret Pueblo society, and he "stressed parallels between Indian religious rites and spiritualism or séance gatherings" (Hinsley and Wilcox 1996:31). But secrecy had the most potent value for its believed insight into the past because "its most salient characteristic—and its greatest value—was the presumed lack of change through generations, for in its pristine insight and instruction lay its profound power to regulate society and the source of . . . their spiritual strength" (1996:31).

As a result, anthropologists gave what they perceived to be the unique and elemental integrity of Zuni culture an exalted value to science and proceeded to seek access into the very areas they lauded the Zunis for protecting and keeping intact. Throughout their time in Zuni, they focused on esoteric realms because "the keys to this religious system would unlock the riches of Zuni life and knowledge" (Hinsley 1983:57). They viewed religion as a means to clarify the differences between themselves and the people of Zuni, and anthropology became the method that would make these secrets part of an "objective" scientific investigation that in turn would make them accessible to interpretation by a wider audience.

Although anthropologists were part of a new discipline that had yet to develop experientially based ethics, the majority of them in the nineteenth century operated within post-Enlightenment empirical rationalizations as the key to understanding the world. By subscribing to the belief in the necessary separation of subject/object and mind/body, as well as to the conviction that all knowledge, once organized coherently, would contribute to the concordance of one great system of knowledge, they hoped to use science to aid the progress of civilization. The lack of discussions on the ethics of unearthing esoteric knowledge in Zuni must be viewed in light of these paradigms. Cushing, Stevenson, and others aspired to open up arcane practices and previously unobtainable knowledge, hoping to achieve recognition as the first to add the secret knowledge of an ancient society to the comprehensive body of scientific knowledge.

Technology and the Embodiment of Knowledge

Cultural historians, with a heightened focus on issues of representation and the consumption of the "other," have explored how Anglo-Americans created cultures of the imagination to meet shifting political and social agendas in the United States (Berkhofer 1978; Dilworth 1996; McFeely 2001). The condition and analytical stance identifying these tropes, however, are dependent on collapsing perspectives previously separated by a century of evolving ideologies—namely, making the shift from the Victorians' faith in their ability to duplicate reality and transform the mysteries of the world into accumulated concrete facts to the twentieth-century illuminations of the colonial fantasy of empire and of the polysemic performances and interpretations of knowledge. In effect, anthropologists need to think differently about their subjects and the knowledge systems that they have used to make sense of them. Anglo-American fascinations with Zuni may have created timeless images of "ancient" peoples, but these Zuni/Anglo entanglements are neither ahistorical nor purely theatrical, but have resulted in concrete, physical progeny such as the photographic collections now housed both at the Smithsonian Institution and at the museum in Zuni. The aim here is to look at how anthropologists have viewed reproductive technology and inscription, an issue explored through the ways in which Stevenson, Cushing, Bunzel, and Hodge used these duplicative processes. Prior to the call to recognize that cultural ways of knowing are socially and individually constructed was the belief that humans' replication and control of the natural world channeled the process of progress, giving power to those who understood the potency of technology and reproduction and utilized this potency to its maximum.

If we look at the origins of models and replicas within the field of science, we find that cabinets of curiosity often housed miniature models of architectural accomplishments or technological inventions (Impey and MacGregor 1985). These models were displayed alongside models of the natural wonders of the world, the two attesting to the powers of humans in harnessing their natural environment and to the powers of God as creator. Models and replicas were seen as effective ways for their creators to embody scientific explorations or the mastering of technological knowledge or both. Along with demonstrating an increased interest in the inner workings of the natural and industrial/mechanical world, models were also used as a way to explore these phenomena in exaggerated scales—no doubt influenced by the minutiae of the world opened up by the microscope and the grand expanses of the world laid out by the transect and map. Similarly, the replication of an artifact or specimen and the plethora of ways of inscribing and materializing ideas advantaged scientists with mobile, possessory, consumable forms of knowledge. Photographs, models, and replicas were and continue to be considered concrete and stable forms used to explore the physical shape of the body of scientific knowledge.

The creation of miniatures and models of objects for museums was a common practice in the nineteenth century. Replicas were also often used by anthropologists to experiment with how things were made, and these duplicates became part of teaching collections and educational displays, where scale might need to be altered for instructional and practical purposes. It has been noted that Cushing was "renowned for his skill at replicating artifacts using traditional Indian technology" (Merrill, Ladd, and Ferguson 1993:540). In a well-documented example of the duplication of Zuni paraphernalia, Cushing created a facsimile of an Ahayu:da, or Zuni War God, and restored a series of associated offerings as a gift for Edward Burnett Tylor, the curator of the Pitt Rivers Museum at Oxford University, who donated them to the museum in 1911.

Cushing was remarkable for his ability to blur the line between fact and fiction, between romance and realism, and between the original and the replica. He is intriguing not only for the recognition he received for the accuracy of his replicas of Zuni paraphernalia, but also for his attempt to transform himself into a member of the Zuni tribe. His entrance into Zuni life began a process of cross-cultural initiation of both Cushing and the Zunis, wherein Cushing was employed for his knowledge of Washington and he used his companions for their knowledge of Zuni religion. It is also possible that Zunis made Cushing a Bow Priest so that he could help protect the farming village of Nutria from the land grab by officers at Fort Wingate, which he did by enlisting Sylvester Baxter to publicize these encroachments. However, Cushing did not want merely to obtain or collect esoteric knowledge; he seemed to want to become a part of the knowledge-producing system of Zuni and to replicate this knowledge for an Anglo-American audience, possibly as proof of his intimacy with Zuni society and his ability to master it. In making models and replicas and in dressing up in Zuni regalia, he both personified and embodied Zuni knowledge making, but he also established himself as authoritative through his supposed position within the Priesthood of the Bow.

Access to this knowledge, however, proved exceedingly difficult for Cushing. During his first stay in the Pueblo following the BAE expedition in 1879, he encountered a substantial amount of disapproval and suspicion from the community toward his attempts at transforming Zuni ceremonies and knowledge into sketches:

> When I took my station on a house-top, sketch books and colors in hand, I was surprised to see frowns and hear explosive, angry expostulations in every direction. As the day wore on this indignation increased, until at last an old, bush-headed hag approached me, and scowling into my face made a grab at my book and pantomimically tore it to pieces. I was chagrined, but paid no attention to her, forced a good natured smile, and continued my sketching. Discouraged, yet far from satisfied, the natives made no further demonstrations. (1979:60–61)

Following this incident, the Zuni governor requested Cushing not to observe the ceremonies that were to be held the following day. Although Cushing was instructed to leave his books and pencils behind, he was adamant that he attend the ceremonies. An impromptu council meeting was held, after which he was warned, "[I]f you put the shadows of the great dance down on the leaves of your books today, we shall cut them to pieces" (1979:60–61). In a "doubtful game of bluff," he threatened the council, who recoiled, and he took the opportunity to escape to the dances in the plaza. He later wrote, "[A]lthough they followed me throughout the whole day, they did not again offer to molest me, but the people gathered so closely around me that I could scarcely find opportunity for sketching" (1979:60–61).

Cushing's intimacy with religious ceremonies and his in-depth field-work provided unparalleled insight into Zuni cosmology; he wrote extensively on Zunis' belief in objects as animate beings. Yet he paid little or no attention to the taboos linked to the prescribed treatment of these objects or to the restrictive system that controlled the duplication of knowledge. In disregarding the significance behind the replication of religious symbolism—an act reserved for the specific caretakers of this knowledge—he also omitted to acknowledge how reproduction and duplication were processes recognized by Zunis as absorbing power:

> Among my drawings was the portrait of a pretty girl. An old white headed grandmother, looking the sketches over one day, recognized this. She shook her head, frowned, and, covering her face with her withered hands, began to howl most dolefully, leaving me abruptly and disappearing into a room adjoining the governor's. At intervals, during the remainder of the day, I could hear her talking, scolding, and sobbing over what she regarded as a great misfortune to her family. (Cushing 1979:61)

Replication may reproduce the power of the original into the duplicate. It may also allow control over the duplicate or vessel, such as with fetishes. In the case described here, the drawing of an individual's likeness can be considered an attempt at obtaining control over a person and therefore an act of sorcery. In discussing Cushing's use of replicas such as those of the Ahayu:da, Zuni anthropologist Edmund Ladd argues that we need to ask the fundamental question, What is real when judging a model or replica of an object? (Merrill, Ladd, and Ferguson 1993). The Ahayu:da and associated paraphernalia given by Cushing to Edward Burnett Tylor at the Pitt Rivers Museum was, according to Cushing, such a faithful replica that it could be considered a scientific specimen. Although in scientific terms the Ahayu:da was a duplicate useful as an example of a particular practice, it also held immense political powers and was designed by Cushing to cement his professional relationship with Tylor and to demonstrate his intimate knowledge of the esoteric religious society of the Priesthood of the Bow, thus illustrating that even in Anglo-American terms it was at the time of its manufacture understood to hold power, even if this power was expressed only as academic collateral.[9]

After his return to the BAE, Cushing publicized his work in travel journals in order to raise funds for further research in Zuni. Consequently, he published material that brought Zuni into the public eye and Zuni religious knowledge and philosophy to a wide audience.[10]

Cushing's ethnographic practices still evoke strong responses today. His work has been continually assessed and reassessed for its role in determining anthropological methods, Zuni history, and the dissemination of esoteric Zuni knowledge. He is remembered as a pioneer ethnologist who influenced many others. According to Fred Eggan, Cushing's work on Zuni philosophy inspired Durkheim's and Mauss's conceptions of culture; similarly, Lévy-Bruhl found in Cushing's writing "a rich source both of insight and of documentation basic to the development of . . . his theory of primitive cognition based on 'collective representations'" (Eggan 1979:18). As noted earlier, Cushing is also recognized as the first field ethnologist to develop participant observation as an anthropological method (Brandes 1965; Pandey 1972; Cushing 1979; Mark 1981; Hinsley 1983). He is remembered as "Kushy" by the people of Zuni, many of whom saw his publication of Zuni religious knowledge and his replication of masks and war gods as a betrayal of the Zuni leaders who had incorporated him into Zuni religious life (Crampton 1977). They viewed his early death—reportedly from choking on a fishbone—as punishment for his dissemination of esoteric knowledge (Hughte 1994).[11] Clearly he is remembered by both the Anglo-Americans and the Zunis as having highly developed creative powers for producing and reproducing knowledge.

If we look at another example of the use of replicas within scientific research, we can see that the belief in the transformational powers of duplication is nowhere so apparent as in the Victorian approaches to photography. From its inception in 1839, photography was viewed as a valuable scientific tool that would assist in the collection of data, and it was quickly taken up by explorers and anthropologists as a way to transport accurate visual data back from the field. In the 1892 edition of *Notes and Queries on Anthropology*, the joint editor, Charles Hercules Read, encouraged the use of the camera, noting that "by these means the traveler is dealing with facts about which there can be no question" (Garson and Read 1892:87). As facsimiles of the world, photographs were the most reliable recording devices of visual information that could be easily transported.

Matilda Coxe Stevenson's thorough methods and desire to collect the maximum amount of information within any given context led her to rely heavily on the use of the camera within fieldwork. By nineteenth-century standards, she forged beyond the majority of her contemporaries to produce a vast collection totaling nine hundred images, showing exhaustive, almost filmlike sequences of ceremonial activities, technology, and daily life (Isaac 2005b). Her correspondence with the BAE shows how she was consistently explicit in her use of the term *series* when referring to the documentation of photographic subjects. One example of this use of the term appeared in her field report for the month of February 1904, in which she stated: "I have observed among the dances which are frequent at this season, two which I have not seen before. I made a series of photographs of them."[12] Later in the same field season, due to her lack of film, she complained because she was prevented from producing a "complete series of views of the summer solstice ceremonies."[13] Her choice of the phrase *complete series* indicates that she planned to create a systematic and cohesive visual record that would probably have followed step by step the numerous events that formed the summer solstice ceremonies: "I am forwarding under separate cover the three proofs you sent me, with the titles attached to the back. You will please read all that I have written on the back of each illustration. . . . If I may be allowed to criticize, I will say that I do not think the dancers in one of the plates, would be satisfactory as merely the backs are shown. . . . I have many fine photos of the dance represented. The one you sent me was taken to show in a series of the dances of the rain makers."[14]

After the development of the Kodak box camera by Eastman and with the assistance of May Clark, her stenographer, Stevenson consistently experimented with photographic equipment, showing her interest in exploring the various ways in which it could facilitate research in the field (Isaac 1995, 2005b). She valued the camera for its ability to transform visual events into permanent facts, but also as a hidden eye, an indiscernible tool for observation that she could use to record ceremonial activities secretly:

> The camera furnished me by the Bureau is not suitable for my work except where I might take inanimate objects. It is all right where time is no object and there is no opposition, but the camera is too large for me to slip up my sleeve until the all important moment. The greatest tact, and quickest manipulation of the camera is necessary in securing ceremonials and other animate pictures. Knowing that I could not

succeed with the camera given me, and appreciating the importance of success, I obtained the one from Mr. Moore entirely upon my own responsibility, and I am quite willing to pay for it personally.[15]

We know, however, that Zunis were aware of the use of the camera to record ceremonies and that individuals attempted to prevent photography in the Pueblo. In the same way that Cushing was reprimanded for sketching the ceremonies, Stevenson's interest in photographing religious ceremonies and paraphernalia was met with grave disapproval in Zuni and resulted in factional differences as to who had the right to control the photographic duplication of knowledge: "While the priests and other high officials favored photographing the ceremonials—in fact, seemed eager to serve the expedition in every way—the populace were so opposed to having their masks and rituals 'carried away on paper,' that it was deemed prudent to make but few ceremonial pictures with the camera, and the altars and masks were sketched in color by the writer without the knowledge of the people" (Stevenson 1904:17). Although Stevenson recorded here that it was the "priests and other high officials" who gave her permission to photograph the ceremonies, it is possible that the Zuni governor and tribal council gave the permission in order to facilitate diplomatic relations with the U.S. government and that the priests did not necessarily agree with this decision. Holman has also used this excerpt from Stevenson to argue that she "created a false dichotomy between 'priests and other high officials' and 'the populace,' and underestimated the extent to which authority over religious matters in Zuni is divided among individuals" (1996a:112). Stevenson's focus, however, was on defining scientific codes rather than on Zuni guidelines for behavior. In determining anthropology as a new science that would facilitate the building of a complete archive of Zuni knowledge, she proceeded to intrude into religious spheres. Even when confronted by clear social codes that condemned this behavior, she chose to view her pursuit of religious knowledge as a valid scientific endeavor. In her ethnography on Zuni religion, she recorded an encounter that revealed the conflict that this pursuit caused within the Zuni community:

Although the writer occupied the upper storey of the ceremonial house and her door opened upon the roof to which members resort, on account of the superstitious dread of the powerful medicine of this fraternity, entertained by inmates of the house, great efforts were required to secure photographs on the roof and to enter the ceremonial chamber, in which the writer spent most of the time during the several days' ceremonies. We'wha, a conspicuous character of Zuni, was untiring in her efforts to detain an old father below while the writer secured photographs on the roof, and several times released her when the father had barred the door of her room with heavy stones. The wrath and distress of the old man knew no bounds, and he declared that the writer would bring calamity to herself but also to all the household. (1904:463)

Although Stevenson was also aware of the consequences her informants faced if they gave esoteric information to her, she persisted in retrieving what she considered scientific data. In an account of her visit to Kołuwala'wa, Zuni Heaven, she commented on the tensions that developed between her and her Zuni guide, on whom she had to use "extreme persuasion" to induce him to take her to this sacred place. She quoted him as saying, "If you insist on going, I will show you the way, but I shall offend the gods and I shall surely die" (1904:154–55). Following this episode with her guide, Stevenson recorded the treatment of Zunis who ignored the protocol for visiting the sacred lake: "The punishment for visiting the lake without the permission of the Ko'mosona is not only death within four days by the anger of the gods, but severe corporal punishment and perhaps death by the order of the Ko'mosona" (1904:154–55). Curiously, she also assumed the same detailed recording system for her antagonistic interactions with her informants, and although she turned her observations into insights into Zuni philosophy, she herself remained external to the logic of this system. She never used these conflicts with her guides to question the purpose of the restrictions and therefore the value given to responsibility toward knowledge.

Anthropologists' continued persistence in trying to take photographs in Zuni created increasingly more volatile conflicts as photography began to play a major role in the relationships between Zunis and visitors to the Pueblo. From 1917 to 1923, Frederick Webb Hodge, a staff member of the National Museum of Natural History (NMNH) at the Smithsonian, working under the aegis of the Museum of the American Indian, led extensive excavations during the Hendricks-Hodge Expedition, which systematically documented the Pueblos of Hawikku and Kechiba:wa.[16] Hawikku was the first Zuni village besieged by the Spaniards in 1540, when Coronado attacked and later occupied it. The Hendricks-Hodge Expedition carried out excavations that uncovered approximately 370 rooms, 1,000 burials, and an assemblage of roughly 20,000 artifacts, most of which were shipped to the NMNH in Washington, D.C.[17] According to Holman, "Hodge's archaeological techniques—stratigraphic excavation, systematic recording of rooms, features, artifacts, in situ photographs, and ethnographic analogy—were sophisticated for their time and facilitated the recovery of thousands of artifacts and their related documentation."[18] As part of the rigorous documentation techniques, Owen Cattel and Jesse Nussbaum proceeded to take 11 films and 1,600 photographs of the excavation and of ethnographic subjects, such as the manufacture of pottery, which are now considered one of the largest systematic visual collections assembled in that period. Hodge believed strongly that he should preserve Zuni ceremonies for future generations of Zunis:

> That the ceremonies of the Zuni people should be recorded accurately there is no question. I believe the best way to do this will be to make those who have the knowledge of the ancient beliefs realize the importance of preserving them on paper by means of photographs. . . . If the wise old men and women could be induced to break down their prejudice about talking of the religious beliefs and ceremonies the younger men who are competent to do so should write down what they have to say. It takes a great deal of ability to do this, as the beliefs and ceremonies are very intricate and not easily written down so that they can be understood. (quoted in Holman 1996a:113–14)

Hodge received permission from Zuni government leaders to film parts of Zuni culture, namely adobe making, pottery construction, and bread baking. He also received permission from the "progressive" faction to film the Sha'lak'o ceremony and the pilgrimage to the Great Salt Lake. In addition, he and his cameraman, Cattel, filmed parts of the Zuni summer rain dances and the sacred pilgrimage to Ojo Caliente. A Zuni group that became known as the "conservatives" were outraged, resulting in the confiscation of the cameras and film, an event that has led to two versions of the story—one in which the cameras and film were destroyed and a second in which the film survived (Parezo 1992). It was this particular event that led to more visible factions in the Pueblo and heightened animosity toward anthropologists.[19]

In addition to models and photographs, the textual inscription of knowledge also holds significant keys to understanding the contexts in which knowledge has circulated beyond Zuni. Anthropologists Ruth Bunzel and Ruth Benedict arrived in Zuni shortly after the incident with Hodges's crew and the struggle over the control of reproductive technology. Their arrival was met with diffidence due to the political tensions and the continued suspicion of the inappropriate circulation of knowledge by non-Zunis. Bunzel reflected on this episode later, as well as on the level of privacy that Zunis tried to maintain during her fieldwork: "In Zuni I encountered informant resistance at all levels. Those whom I interviewed for data on economics and social structure were afraid that their neighbors would think they were telling secrets; those who were willing to talk about religious matters feared supernatural punishment" (1952:xix).

Although not the first anthropologist to record the rationale behind the Zunis' fear of having their religion recorded, Bunzel seems to have reflected on this topic in more depth. Following a long-term relationship maintained with the Zuni elder Dick Tumaka, she recorded his words to her on his death bed: "it is true I will die because I have given away my religion (the esoteric texts he had dictated to me) and I have nothing with which to defend myself" (1952:xix–xx). She recounted how he did in fact die a few days later and how rumors circulated about his being a sorcerer and his death a result of betraying secrets.

Unlike Stevenson, who rationalized that the recording of Zuni material would aid science, Bunzel argued that it would aid Zunis because much of it was not being learned or passed down in the Zuni community:

> I think I eventually convinced them that it was to their advantage to have these rituals recorded. They would complain that the boys didn't want to learn. It takes a whole winter to learn one of these long chants and then the men who have to perform them have to come every night to the man who is the owner or keeper of a ritual and they have to learn from him. It takes hours to perform. To learn these things letter-perfect takes a long time. I convinced them it was to their advantage to have them written down and preserved. Since they complained about how the young men didn't want to bother with elaborate ceremonies I said, "You have them written down in the books and then you have them forever." (quoted in Parezo 1992:xxxii)

Years later in an interview with Parezo and Hardin, Bunzel stated that she firmly believed that the Zuni gained from recording the information.

According to Bunzel, the exactness of her description and the Zunis' agreement with this accuracy turned their oral beliefs into a canon—religious writings regarded as definitive.

Current anthropologists appear sympathetic to Bunzel because they believe her methods to be less intrusive: "Bunzel neither took photographs of esoteric ceremonies nor tried to gain access to kivas as had earlier anthropologists such as Cushing and Stevenson. She was extremely sensitive to the role of the intruder and constantly questioned her conflicting loyalties to science and to the people with whom she worked—people who had resisted discussing certain areas of their life" (Parezo 1992:xxxi). Zunis' perception of the act of duplication, however, does not differentiate between different types of inscription—photographic or textual; they see both as transforming powerful knowledge into another form or vessel.

Innovations in technology did not just open up the American West; they also created new forms of knowledge, and unique new cultures were born out of the joining of previously separated geographical and intellectual territories. Victorian technology such as the railway and the telegraph had introduced innovative ways of processing and transmitting knowledge, making "it possible for people to imagine knowledge of things not sequentially but simultaneously" (Richards 1993:4–5). From a Zuni perspective, for instance, the photographs generated by new technology now required the imposition of a control that reasserted the photographs' place within a religious hierarchy of access and that prevented the images from being viewed outside the circles that dealt with the knowledge depicted.

Zuni Responses to Anthropology

Outsiders' prolonged and intensive quest for Zuni religious knowledge has also produced changes in how these visitors are both perceived and received within the Pueblo. According to Pandey, Stevenson's vigorous and persistent intrusion into religious societies caused much of the current antagonism toward anthropologists in the Pueblos (Pandey 1972). Non-Zunis' interference has also resulted in the alteration of the Zuni political processes and the increased formation of political factions (Pandey 1967). Roscoe argues that the majority of anthropologists working in Zuni were "outcasts from Anglo-American society," and therefore, "as the history of the fascination of Zuni reveals, the act of investigating another culture always entails a particular ethical and moral stance." Consequently, "the idealistic representations of pueblo life have not passed without impact on its subjects" (1991:xvii). Whiteley suggests that there have been both ambiguity and contradiction within the representation of Pueblo culture, and that the professionalization of anthropology has had negative impacts on its subjects: "the reasons for indigenous resistance to cultural commodification by academic ethnography are several . . . but at base they are the result of the social and political estrangement of anthropology as a research-university discipline from the perspectives and situated interests of its subjects" (1998:6). Once Zunis learned of the degree to which esoteric knowledge had been circulated to a broader audience, many chose to defend publicly their right to fiercer and more adaptive levels of control. Over the past hundred years, this process has culminated in the overlapping of both Zunis' and anthropologists' interests and has created competing claims over the use of esoteric knowledge and paraphernalia—a process that has continued with repatriation and the negotiation over the ownership of religious objects in museums.

Zunis have continually objected to the attempts made by anthropologists to sketch or duplicate religious imagery. Although Cushing, Stevenson, and others recorded the disturbances created by their attempts to secure religious information, none of them sought to elucidate the premises on which these reactions were based or to acknowledge Zunis' requests to respect their own system for the control of knowledge. This decision has molded the conflicts between scientific endeavors and Zuni religion as valued in Zuni terms. Cushing sought entrance into the Priesthood of the Bow and commended himself on overcoming all the challenges that had previously prevented him from penetrating the very core of Zuni life. Similarly, Stevenson continually fought to enter the kivas, using her status as a government anthropologist as justification. Bunzel rationalized her endeavors as the need to record this knowledge for Zunis, rather than for science. Although they used varying approaches, they all forged the view that anthropology was not just the study of a group of people but a key that could uncover religious knowledge and bring to light previously unexplored territory, even when against the expressed wishes of those being studied. In the case of Cushing and Stevenson, they believed this process of transforming Zuni knowledge into scientific knowledge would help them uncover the code to interpreting a collective human history.

Cushing and Stevenson's aim to obtain esoteric knowledge and to publish what they evaluated to be the unique elements of Zuni culture be-gan an era that glamorized Pueblo religion—an era that continues today and affects how the people of Zuni perceive the nature of the outside observer. As more and more researchers and ethnologists sought access to the esoteric realms of Zuni society, community members developed new means of exclusion to prevent outsiders from gaining access to or observing religious ceremonies (Lyon 1988). Zuni citizens became in-creasingly aware of the different accounts found in the various publica-tions and representations of Zuni history and culture. In recent years, observation of how the people of Zuni have responded to the research carried out by anthropologists has been given more prominence in eth-nographic literature (Pandey 1972; Hinsley 1990; Roscoe 1991; Ladd 1994). The highly visible presence of anthropology in Zuni has also affected how the community views itself, specifically in terms of attitudes about the control and transmission of knowledge.

In Zuni today, visitors are prohibited from taking photographs and from making sketches or tape recordings of religious ceremonies. In addition, to be able to carry a camera when visiting the Pueblo, visitors must purchase a permit that designates which areas and objects cannot be photographed. Other Pueblos have also set up this public system of control, such as Hopi, where, as Whiteley argues, they are "deeply sus-picious of *any* graphic representation of their culture, particularly ritual knowledge and practice" (1997:187). As a result, "all villages have featured signs prohibiting photography, note taking, painting, and sketching" (187). Unfortunately, as Loren Panteah (1995b) argues, visitors to Zuni have continually attempted to take photographs, regardless of the notices posted around Zuni with instructions not to photograph, draw, video, or tape-record religious ceremonies: "Over the past years, a lot of visitors came and watched our religious dances. Since our dances are so unique and colorful, it intrigued people enough to write books on Zuni about our religion and our kachinas without permission."

Anthropologists have always held a controversial position in Zuni (Pandey 1972), but more recent incidents illustrate how Zunis have sought to maintain control over the research carried out in the Pueblo. In the 1960s, Dennis Tedlock documented Zuni oral traditions, an inter-est that led to almost thirty years of work in the Pueblo. Subsequently, his wife, Barbara Tedlock, carried out research on the aesthetic struc-ture of Zuni life as expressed in prayers, art, and dance. Her publication of her personal experiences in Zuni, *The Beautiful and the Dangerous:*

The sign at the entrance of the Middle Village providing protocol for visitors, Pueblo of Zuni, 1997.

Dialogues with the Zuni Indians (1992), became one of the most controversial of the ethnographic studies of Zuni. She chose to publish much of her private exchanges in the community—in effect, sensitive personal information about the families with whom she had worked. Although the names had been changed, many Zunis commented on how it was possible to make identifications. Subsequently, the book initiated heated discussions within both the Zuni community and the American Anthropological Association. These discussions addressed the purpose and nature of anthropology and fieldwork, as well as the need for guidelines on fieldwork research. The Pueblo of Zuni now requests researchers to consult with the council when designing or publishing fieldwork projects.

Managing sensitive knowledge has also become a professional occupation in Zuni, such as through ZHHPO. In addition, anthropologists at Zuni can clearly be seen to be working for Zuni rather than on projects propelled by external interests. In the 1970s, a shift occurred in how the religious leaders and the tribal council controlled the juxtaposition of anthropological and religious interests in Zuni. With the tribe's decision to pursue the Zuni land claims cases in court, a legal identification of the history of Zuni land use resulted in highlighting the importance of particular areas for the survival of religious practices. In addition, the development of new cultural resource-management programs and the tribe's desire to protect ancestral sites led to the creation of a new forum for collaborative projects with non-Zuni researchers. These work teams of researchers and religious leaders helped form ZCRAT and resulted in the tribe's considering the implementation of guidelines that would help manage sensitive information. Apart from consulting with tribal members and the anthropologist Edmund J. Ladd, the tribe hired outside anthropologists to help prepare research for the land claims and legal cases against the U.S. government. These researchers used the knowledge they gathered to achieve goals set by the Zuni tribe instead of pursuing scientific objectives dictated by the discipline of anthropology.[20]

Following the Zuni land claims cases, Richard Hart, Cal Seciwa, and T. J. Ferguson proceeded to organize the Zuni History Conference in 1989. This conference brought together an interdisciplinary panel of researchers who had been working with religious leaders and community members to collect expert witness material for the courts. During the conference, participants presented to the community the historical, anthropological, and archaeological information that had resulted from the land claims cases. It was one of the first attempts to build a comprehensive forum for Zunis to have access to the research conducted in the Pueblo over the past century. The presentations at the conference also resulted in the publication of a free tabloid titled *Zuni History* designed specifically for members of the community. After the claims cases were decided, a second edition was published, *Zuni History: Victories in the 1990s* (Hart and Ferguson 1991).

Although in the nineteenth century the rapid industrialization and expansion of the United States fuelled anthropologists' concern about the survival of traditional societies, the methods and technology they introduced to the discipline as tools for "salvage ethnology" also intensified the problems facing Native individuals who were responsible for maintaining the preexisting systems for the transfer of knowledge. From a Zuni perspective, these new methods not only recorded their knowledge but also absorbed it and disregarded the Zunis' responsibilities as teachers. Anthropologists ignored the importance of the processes involved in maintaining oral traditions and misunderstood how the exclusive nature of the knowledge had guaranteed its survival. The opening up of esoteric knowledge to the world brought dilemmas to its performers or guardians. Community members came to distrust those individuals who had shared this knowledge and, more specifically, those who had participated in its documentation. Furthermore, the methods that researchers hoped would preserve the ceremonies also endangered the social network that maintained them. This process subsequently triggered internal debates about the value and control of the contexts in which this knowledge was maintained.

We now know that there is substantial dissonance between Anglo-American and Zuni ideas about the act of duplication. Within scientific paradigms, a replica is successful if it is accurate to the original, thus aiding science in creating a stable concrete fact. In Zuni terms, however, not only does the replica embody the knowledge, it is animated by it. Early accounts from Cushing, Stevenson, Hodge, and Bunzel underline these conflicts.

For more than a century, anthropology at Zuni forced a continually shifting relationship between Zunis and the visitors, who represented the changing science of ethnology. This history provides a unique opportunity to look at how the grand organizing paradigms played out on the ground in Zuni and how individual anthropologists participated in their assertion or dismissal. In the same way that entropy and the disintegration of data were accepted as phenomena working against the collectivity of knowledge (Richards 1993), anthropologists eventually abandoned the evolutionary frameworks because of their inability to prioritize or explain data. These universalizing theories had resulted in the collection of a plethora of objects, physical measurements, human remains, and languages—all assembled within the hierarchical ladder of social evolution. In devising a schema to compare different cultural traits and technologies, however, anthropologists largely ignored the internal coherence of each society. The sheer volume of data required new methods of organization—a shift that eventually came with Boas's regional approach that was designed to focus on individual cultures. Although this approach was not articulated as "Boasian particularism" and "cultural relativism" until much later, the dissatisfaction with the theories of social evolution elicited anthropologists to explore frameworks that allowed for the possibilities of the plurality of knowledge systems.

As Zunis became increasingly aware of the ways in which their culture had been presented to external audiences, they developed strategies to engage with and control these inscriptions. As explored in the following two chapters, the decision to develop the A:shiwi A:wan Museum and Heritage Center provided community members with an opportunity to experience Anglo-American museum concepts firsthand by exploring the role of anthropology, collections, and reproductive technologies, such as audio and video recordings, as well as how they articulated or conflicted with Zuni cultural values.

4
Negotiating Local Values
The Origins of the Zuni Museum

The idea of establishing a museum in Zuni first surfaced in the 1960s during the tribal administration of Governor Robert Lewis. The son of Margaret Lewis, who over the years had hosted a succession of anthropologists, Lewis had grown up familiar with these visitors to Zuni, and he subsequently developed a long-term interest in the archaeological and anthropological research that focused on his own culture.[1] In 1965, his administration orchestrated the development of the Zuni Constitution as a means to assume more control over tribal government and to absorb the portion of civil affairs that were held under the BIA. As part of this scheme, between 1971 and 1974 the tribal council conducted a needs assessment survey in which high school students took questionnaires door to door around the Pueblo. Georgia Epaloose, a member of the museum board, recalled that "when we [were] going around with the survey, one of the things the [elders] noticed was that the use of the [Zuni] language was becoming very limited. . . . A lot of them were saddened. One of the questions they asked was, 'What would help preserve a lot of our traditions?' . . . . Those that did have ideas on the museum said, 'We could have something like a museum, so that when you kids go out and get educated and come back, you would be able to re-learn a lot of the Zuni.' "[2]

The concept of a museum also became closely linked with the council's reorganization of civil affairs and programs for economic development. The introduction of a museum was seen as an opportunity to address the way in which Zuni material culture—both archaeological sites and artifacts—had been curated or controlled by outsiders and how the priorities of research had not benefited the Zuni community, either culturally or financially.

As noted in chapter 1, these years of political change in Zuni are also closely linked to the Lyndon Johnson years in Washington, which generated the plan to build the Great Society (Ferguson, Hart, and Seciwa 1988). According to Califano, "what Lyndon Johnson was about during his presidency was social and economic revolution, nothing less" (Califano 1991:209). Within the new policies of the Lyndon administration, agencies such as the Office of Economic Opportunity and the Community Action Program (CAP) revolutionized tribal government, leading the way for self-determination. In particular, CAP was designed to develop community initiatives that would "reform institutions by empowering the poor" (Matusow 1984:245). Pueblo anthropologist Alfonso Ortiz notes that CAP allowed Native Americans to sidestep the BIA for the first time and apply directly to Washington for funds (Ortiz 1986:220). In his review of federal Indian policy, Castile argues that although CAP did not reduce the poor economic conditions on the reservations, they did in fact allow for the development of the structures of self-administration (Castile 1998:33).

Because federal funds were also available for archaeological research in the 1970s, Zunis began to see this type of research as a source of economic development. Governor Lewis not only encouraged and endorsed archaeological research in Zuni but also sought to develop it as a Zuni endeavor. In the late 1960s, the BIA had funded the excavation of a series of sites uncovered by road works in Zuni, contracting with outside institutions to carry out the excavations. In 1974, in order to assume control of excavation funds, the Lewis administration developed the Zuni Conservation Team, which by 1978 had become so successful that the governor and tribal council established the Zuni Archaeology Program (ZAP) (Anyon and Ferguson 1995).[3] The museum was viewed as a potential complementary adjunct to the archaeological program that would also provide professional training for Zunis to interpret and protect their own cultural resources and encourage economic development. A year after the resolution supporting the archaeology program was passed, another resolution confirmed and formally recorded the council's commitment to assuming responsibility for the welfare of the tribe through programs that would address the maintenance of the cultural and natural resources of Zuni.[4]

A new council led by governor Edison Laselute continued to pursue the course set for the museum by the Lewis administration. On November 9, 1976, Laselute wrote to Susan Wagner of the National Endowment for the Arts in Washington, D.C., in the hope of locating funds that would help further the development plans. In his letter, Laselute explained that the particularly rich history of the occupation of the Zuni territories was revealed by the archaeological research: "investigations on the reservation have delineated a cultural continuum of almost 8,000 years. The modern Zuni has a direct link to this past and information regarding this heritage should be accessible to him." The governor also explained that a museum and educational program were an appropriate way to protect these archaeological sites: "Throughout the years these sites have been disturbed or destroyed through illicit digging or development projects . . . sites have been excavated by established scientific institutions, yet the artifacts recovered by excavation are [not] easily accessible to the Zuni people. . . . A museum could provide indirect results regarding preservation and protection of sites through educational displays designed to teach people why sites are important and should be protected."[5]

Laselute also confirmed the tribe's commitment to help encourage economic growth in Zuni: "[A]lso important to the Zuni people is the economic benefit a museum would bring to the community . . . undoubtedly, a museum will enhance the pueblo's attraction to tourists."[6] This aspect of the museum was also pushed by the National Park Service and the BIA, who considered that tourism should be a strong factor in defining the museum. The BIA area director wrote a letter to the governor of Zuni endorsing the plan for a museum and advocating that its development be combined with a submitted National Park Service proposal for an archaeological park at Zuni.[7] Within this particular scenario, the museum would also operate as a visitor center, providing tourists with a more intimate, "authentic," and "in situ" view of Zuni culture than that presented by non-Zunis. In his letter to the governor, the BIA area director stated that "such a facility will certainly be an asset to Zuni Pueblo and the American Public as well. . . . [T]he museum being operated as an enterprise of the Pueblo will also present an opportunity for the Zuni people to explain their past and present culture to the American public at large and to Zuni youth."[8]

The potential economic benefits of establishing a museum were not lost on the members of a community whose income relied heavily on the sale of jewelry. From survey reports in November 1979, "out of 462 responses, 362 were in favor of a tribal museum, 76 opposed and 24 had no comment or were not interested."[9] Arlen Quetwaki, who presented the results of the survey, pointed out that "the majority who were opposed were concerned that the tribe could not afford a museum," although the "positive responses indicate the community wants the museum to be an educational institution for Zuni people, and many people also desire a museum because it would be good for the economy, including jewelry production and tourism."[10]

In 1979, the tribal council, with the help of zap, sought and received a grant from the National Endowment for the Arts to develop the Museum Study Committee, made up of community members who were to assist the consultants, Mimbres & Associates, and the council in carrying out a feasibility study for the museum.[11] In discussing its purpose, the committee argued that although "displays or exhibits developed for tribal members would also be of inherent interest to non-Zunis," the committee agreed in 1979 that "the role of the museum as a Visitor Center should always be secondary to the role of the museum as an educational institution for the Zuni people."[12] The committee's main concern following its creation was to develop a museum sensitive to Zuni ways of interpreting culture and history. In this manner, it shifted the focus away from founding a research museum that would attract non-Zuni visitors, as envisioned by the council, and toward developing a center with local concerns: "The Tribal Museum should be developed by the tribe *to serve the needs of the Zuni people*, and . . . the museum should be geared toward what would benefit the Zuni people the most. Its basic and primary orientation should be 'By Zuni, For Zunis,' with Zuni tribal members being the primary target group for the delivery of museum programs and services," the committee argued in one meeting.[13] This move shifted the control of the museum away from the tribal council's economic agendas that had been fueled by the desire to protect and conserve Zuni heritage and turned it toward the Museum Study Committee's interests in reviving Zuni cultural practices. It was an ideological shift away from archaeology and preserving the past and toward cultural performances and the contemporary political frameworks of identity.

The Museum Study Committee was also concerned about the decrease in the amount of information being handed down to the younger generations, so that the dominant theme of its deliberations became the need to target Zunis who were not receiving knowledge about their culture. In his letter to the National Endowment for the Arts, Governor Laselute pointed out the need for providing educational programs for the youth: "We have come to the realization that, in spite of all the diverse educational facilities, we are not serving our younger generation adequately and purposefully in the area of tribal cultural awareness."[14] This concern continued to surface in the research carried out in the museum development plans. A second feasibility study carried out by Mimbres &

Associates in 1980 argued the need to find appropriate ways of maintaining Zuni culture because "there is apprehension among Zunis that consciousness of traditional culture on the part of the young people is fading, partly because there is little local control over the school curriculum and partly because so much of the visible Zuni culture from past times has been collected by people remote from the pueblo."[15] The committee subsequently focused on designing a museum that would educate the younger generations of Zunis and would follow the appropriate protocol for the treatment of Zuni knowledge and material culture.

Concurrent with the development of the Zuni museum, the council and Bow Priests were successfully campaigning for the return of the Ahayu:da, War Gods, which had been held as part of museum collections around the United States (Merrill, Ladd, and Ferguson 1993; Ferguson, Anyon, and Ladd 2000). In addition, institutions that had large collections of Zuni material culture had also taken an interest in the development of a museum in Zuni: "private collectors and institutions such as the Smithsonian have declared they will loan or return valuable artifacts to the tribe if the Zunis establish a proper facility for the care and maintenance of such precious items."[16] With the repatriation process in mind, the Study Committee made it clear to external agencies and museums that many of these objects were not suitable for exhibition in Zuni. It became apparent that individuals who were developing the museum would also need to negotiate carefully with religious leaders and community members over what were appropriate objects for display. The Museum Study Committee determined that "the care and maintenance of religious and sacred objects was [sic] the responsibility of the religious leaders" and that artifacts the tribe recently recovered were returned not for the museums, but to use in the religious system. "[S]uch artifacts do not belong in any museum, especially a tribal museum at Zuni." Committee members also felt that a protocol was necessary to determine what type of knowledge could be made accessible to the Zuni public and agreed that "the museum exhibits and educational materials should be screened to make sure that only appropriate objects and ideas were interpreted, and that the museum did not violate any cultural beliefs."[17]

The tribal council was also concerned with the issue of non-Zunis' gaining access to esoteric information through the museum. In 1979, the tribe contacted the Colorado Council of the Arts in order to gain advice on dealing with the esoteric or sensitive areas of Zuni knowledge within the context of a museum. The Council of the Arts report recommended that an area should not be set aside for viewing by Zunis only, but that "the museum should be open to everyone, including non-Zunis."[18] There is a hint that the council may have been considering the inclusion of such a space in the Zuni museum. The external consultant's understanding of the purpose of a museum in Zuni was clearly more closely aligned with Anglo-American aesthetics and expectations about the function of museums, as shown by the suggestion to the Zuni council that "[t]he concern for privacy, for example of religious objects, has been dealt with before in different places and museums. These museums have found that if these types of objects were put on display without telling the people their purpose, very little was lost as far as secrecy is concerned. It should be noted that you are not obligated to tell the visitors what the exhibits mean."[19]

It appears that a number of external consultants wanted religious aspects of Zuni culture to remain an integral part of the museum, a preference that can be attributed to the interest that non-Zunis and tourists have continually held for the religious and ceremonial facets of Zuni culture. Beyond the wish to have displays about the religion, non-Zuni planners also apparently expected that Zunis should draw from the religion in determining the nature of the museum. Mimbres & Associates addressed in their 1980 feasibility paper what they perceived to be the strength of Zuni identity—Zuni religion—and therefore what should be part of the museum:

> A museum becomes a tool for community identity, a "consciousness raising" institution. Visual materials should connect to outside community events and help provide the understanding by which the past illuminates the present and future. At Zuni, this linkage is maintained by other institutions as well, particularly through religious ceremonials, so that a museum, rather than being inspired by outside or "Anglo" ideas, should find its verification for collections and displays, and for its design and theme from existing community cultural forms.[20]

Museum staff members would have to negotiate within the community about what it believed to be appropriate for the museum, as well as between Zunis and non-Zunis regarding how much knowledge should be accessible to non-Zunis. The museum's role as a space that would privilege the process of mediation was also an expectation echoed by consultants Castillo & Associates, who helped set up the museum according to the planning team's requests: "development is to follow an innovative concept of utilizing the museum as a focal point of a broader 'cultural center' of the Zuni people. The museum will be designed and programmed to provide a unique forum of both cultural awareness to non-Zunis of the region and transmission of tribal heritage from one generation of Zuni to the next."[21]

During much of the 1970s, the tribal council and the BIA concentrated on the development of economic projects linked to tourism, but by the late 1980s community members voiced their concern regarding council decisions to give tourists access to sacred sites. In 1989, the community requested a referendum on the tribe's involvement with the proposed Zuni-Cibola National Historical Park to be developed on reservation lands. By eventually rejecting this proposal, community members clearly voiced their concern over the use of ancestral sites as tourist attractions and over the development of a museum that, according to the park plans, would have also served as a visitor center for tourists. This referendum marked a significant shift in the way tourism was handled within the tribe and subsequently in the direction that the museum would take. From 1989 on, the new policies regarding tourism reflected the community's desire to restrict visitors to the Pueblo rather than to encourage the growth of tourism. Many of the early planning meetings for the park had not sought to incorporate religious leaders' views, so when it became known that the park would give tourists access to four ancestral sites—one of which was an active shrine—a number of religious leaders joined forces to prevent the park from being developed.[22] Former ZAP director Roger Anyon told me in 2000, "The issue of the park galvanized the religious leaders and actually set the events into motion that led to their greater visibility in Zuni political affairs."[23] The decision to entrust religious leaders with the role of paid consultants for the tribe shows the dramatic shift in ideology wherein priests were presented as both prominent and legitimate cultural leaders to the outside world. In addition, the overlap between secular government and religious leadership in Zuni was justified within the national political arena.

The Museum Study Committee then requested funds that were left over from the Cibola planning grant. In a 1997 interview, a Zuni museum board member declared that although the community had defeated the whole issue of the National Park Service coming to the reservation,

[a] large portion of the community realized that we need to . . . preserve the ruins out there, not necessarily [through] tourism, but just preserve them. At the same time they realized that we will need to have a mechanism or institution in the community that would educate or be a repository for all those things that are not religious or sacred. The main thing behind collecting and archiving all this information . . . is to let the kids know what their traditions are . . . also [to] perpetuate the language.[24]

Subsequently, the planning for a museum continued to move ever farther away from ideas about archaeology and the curation of objects and instead evolved toward an institution that would give ascendancy to Zuni values, thus encouraging the education of younger generations in a culturally appropriate manner.

An important turning point came in 1982 when the Zuni Cultural Resources Enterprise and the Zuni tribal council received an Administration for Native Americans grant to train board members and staff for the proposed museum. At this juncture, the Museum Study Committee, the newly appointed board, and staff became known as the Zuni Museum Project. During this phase, a series of exhibits was developed to keep programming going as the tribe moved closer to establishing the final concept for a museum. Prior to the Administration for Native Americans grant, the Museum Study Committee had supported researcher Jane Young in designing a rock art exhibit at the Zuni Tribal Fair. From 1983 to 1990, Margaret Hardin, from the Los Angeles County Museum, in association with the Pueblo of Zuni and the Heard Museum, curated an exhibit on Zuni pottery—The Gift of Mother Earth: Ceramics in the Zuni Tradition. Rose Wyaco, who later became the first Zuni director of the museum, also mounted two exhibits titled Zuni Farming Villages and Zuni Pueblo: Then and Now.[25]

Another pivotal point in the history of the museum came with the decision to establish it as an independent institution that would operate separately from tribal government. In an interview in 1997, former director Nigel Holman presented his perspective on why the museum eventually chose to pursue independence from the tribal government: "the idea is that the museum needed to be independent of the tribal council in order to be part of the community, so it wouldn't be at the mercy of the tribal council, and that all of the community could feel that it was their museum, rather than it being the ruling group or the tribal council's museum."[26] A committed and long-term exploration began as to what kind of independent institution might also be sustainable in a small community such as Zuni.

Redefining the Museum: The Zuni Ecomuseum

The different visions for the museum can be used to highlight both the diversity of the perspectives in Zuni and the complexity of the relationships that developed with non-Zuni external parties. These ideas were so disparate that in an undated and unsigned museum feasibility report, it was stated that "when either Zuni planners or the Consultant use the word 'museum,' there is no agreed-upon concept of the institution that is to be developed."[27]

Zunis also began to question the museum concept itself and its relevance to Zuni culture. Negative and more rigid readings of museums surfaced from community members who had previously been excluded from these institutions or who viewed them as products of markedly different Anglo-American cultural practices. Opinions were aired that depicted museums as "elitist institutions" that were "generally started by wealthy individuals who had amassed collections of art, cultural artifacts or objects of everyday life, or natural history or botanical specimens."[28] From a Zuni perspective, the conventional or "traditional" Western museum collected objects as a way to preserve culture and thus was grounded in the past meanings of these objects rather than in how they related to current practices or their use today.

Another criticism was that in the care or organization of objects, conventional museums did not distinguish between sacred objects that people rarely came into contact with and those objects that were a part of everyday Zuni life. During the long-term collaboration with the Smithsonian Institution that was by and large initiated through the process of repatriating the Ahayu:da in the early 1990s, religious leaders from the Deer and Bear clans in Zuni worked alongside Smithsonian curators to discuss the nature of the collections. The religious leaders exposed the Smithsonian staff to Zuni philosophy relating to the objects' original contexts and care. Although the case for repatriating the Ahayu:da was centered around issues of cultural patrimony, the Smithsonian staff also initiated various publications that examined the differences in Zuni and Anglo-American approaches to material culture (Merrill, Ladd, and Ferguson 1993). The Smithsonian anthropologists and curators, William

Merrill and Richard Ahlborn, also explored the history of the representation of Zuni religious objects within the Smithsonian and some of the perspectives Zuni visitors shared about the collections, and they argued that "Indian people who visit museum collections frequently are shocked by the techniques that museums routinely employ to preserve items that are of great religious significance for them" (Merrill and Ahlborn 1997:176). In addition to being concerned about the techniques used to preserve objects, such as fumigation, Zuni visitors were "dismayed to discover that religious objects are stored among more mundane materials and that anyone accessing the collections has access to such sensitive objects, which in their own societies are available to only one or a few individuals" (Merrill and Ahlborn 1997:176).

As described in the previous chapter, there is also a history of Zunis' discontent with the manner in which Anglo-Americans portrayed and interfered with their religion. Finding visible evidence within the nation's capitol of these misconceptions about Zuni culture triggered an immediate and formal response from the tribal council and religious leaders about the appropriate treatment of religious paraphernalia. These sentiments formed the basis of discussions about the direction of the Zuni museum and the need to address the correct treatment of objects. In 1975, the tribal council had hired architects from Castillo & Associates of Albuquerque, New Mexico, to draw up a series of plans for the museum. The finished drawings included an auditorium designed to replicate a kiva, or ceremonial house, and a display of kokko, or kachina, masks, which were arranged in glass cases that were intended to line the surrounding walls. These masks, however, have always been housed by families in the Pueblo or by religious societies who are assigned as guardians or caretakers. From a Zuni perspective, the masks are not representations; they are animate and vital embodiments of the kokkos, and their care is the distinct responsibility of chosen individuals. In addition, the masks are seen by other community members only during the ceremonies in which they are worn. In the 1997 interview, former museum director Nigel Holman used these architectural plans as an example of how external consultants, when relying on ideas stemming from Anglo-American museums, misrepresented Zuni values: "The classic renditions were ones [where] you could see all these masks in cases. These were done in the early 70s. . . . I always used it as an example of what we weren't going to be, because we would never have masks in cases. . . . There were modified versions of those drawings that were clearly the tribe saying 'this isn't going to work.' The consultants and their artists clearly didn't understand it."[29]

The Museum Study Committee became concerned about the future role of collections in the museum and how the community would respond to the display of objects of a religious nature. The Anglo-American model for museums fails to reflect Zuni values by giving priority to practices aimed at preserving objects and by adhering to access policies that do not reflect Zuni religious hierarchy or an individual's responsibilities for the care of objects. In a 1997 interview about the origins of the museum, Malcolm Bowekaty recalled his visits to other museums in the Southwest region, many of which he felt were inappropriate models for the Zuni museum: "[This museum is] not going to be a museum in the sense of the Northern Arizona Museum, where you have a lot of artifacts. It is not going to be the same as Mesa Verde where, in the past, they have displayed a lot of human remains."[30] Museum staff member Vernon Quam also identified what he felt was the community's reaction to the Anglo-American idea of a museum: "I think when the word *museum* comes up, it scares people because they think a museum is just a place where you see objects or a place where it is dead—there is nothing but objects in a quiet room."[31]

Similar discussions had taken place within the Ak-Chin tribe in Arizona, where the discovery of archaeological sites had also triggered an emotive discussion within the community about the need to preserve and educate the younger generations about their heritage. The Ak-Chin also objected to the conventions of Western museums as storehouses of objects divorced from everyday life, and they too looked to alternative museum models that could help resolve some of the conflicts that had risen between the two cultural systems. With the guidance of Nancy Fuller from the Smithsonian Institution, the Ak-Chin Him-Dak Eco-Museum was established as the first tribally operated ecomuseum. Fuller had argued that the ecomuseum concept was suitable to Ak-Chin because it was concerned with "integrating the family home with other aspects of the community, such as the natural environment, economics, and social relationships" (1992:328).

The concept of the ecomuseum was pioneered by the French museum professional George-Henri Rivière in the 1980s. Rivière (1985) believed that museums should approach culture from a holistic perspective, which included the ongoing practice of tradition and not just the interpretation of the objects that manifest these traditions. As director of the

International Council of Museums from 1948 to 1965, he was influential in establishing the UNESCO cultural heritage program and for forging international links between museums. His inspiration for the ecomuseum also highlighted his desire to link small communities with museum professionals, to encourage the exchange of specialized knowledge, and to provide local experts with authority at the international level. Rivière argued that the museum should be a forum for self-exploration: "It is a mirror in which the local population views itself to discover its own image, in which it seeks an explanation of the territory to which it is attached. . . . It is a mirror that the local population holds up to its visitors so that it may be better understood and so that its industry, customs and identity may command respect" (1985:182).

In a comparative critique of conventional museums and ecomuseums in France, Poulot suggests that ecomuseums are a part of a movement toward institutions designed to develop self-awareness among community members. Their adoption in France has meant that "the ecomuseum has indeed participated in reshaping the social uses of 'heritage' in French society" (1994:77). In his definition of the ecomuseum, the focus is on current practices rather than on the interpretation of the cultural products or material culture of a society, and he suggests that "the aim . . . is to make society aware of the wealth of resources it unknowingly possesses; the old task of salvaging and recording has been replaced by the business of discovering and interpreting culture" (77).

Undoubtedly, ecomuseums are political vehicles. They have tended to represent community and rural concerns and the advocacy of local rights over national interests at a time in which many of these communities have lost control of their local environments. Peter Davis points out that the prefix *eco-*, derived from the Greek *oikos*—a house, living space, or habitat—has strong political origins in the environmentalism movement of the 1970s and 1980s (1999:7). With this environmentalist viewpoint, those who developed the first ecomuseums advocated a holistic view of the landscape as opposed to the limited traditional Western definition of land based in notions of property or nationalist governmental control, such as with national parks. For communities that do not operate according to the latter values, the ecomuseum provides an organization that can foster their local view of the landscape. Davis argues that "a new philosophy is needed that leads to the empowerment of local communities, providing them not only with a mechanism for rescuing an artifact, a habitat or a way of life from loss or destruction but also a means of expressing a deep conviction to preserve and deepen a sense of place" (1999:21). These concepts have become part of the evolution of the movement to protect the environment, preserve cultural ways of life, and provide programs for cultural revitalization. In this way, from the Western viewpoint, ecomuseums can be equated with the movement that venerates the past and seeks to counterbalance the changes brought about by industry and a corporate agenda. Zunis perceived the ecomuseum from a different perspective, however, seeing it as a concept that would allow them to leave Western agendas altogether. Interestingly, this collaboration between Zunis and ecomuseum advocates might be viewed as one in which Anglo-Americans encouraged Zunis to separate themselves from Western ideals and practices.

In 1989, Fuller led a delegation of members of the Ak-Chin tribe of Arizona to Zuni as part of a tour sponsored by the Smithsonian Institution. The Ak-Chin representatives met with the group that was part of the Zuni Museum Project and discussed their own decision to develop an ecomuseum at Ak-Chin, a "community-controlled and community-based museum."[32] During their visit, they provided Zuni museum board and staff members with literature about ecomuseums, including the excerpts from Rivière given here.

The idea of a museum as an institution that would allow for the exploration of one's own culture appealed to the museum board. Following the visit of the Ak-Chin delegates, the board decided to draw from the ecomuseum approach because it allowed them to find ways of integrating traditions from preexisting spheres of knowledge with the current issues facing the younger generations. It was also a model that gave emphasis to everyday practices in a way that would not have been possible within a conventional museum. It would allow them to mirror specific Zuni values and to maintain the cultural context of knowledge. According to Anyon, one of the most appealing aspects about ecomuseums is the concept of continuity: "they do not deal only with the past. . . . [T]he ecomuseum makes the links between the past, the present, and the future, and shows a community in evolution."[33] Board member Georgia Epaloose stated in 1997 that, to her, an ecomuseum represented "more than artifacts, . . . [we are] using the then to understand the now . . . rather than using the past to see how we were."[34] Regarding the relationship between the museum and the community, board president Malcolm Bowekaty explained to me that an ecomuseum "is part and parcel of the community. . . . [I]t is a very dynamic living thing, as opposed to a static thing . . . a repository for artifacts or a lot of material . . . from the culture that you are trying to preserve."[35]

On learning about the ecomuseum concept and deciding to apply it within Zuni, the board referred to this model as a "significant breakthrough," hoping it would bridge the gap between Anglo-American museum practices and those desired by the Zuni community. It would provide a forum devoted to exploring Zuni history and culture as an ongoing process, with an emphasis on the interpretation of culturally or geographically specific practices and their relevance to the present. As Anyon wrote in 1993,

> While conventional museums are a concept alien to Zuni culture, it was recognized that the ecomuseum approach was compatible with many traditional Zuni ideas. For instance, ecomuseums take a holistic view of society, emphasizing the relationships between the community and the land, the Past and the Present, and the Present and the Future. Ecomuseums are community directed. They exist to promote cultural preservation activities throughout the community (in homes, schools, and the workplace) rather than to corral them into the confines of a specific museum location.[36]

Because the ecomuseum model gave the board members the freedom to explore Zuni values, they also used it to push ideas about the informal nature that they hoped their institution would adopt. This definition of the term *ecomuseum* is clear in the architectural program for the museum drafted by University of New Mexico architects Cherry and See, wherein the museum "is to be an 'ecomuseum,' a museum without walls. . . . The notion of a museum without walls is intended to indicate that many of the exhibits and teaching activities will be happening in the community itself."[37]

The attraction of ecomuseum practices also came from the concept's promotion of the use of community members as the central resource, rather than a focus on collections and the display of material culture. This approach allowed flexibility in developing programs that would draw on local expertise instead of outside support from researchers. In criticism of the Anglo-American ideas of museums, the museum board was concerned that a reliance on archaeological artifacts would locate the display of Zuni culture in a Western format, thereby concentrating only on the past structure of Zuni life. In the choice to identify with this specific aspect of an ecomuseum, the Zuni museum created a value out of not having collections. In the early 1990s, the museum produced a brochure to educate both the community and outside investors about its unique nature, stating that it was "neither a temple, [n]or a storehouse."[38] In a 1991 article for the free newspaper *Highway 53 Express*, Holman explained what an ecomuseum in Zuni would represent to the community:

> Most people have visited museums somewhere. The likelihood is that these have been traditional museums where the main focus is on exhibits of artifacts in glass cases. You are there as a guest—often a paying guest—and you have little opportunity to talk to the curators and to tell them of your feelings toward the museum and the work it does. Ecomuseums are different. The main focus in an ecomuseum is PEOPLE: the visitors, the people whose lives are portrayed in the exhibits, and the people whose job it is to manage the museum. Visitors come to the museum as PARTICIPANTS in the main goal of the museum—that is to preserve the culture of the people of Zuni for the people of Zuni themselves.[39]

The issue of collecting material culture also required careful negotiation. Although the idea of a museum had in large part grown out of the tribe's involvement in developing its own archaeological program, collecting artifacts was a cause for concern. There were, of course, practical considerations, such as the high cost of curating collections. The original intent of a museum had been for safekeeping of artifacts, but, as we have seen, the Museum Study Committee shifted away from this agenda by the early 1980s and started to discuss other options. The committee subsequently was forced to leave collections in the care of national institutions: "the tribe cannot afford a large storage capacity in the museum. The cost of curation is very expensive, and there was general agreement that the museum should try to minimize its collections. Other museums holding large Zuni collections should be encouraged to continue to care for and maintain these collections." The Museum Study Committee had extremely pragmatic concerns about the cost of curating collections. At the time, it was much easier to get funds to erect a building than to pay for staff and operating expenses. The committee wanted to make sure that the tribe would not end up with a museum building and no means to pay for community programs and operations.[40] With the help of Zuni tribal member Edmund Ladd, who was an ethnologist at the Laboratory of Anthropology in Santa Fe, the Museum Committee requested and received permission to acknowledge the Zunis as owners of the objects and the laboratory as temporary caretakers. In the event that the Zuni museum mounted exhibits, these objects could be brought to Zuni for display. In addition, it was decided that permanent displays such as those found in large museums were not appropriate for a local museum because community members who frequently visited the museum would lose interest if the displays did not change.

The decision to move away from the collection of material culture is one of the outstanding aspects of the museum in Zuni because its original function had been to preserve Zuni artifacts by Zunis for Zunis. It is possible to consider, however, that the politics of the ownership of historic objects from sacred sites, where questions might arise regarding the proper authority for care, would delay or deter the museum from actively seeking collections. Many Zunis also saw museums as graveyards focused on the detritus of the dead rather than on the concerns of the living. Nonetheless, the Zuni museum is not alone in the decision not to have collections. A number of indigenous museums, often referring to themselves as cultural centers, have chosen not to focus on objects. This shift begs for further comparative research on the role of material culture in perceptions of the preservation and communication of history, and these new institutions will most likely reveal a diversity of methods, whether visual or aural, for the transmission and maintenance of history.

Thus, the emphasis in Zuni shifted away from the curatorial interpretation of material culture and was instead placed on the people who owned or were responsible for local knowledge. This aspect of the eco-museum model directly related to the Zuni people's desire for the museum to mirror the long-established and time-honored oral traditions responsible for most of the transmission of knowledge in Zuni. Tom Kennedy, the director of the A:shiwi A:wan Museum from 1995 to 2003, proposed that community members, who took care of objects through their religious responsibility and rights of inheritance, could be viewed as the official curators: "everyone in this community is a curator and maintains their portion of the community's treasure. Many of these were handed down from their forefathers and some of them are things that are just now developing the cultural value that they have."[41] The crucial factor in this shift in emphasis was the acknowledgment that community members responsible for the care of objects of cultural importance are also the caretakers of the knowledge about the significance and history of these materials. In the search for new ways to care for objects outside "traditional" Anglo-American ideology, the relationship between a person and an object would be viewed as the provenance of that object. According to Kennedy, the ecomuseum concept allowed for these specific requirements in the care of objects: "[By] using the concept of an ecomuseum . . . we can go to whomever in the community and ask either to borrow the objects and the stories that come along with it, to share with the rest of the community, or to tap into their knowledge base that they have in their head. At the end of the time, if they so desire, the objects go back to them."[42] Similarly, a Zuni museum board member suggested to me that the museum should assume a portion of the responsibility for maintaining this information, thereby drawing an analogy between personal memories held by individuals and collective memories held by an institution:

> The museum takes a similar role because we are going to be a repository for a lot of information. I think there will come a point in time when we will need to do a lot of what we are doing here—the taped information. In some future time, the value of that will be recognized. We won't have all those people that are very knowledgeable. They are going to be long gone. So there's going to be a lot more people . . . saying we need this type of information. Then there will be the next phase where those people who are initiated can listen to this, or if people are very sincerely interested in this, we'll do some sort of presentation.[43]

Although a museum of any form was still a foreign concept among the Zunis in the 1980s (and perhaps still is today), the board envisioned that an ecomuseum would assist them in determining what the Pueblo of Zuni wanted from a museum. Kennedy also remarked on an ecomuseum's ability to evolve with a community: "the ecomuseum asks what can we do to recombine all these variables into something that works for us—that makes us a better society in the future." He felt that with this approach, the community's response could be used to determine the design of the museum. Similarly, he thought it was a more sympathetic approach for a population that had not previously operated a museum: "the museum tries to respond to needs and tries to serve the community. . . . Museums in this community are somewhat of a new thing. I don't think, by and large, that the majority of the community really know what it is that they want in a museum because the concept is still quite foreign."[44]

If we look back at the history of the museum, we can see how both the Museum Study Committee and then subsequently the board were provided with the opportunity to examine what they felt were the issues facing the community. They considered which aspects of Zuni culture should be adopted and fostered within museum programs. This mode of self-exploration was eventually institutionalized as part of the functions of the museum itself. The exploratory forum used to determine the theoretical foundations of the museum would also benefit the Zuni youth by giving them the opportunity to look at their own culture and identity.[45] This reflective process also involved interpreting the dynamics behind particular aspects of contemporary Zuni life, which required insight into the relationship between the past and the present, as well as into the relationship between Zuni philosophy and Anglo-American culture. Other important relationships surfaced, such as the dynamics between the younger and elder generations of Zunis and the differences between the public and private spheres of knowledge. The museum thus sought to develop programs that identified and acknowledged appropriate ways of balancing the different values exhibited in these relationships.

Becoming the A:shiwi A:wan Museum and Heritage Center

The naming of any institution is a deeply political process, and the naming of the Zuni museum was no exception. In searching for a title, the phrase "the Museum of the Zuni People" was initially used. According to Holman, however, this title gave an ambiguous role to the Zuni community, who wanted to clarify whether Zunis were the subjects or owners of this organization. By 1992, the Museum Study Committee and the Zuni Museum Project had become the A:shiwi A:wan Museum and Heritage Center. The board chose "A:shiwi A:wan," meaning "Belonging to the People," to describe an institution that was specifically for Zunis. The addition of "Heritage Center" was considered crucial to foster the development of an institution that did not rely on the concept of a "museum" focused on object display, but implied a "center" that would involve the community in traditional activities. According to Anyon, the term *museum* was retained in the title because "the organization had to interface with the outside world on many levels, one of which would be fund-raising. Simply having the word *museum* in there would be a clear, meaningful signal to non-Zuni outsiders."[46] By the time I was working in

The courtyard of the A:shiwi A:wan Museum and Heritage Center, Pueblo of Zuni, 1997.

Zuni, however, the museum director, Tom Kennedy, was using the name "A:shiwi Center," and he argued that this change was necessary because the term *museum* held negative connotations within the community. The rapidly changing titles for the museum bore evidence that its position in the community would have to be carefully negotiated.

Throughout the 1980s, the Museum Study Committee and the Zuni Museum Project encouraged professional training for Zunis working for or associated with the museum. As a result, Rose Wyaco, Otto Lucio, and Joseph Dishta received training through the American Indian Outreach Program at the Smithsonian in Washington, D.C., interning at the NMNH.[47] In order to develop exhibits and to design teaching programs for the museum's opening to the public in the early 1990s, JoAllyn Archambault, director of the Outreach Program, assisted in setting up what became known as the "Zuni Catalog Project." This project was a comprehensive compilation of Zuni objects and materials housed at the Smithsonian Institution. These records were also designed to be the basis of what was simultaneously known as the Zuni Archive Project, which was also receiving records and administrative support from the Zuni Cultural Resources Enterprise with the idea of developing a tribally operated archives and records repository (Anyon and Ferguson 1995).[48]

One of the central functions of the Smithsonian section of the project was to facilitate the work of staff trainee Otto Lucio to duplicate the vast collection of photographs held at the NAA, taken by anthropologists in the nineteenth and early twentieth centuries. The majority of photographs were by the anthropologist Matilda Coxe Stevenson, but the collections also included images taken by Smithsonian photographers, such as John Hillers, who worked for the Mindeleff brothers. In addition, the NAA collection included the work of commercial photographers such as Ben Wittick and Tom Mullarky.[49] The duplicate prints totaled approximately three thousand images, which were transferred to the Zuni Museum Project in 1989 and subsequently formed the first collection of the A:shiwi A:wan Museum and Heritage Center.

In 1992, the exhibit The Pueblo of Zuni as Seen Through the Eyes of Pioneer Photographers from 1879 to 1902 was the first to be hosted by the newly named A:shiwi A:wan Museum. It consisted of a selection of these duplicate prints from the Smithsonian, revealing the visual legacy created by visitors who had documented life in the Pueblo. The brochure for the exhibit stated,

> Since the first encounter between the people of Zuni and Francisco Vasquez Coronado in 1540, we have been welcoming hosts to many visitors. We have contributed to the lives of these visitors by sharing our way of life with them. In return, many visitors have contributed to our lives. The contributions of visitors have taken many forms. Sometimes the benefits were economic in nature, and were felt immediately. The photographs in this exhibit represent a very different contribution, and one which is only now being felt—one century after the visitors responsible left our community. It is only now that these images are available for the Zuni people themselves to view and to learn from.[50]

The staff curating the exhibition—Rose Wyaco, Otto Lucio, and Nigel Holman—also pointed out in the brochure that the images shown should be seen as selected out of the "thousands of scenes which could have been recorded on any one day"; they pointed out, moreover, that visiting photographers often chose images that represented "tradition" and avoided those that revealed change.[51] The negotiation between tradition, continuity, and change became the main theme around which new exhibitions were centered.

What I find fascinating about this exhibit is not so much that community members formed new relationships with their past through the photographs, but that as religious leaders became aware of photographs depicting esoteric subjects, they were able to communicate their concerns regarding the display of such photographs and, through negotiations with the museum, gain a higher degree of control over the use of these images. This process challenged me to question how new visual material, such as photographs, was being absorbed into the Zuni system for the control of knowledge. The issues over control created a marked controversy with the Smithsonian advisors, who had intended all the photographs to be available to the Zuni public. The religious leaders conveyed their apprehension that many of the images showed esoteric practices of the religious societies and therefore should not be available to uninitiated Zunis and especially to non-Zunis. The Zuni museum chose to take an active role in helping the religious leaders determine the nature of the photographs. Between 1992 and 1996, Holman, with assistance from the Lila Wallace Reader's Digest Fund, developed a program in which ZCRAT members screened these images and separated out those photographs that contained sensitive information. As mentioned previously in chapter 2, these images were then transferred to the ZHHPO. Thereafter, only initiated members of the religious societies were given access to the photographs. This action was not aimed at outsiders but was directed toward controlling information available to community members. Although the museum staff did not broadcast these curatorial decisions to the community, they eventually intimated that religious leaders influenced the level of knowledge that can be available within Zuni and in what context it is transferred.

Although in the 1990s the advisors from the Smithsonian expressed concern over differential access policies for the viewing of photographs at the A:shiwi A:wan Museum, these policies came into play at a national level with the opening of the National Museum of the American

Indian in Washington, D.C., illustrating that the religious leaders of Zuni played a part in breaking new ground for similar groups that eventually demanded recognition of their specific knowledge systems and social hierarchies.[52]

A subsequent exhibition, Then and Now (1993), resulted from a collaboration between the museum technician, Otto Lucio, and the photographers of the California-based Batista Moon Studio. The exhibit displayed current images of the Pueblo alongside the historic images from the Smithsonian. Creating a new visual document of the Pueblo, however, required a particular protocol. In correspondence with the newly formed ZCRAT, Otto Lucio assured the religious leaders that this project would be respectful of the customs that surrounded the treatment of religious subjects: "This 'future photographic exhibit' is not interested in photographing any religious shrines, activities, or dances. . . . I am not interested in photographing any activities that relate to our native religion. I know the concerns, the safeguards, and the consequences. Therefore, I have made it clear to Batista Moon Studio that no photographs will be taken during times of religious practice and meditation."[53]

The Zuni museum trajectory thus far reveals its tendency toward exclusivity in order to meet the Zuni community's needs. First, there was the shift away from catering for tourists, then the move away from the care of objects, and, finally, the establishment of differential access policies that distinguished between initiated and uninitiated members of the religious societies. The projects that engaged the religious leaders in discussions over the use of photographs were the first program initiatives to highlight the need to mediate the type and level of knowledge provided both to non-Zunis and to the Zuni community. Underlying these decisions to establish the museum, as one that would follow Zuni cultural ways, was also an exploration of Zuni culture and the challenges the community faced from changes taking place in the Pueblo. As explored in the next chapter, the social hierarchy in Zuni that prescribes access to privileged knowledge has caused tensions within a community now demographically dominated by the younger generations. Individuals must mediate between the traditional means of accessing knowledge associated with exclusionary rights and the changes to the Pueblo that have forced younger, externally educated generations to explore their identity and their role in facilitating the transmission of knowledge to future generations.

5
Finding the Middle Ground
The Museum as Mediator

The conversations I had with people at the A:shiwi A:wan Museum frequently began with heartfelt concern about the difficulties facing the younger generations in the Pueblo. A picture was presented to me in which young Zunis are continually besieged by the Anglo-American cultural values that prescribe particular ways of life as "successful," such as practicing law and doing business. These messages are eroding the Zuni cultural values that conventionally give money and external hierarchies a less essential and indeterminate role in Zuni. If Anglo-Americans believe that they hold the means for the correct way to structure one's life, Zuni culture is automatically positioned in a negative light. At a young age, Zunis are thrust into a world in which the externally imposed critique of their culture is unavoidable. Museum board member Georgia Epaloose argued that these competing messages from Anglo-American society are extremely detrimental to the self-esteem of the younger generation: "Too many things are coming in [and] influencing our young adults. [They] are constantly telling them: 'What you have is not good enough. You must get Nikes because that's the best on the market.' . . . Or, 'to be successful you have to become a corporate lawyer, be a CEO.' They're being bombarded with that kind of message. Some very up front, some very subliminal."[1]

One of the most important defining factors about the museum is that its character was influenced largely by college- or externally educated Zunis, all of whom chose to join with other like-minded individuals to build an institution that would explore the contemporary issues facing the younger generations. Many Zunis who became staff and board members had left the Zuni reservation for educational or professional pursuits and experienced a level of sensitivity about their culture that motivated them to view their identity through both internal and external lenses. Zunis define themselves primarily according to their family and clan affiliations, and secondarily through their accumulated and continuously changing religious responsibilities, but many have also accumulated experiences outside of the Pueblo that bring into sharp relief cultural differences between Zuni and Anglo-American ways of life.

This chapter explores how during the 1990s the museum staff and board members shaped the museum in order to meet the challenges presented to the community by changing social conditions. Many Zunis were extremely concerned about future opportunities for their children, both within their own culture and in Anglo-American society. Our starting point is recognizing the predicaments linked to defining Zuni identity as articulated by those working in the museum. In questioning the locus of empowerment within the community, I asked, Who in particular highlighted these dilemmas, and how did they undertake the challenges associated with the exploration of Zuni identity? The museum staff's critique of Zunis' identity, impelled by growing fears of an increasing gap between elder and younger generations, led to open discussions of the complexities involved in institutionalizing traditional knowledge and in reconciling internal and external views on Zuni culture.

As noted, many of the museum founders had spent time away from Zuni, and they returned home with a passionate belief in the importance of comprehending and appreciating their culture. Georgia Epaloose asked, "What is it that makes us unique? What is it that makes us Zuni?"[2] This mode of self-exploration was seen as a critical perspective that would help the younger generations understand their world and, of especial importance, reach a deeper awareness of the historical processes embodied by Zuni religion and culture. Malcolm Bowekaty commented, "I think a lot of times people go back to the traditions and the religion and the reasons why we practice what we practice. Once kids realize there are some things to be very proud of, that will enable kids to really look at it in a very strategic and intelligent fashion, and they can decide whether they want to be in a vein where a lot of negative things are incorporated, or whether they want to take a pro-active stance and say Zuni needs to be preserved."[3] Bowekaty and Epaloose conjectured that if they could assist the younger generation in thinking critically about these cultural choices, the youths might make informed decisions and choose Zuni philosophy rather than Anglo-American conceptualizations of the world. According to Bowekaty,

> I think they also need to realize that a lot of negative things we inherit or adapt from the larger culture are very useful because it allows us to make judgments. It allows us to realize if we are making criticisms

against the negative things that we have inherited from the dominant society—there are responsibilities attached to that. If we realize that, then we have to start making changes within ourselves or within our own families or with the community—saying, "These are negative things, how do we correct that?"[4]

Poulot suggests in his comparative analysis of the theoretical concerns of ecomuseums that these local institutions rely on the process of drawing out the cultural wisdom that everyone possesses but too rarely is aware of, so that they become vehicles for self-discovery (1994). The ecomuseum concept therefore interested the Zuni museum founders as a forum for self-discovery and the investigation of the dynamics of Zuni identity. Epaloose suggested to me that the museum should be an institution "that we can use to structure and understand who we are [and to identify] the perception of how we see things and how we do things. . . . We are here as a vehicle to help you understand yourself, where you come from and where you're going."[5] Board members also argued that the museum could help mitigate external influences within the Pueblo and "help Zunis identify what is important for us to look at . . . and . . . really reaffirm that it is okay to be who we are."[6] The museum, Epaloose commented, would play a dynamic role in substantiating Zuni values: "The museum needs to start having activities more frequently to constantly reaffirm, and have the community, and have the youth realize that it is okay who we are—and help our young people to see that there's a choice there and help them make the best positive choice for themselves individually."[7]

Once the level of marginalization of some younger members of the tribe and the dissonance between the generations had been identified, there was a desire to bring into the museum these extremely sensitive and difficult issues that were not dealt with elsewhere. Using the museum would make it acceptable to explore issues of identity—a personal activity not previously engaged with in a public arena in Zuni. The museum in this particular frame of reference became a forum for intellectualizing Zuni identity, or, as Poulot (1994) argues, a place for defining "rhetorical coherence" in some of the shifts in cultural values that were being differentially experienced by the community.

The programs that were established in the museum reflected the desire to develop a vehicle for self-exploration and reaffirmation of Zuni cultural values. Holman, in the time that he was director (1990–95), sought grant money from the Seventh Generation Fund to initiate specific staff positions for what became known as Tradition Bearers—a program that relied on elders in the community who were accomplished mentors within the long-established system for the transfer of knowledge. From 1996 to 2002, when funding terminated, such a position was held by Rita Edaakie, who had experience in teaching younger children in the Zuni Public School District, where she worked as a foster grandparent to instruct and encourage children to read in the Zuni language. In an interview, she talked openly about her desire to teach younger generations about their history and traditions:

> The project that means the most to me is teaching the children of what are our traditional ways—the traditional cooking and what ingredients would go into a meal. At the schools, too, they want to know some things that they have been studying about corn and what it means to them, pertaining to one individual corn. So I have gone into the schools teaching them what they want to know. Most of my teaching is about our traditional ways and how to go about obtaining our history.[8]

Edaakie also communicated her concerns that children needed to learn fundamental social roles and responsibilities, and that if they were left without parents or guardians to guide them, she wanted to be there for them: "the children, they need to know what knowledge we had in growing up and what the teachings were and how to go about our religious doings. So they would know if all of a sudden they are left behind and don't have anybody to turn to."[9]

In their efforts at the museum, staff members were attempting to reach those youngsters who were not receiving the familial knowledge associated with traditional Zuni culture, but they were careful not to intrude on areas that were understood to be the religious leaders' responsibility. If we look at Edaakie's position as Tradition Bearer, her role at a basic level combines Anglo-American and Zuni expectations regarding the transfer of knowledge. Her approach to this role brought together Zuni perceptions of the significance of oral tradition and Anglo-American expectations about easily accessible information. She was in many ways a surrogate grandmother. This methodology represented the museum's decision to engage the Pueblo children in their traditional practices; it recognized that such practices were usually situated within a restricted or familial arena of access, and it combined this approach with one that was open to sharing knowledge. This environment was considered crucial in order to reach the children who may not have been catered to by the more exclusive preexisting system.

There was also apprehension among many community members and museum staff that children did not always receive knowledge about their clan affiliation. In 1997, Vernon Quam, the museum community coordinator, initiated family activities such as storytelling and traditional games. The most popular activity was the one he designed to teach about clan identity. Using his contemporary knowledge of current membership, Quam illustrated how there were twelve active matrilineal (exogamous) clans into which a child could be born and that would determine his or her kin relationships within the community. Clan recognition is used in Zuni as a form of introduction. An individual announces his or her maternal clan first and subsequently the paternal clan, using the expression "child of" to explain that the paternal clan is being named (i.e., he or she belongs to the Sandhill Crane Clan [maternal] and is a child of the Dogwood Clan [paternal]). Quam helped children identify which clan each belonged to and then assisted them in painting their clan symbols on swatches of cloth, including the Zuni language term for each clan alongside an illustration of the animal or plant associated with that clan. These activities have become popular among children and parents, who request for it to occur at a number of museum events.

Tradition, according to Zuni expectations, is understood as practices that are transmitted intentionally from elder to younger members of the community in order to define an individual's specific social role and to affirm generational links. From my perspective as an observer of the current modes of perceiving tradition in Zuni, I focused on the instrumentality of tradition in negotiating the relationship between the past and the present, or, as Georgia Epaloose argues, in "using the then to understand the now."[10] The most widely recognized research to interrogate our previously unquestioned ideas about tradition is Eric Hobsbawm and Terence Ranger's (1983) examination of "the invention of tradition." They look at the ways in which nations use ceremonies and public institutions to validate present social arrangements through reference to a past way of life, the origins of which are so remote that they apparently need no justification. Marie Mauzé, however, questions this combined use of the terms *invention* and *tradition* and the confusion it creates "because we sense that these terms go "beyond usual anthropological discourse to entail political and ethnical positions" (1997:4–5).

A clan identification game in the A:shiwi A:wan Museum and Heritage Center, 1997.

Many see the combination as a way of disempowering indigenous communities who are employing the term *tradition* in their political battles against colonizers.

It is important to define the use of the term in this context and to address the nature of the politics involved in it. In locating the concept of tradition here as a tool that the A:shiwi A:wan Museum used to explore issues of identity, I would argue that some practices may be relocated into different contexts or modified to suit new circumstances and therefore that there are inventive strategies in using traditional knowledge. Among museum staff in the 1990s, the emphasis, however, was on the notion that these traditional practices had social adhesive powers based on the transmission of knowledge and efficacy in bridging periods of social transition. A useful example of this notion is Rita Edaakie's book *Idonapshe: Let's Eat: Traditional Zuni Foods* (1999).[11] While researching for the book, Edaakie shared with her colleagues at the museum her concerns about the increase in diagnoses of Type II diabetes within the community. This increased incidence posed a major challenge to the community, and Edaakie chose to collaborate with the Zuni Diabetes Prevention Program, which provided a dietary analysis of the traditional recipes. Thus, traditions should be seen to have both internal political power, as in the case of diabetes prevention, and external powers, as in the case of land claims, where preexisting knowledge was used to establish Zuni land use over the past five centuries.

Nevertheless, how does a *new* institution such as the Zuni museum establish community confidence in its ability to teach traditions? Museum staff were faced from the beginning with the daunting responsibility of exploring and identifying which areas of knowledge could be introduced into a public institution. As discussed previously, Zuni religious leaders had interceded in 1992 to resolve an untenable situation, applied their traditional obligations to a novel medium, and controlled the religious knowledge they found in the duplicated photographs donated to the Zuni museum by the NAA. The reverberations from the resulting controversy are still felt in some national museums today, highlighting different expectations regarding the objectification of knowledge. For museum staff, however, the photographs represented an opportunity to explore the traditional paths that defined and controlled the circulation of knowledge. While Nigel Holman was director, he worked alongside Andrew Othole, the cultural preservation coordinator for the ZHHPO, in determining that religious leaders should review the photographs to define appropriate levels of access. In his role as director, Holman had become aware of the problems these images presented to the museum: "More than a [thousand] of these photographs depicted religious ceremonies, and represented a challenge to the museum's commitment to reflect the community's traditional beliefs. Specifically, this included the belief that such photography is inappropriate. More generally, however, it included the belief that such religious knowledge is held on behalf of the community by individuals and that it is inappropriate for it to be known more widely" (1996b:104).

In 1993, Holman submitted a grant proposal to the Lila Wallace Reader's Digest Fund for a project in which museum staff and ZCRAT members could review the photographs and devise a culturally specific system for their curation. As mentioned previously, images of a religious nature were thereafter transferred to ZHHPO to be available only to the initiated members of religious societies. Access was then to be determined according to the particular role an individual played within the religious societies.

Holman explicitly supported the decision to separate the photographs because he believed it was an important first step for a fledgling institution that was coming of age in an environment that emphasized the authority of religious leaders as the repositories for cultural and religious knowledge. "Access to these photographs will, in the future, be based on an individual's need to know. For instance, if an image records a particular location, only those individuals who should be knowledgeable about this location will be permitted to view it. Individuals who need to know would probably also be the only people who could contribute to the documentation of the features and activities in this photograph" (Holman and Othole 1993:n.p.).

The decision to isolate and then transfer the photographs to ZHHPO created controversy, however. According to the accepted philosophy of conventional Anglo-American museum practice, this move represented not only the deaccessioning of collections, but also the application of restrictions not conformable to national guidelines guaranteeing equal access. The museum's agreement to the religious leaders' request also raised extremely pertinent issues that many other museums in the United States were facing. In 1992, the Hopi tribe had sent a letter to major museums across the United States requesting that all photographs and archival material that contained knowledge collected by anthropologists working in Hopi be placed under a moratorium preventing researchers from gaining access. Many museum professionals and anthropologists considered the Hopi letter a call to open discussions about issues of intellectual property and the control of knowledge. A few years later Holman also translated his experience in Zuni for other non-Zunis in order to open up the discussion regarding indigenous modes of control that conflicted with Anglo-American expectations. He published a series of articles to educate the American public and museum community about preexisting systems for the management of esoteric knowledge (Holman 1996a, 1996b).

Holman and Othole, during their involvement in reconciling the different approaches to the photographs, alluded to the museum's need to mediate these disparate cultural expectations of access: "the community's museum and religious leaders have co-operated to the benefit of the entire community by developing a compromise between modern museological principles and traditional religious practice" (1993:n.p.). This cooperative process was crucial in establishing the museum as a participating member of the Zuni community and not an institution for tourists and outsiders that disregarded internal mechanisms for the control of knowledge: "A request from a recognized community group for the museum to adopt a culturally appropriate policy would never be denied. Its stated philosophy and goals require that it be especially responsive to community wishes. Indeed, any other approach would guarantee that the museum in Zuni would become nothing more than a tourist attraction" (1993:n.p.).

The photographs became catalysts that pushed people to recognize and act upon the differentially privileged layers of access to knowledge. Zunis also saw them as entities that embodied the power of their subjects —an especially important factor if they showed religious ceremonies or shrines. As mobile and materialized forms of sacred domains, they needed to be held and maintained by the guardians of these places and practices. According to the Zuni perspective, they were not merely duplications—they held the efficacy of the original. In this view, the interaction between the world, the photographer, and the film does not result in mere representations of the world; images are offspring with as much power as their parents. Although video, film, audio recordings, computers, and the Web provide Zunis with a range of duplicative technology, their use as transformative technologies within public arenas now demands more careful navigation.

The purpose of conventional Anglo-American museums has traditionally been to collect, interpret, and disseminate knowledge. At the same time that their ideology has come under question, especially regarding their exertion of the authority to represent the "other," information and reproductive technology has surfaced as the fastest-growing and most innovative area within the museum world. Although the phrase *reproductive technology* is more frequently employed to describe the methods used to increase human fertility and reproductive success, in the context of my research I use it to refer to technologies that reproduce human knowledge, such as cameras, computers, and tape recorders. I have specifically selected the term *reproductive* because it heightens our awareness of the efficacy that people may or may not attribute to these technologies. These reproductive and representational vehicles are now inextricably linked to ideas about increasing access to knowledge—for example, museum Internet sites, computer terminals in galleries, and databases. As a result, this technology has been equated with the move toward democratizing or increasing visitor access to information, and museums have started to use computers as a way to expand the museum space and to redefine public access.

These new forms of technology have largely gone unquestioned within national museums, but the issues they raised within Zuni elicited animated discussions about the duplication and circulation of knowledge outside of the mentor/mentee relationship. Another development at the museum illustrates these issues. Through collaboration with the Zuni Bilingual Program, the museum installed a computer program designed to teach the younger generation the principles of the Zuni alphabet and vocabulary. Plans were also presented to develop an ongoing repository for video- and audiotapes that would augment the museum's program to collect and transmit local knowledge and history. A number of teenagers had approached staff members at the museum with requests to learn particular prayers. The staff members themselves were comfortable with teaching these prayers, but when a non-Zuni staff member suggested that a computer program be designed that would provide the prayers and corresponding occasions in which they could be used, discussions ensued on the various problems presented by this use of the technology. Staff outlined how the distinct Zuni terminology that defines and structures each prayer usually refers to significant place-names and shrines in the landscape. Children often do not know these place-names or the cultural significance they carry with them. In order for a child to understand the prayer at a mnemonic level, the stories that accompany each place-name would need to be explained and their historical significance outlined. A mentor who is physically with the child would have to assess exactly which prayer is appropriate for the context the child has described and, more important, would have to explain the responsibilities and behavior that accompany the prayers.

Would the museum be able to adhere to the preexisting protocol for the transmission of knowledge while at the same time institutionalizing this knowledge within an open forum? What were the implications of a forum that would operate through a different set of criteria for the maintenance of knowledge—that is, by means of recordings and texts rather than oral storytelling? Reproductive technology offered methods for documenting knowledge that people feared might be lost. It also simultaneously presented a threat to oral traditions by capturing a performance and separating it from its performer, thus defying the expertise of teachers to determine the appropriate context for the transfer of specific knowledge and cheating students out of the highly valued interaction with their teachers. Vernon Quam looked at the overlapping and contrasting values that needed to be reconciled: "We are in an era of modern technology and things have changed . . . but then again, the religion and culture are still intact. We have not lost it. In this time and age, it is appropriate for us to document it in writing and recording—because what if we eventually come to a point where our elders are not here and all that information is being lost? With writing it down, it would be beneficial for future generations to utilize."[12] The mode for transfer, however, was seen as a key issue in maintaining the relationship of the receiver to the integrity of the knowledge—especially in regard to the transmission of religious and privileged knowledge. Quam stated that religious prayers can be handed down only orally and that "it is taboo to write them down." He also stressed that although modes for transmission demand careful negotiation, the need for the active transfer of knowledge is important: "we will really need to practice the sharing of knowledge through oral communication. . . . [I]f we don't share the knowledge—we will lose it."[13]

Negotiating the Role of Tourism in Zuni

Nowhere is the tension between Anglo-American and Zuni approaches to knowledge more pronounced than in the areas of the Pueblo influenced by tourism. The critique of identity within a marginalized and colonized community seeking control over its cultural heritage is not easy and is not necessarily an area to which tourists should have access. There is a paradox, according to Poulot, implicit within institutions that seek to define identity through "rhetorical coherence," yet at the same time also seek to establish a "critical perspective" in order to facilitate self-analysis: "There is an apparent contradiction between, on the one hand, the process of self-recognition, which implies a sort of introversion of the community, a concern exclusively with its own history and geography, and on the other hand, the desire to represent oneself, that is to compose and project images for the consumption of others" (1994:78–79).

How does an institution invite visitors into what the community views as an environment designed to foster exclusive cultural knowledge, but avoid creating a window of voyeurism through which the tourists can observe internal aspects of the society that community members have sought to protect from external curiosity? This question is especially pertinent in Zuni because it draws to the surface some of the issues involved in institutionalizing the layers of knowledge not usually circulated within a public arena. Put differently, the question is, Do you allow outsiders to have access to an exploration of the crises facing the community involving issues of identity? The Zuni museum's primary function is to encourage the transfer of knowledge about Zuni heritage to the younger generations. These specific areas of knowledge, however, are located within a system that discourages access to those who are not participating in the network of social responsibilities.

In an interview with a Zuni High School student, I asked her what she viewed as the museum's role in regard to tourists. Her response focused on the museum's need to screen information for the visitor, and she suggested that "the role would be not to give too much information out. If you give too much information, [the visitor] might . . . steal our Zuni language and Zuni culture. We don't know who the tourists are. They just come and go through our village."[14] Quam also stated, "A lot of the questions I've been asked [by tourists], I couldn't reply to them because some of them [the topics] were very sensitive."[15] Without placing the emphasis on local directives, museum staff would be unable to build the community's confidence in the museum. In the Zuni museum, it was common for visitors to point to a nineteenth-century photograph of the Pueblo that hung in the gallery from 1995 to 1999 and ask if they could be given directions to this particular section of the Pueblo. The photograph depicted the layers of terraced adobe houses of the Middle Village as they were in the 1890s, but this architecture is not current building practice for housing in Zuni today. Museum staff often used this scenario as an example to illustrate how tourists came to Zuni with predetermined ideas about what an Indian pueblo should look like. There was a clear tension between demystifying tourists' misconceptions about the Pueblo and the problems associated with disseminating knowledge deemed to be sensitive. In the case of Zuni, the fear is that tourists will gain un-screened access to historic and sacred sites, as well as to religious prac-tices and associated knowledge.

Nevertheless, the museum does not actively exclude tourists, so they are a part of the audience for which it is responsible—through either the active or passive consumption of knowledge. In 1997, museum director Tom Kennedy and Vernon Quam initiated discussion with the tribal council to convince its members that the museum should operate as the primary orientation center for visitors. In this way, they hoped to engage tourists actively with the protocols that define behavior in the Pueblo. Quam declared that "visitors should use the museum not just as a place to come and understand the history or culture of Zuni, [but] as an orientation center" that would explain to them the appropriate etiquette for their visit.[16] Kennedy placed the museum in the role of mediator between the tribe and non-Zunis:

> I think if the museum took on more of an active role in orienting tours . . . what to do and suggestions of what not to do—of how to be good visitors in this community—that we would provide an incredi-bly valuable service to the community and maybe lessen some of the tensions that exist. That might be . . . a redefinition of our purpose for the community itself, that they will have some confidence that these visitors have come to Zuni . . . [and] to the A:shiwi Center to really learn what we are all about and to learn to be a better citizen within our community. . . . I think we are starting to take that on.[17]

Staff also felt it was their responsibility to provide a service to the com-munity by acting as a control mechanism for the interaction between tourists and the community:

> Just recently there have been a lot of incidents with visitors coming to Zuni, especially during religious events. The tribe could allow us to be the Visitor Orientation Center. We could control the visitor from

interfering with the religious activities going on and keep them away from that area during certain times of the year when there are activities going on. We'll attract them to other places further away from the main Pueblo. We might have a nature walk along DY [Dowa Yalanne, the sacred mesa], or an artisan's tour on this side of the Pueblo. Or we might have a half-day field trip for visitors.[18]

Although tourists were seen as intrusive, it was understood that instilling pride in the younger Zuni generations involved projecting an accurate and positive image of Zuni to the outside world. Georgia Epaloose declared that the museum is the appropriate place for this negotiation to take place: "I think of all the entities in this community, the museum can do the best job of informing the tourist . . . and giving pretty accurate information"; the museum "would be the best resource this community could have in terms of articulating to the larger public of who we are and what we are all about."[19] Clearly, there were benefits to using the internal mode for interpreting Zuni culture and thereby allowing the "outsider" to experience an "insider's" view of life in Zuni. According to Kennedy,

[The museum's role] is an ambiguous role to some extent, because, if you strictly go by the concept of an ecomuseum, that really means a museum for the community first, and that is really the mode that we operate on. In fact our [board] president, Malcolm Bowekaty, said . . . if we do it well for the community, if we do it well for ourselves, outsiders can also benefit from it too. Our main focus is the community, and I think that serves a pretty good function for those visitors to Zuni who are interested in vicariously experiencing the life of the community, and so you do it by seeing these programs that are meant for the community.[20]

Concern about the invasive nature of tourism has therefore been an ongoing discussion in the museum. Between 1993 and 1995, museum director Holman worked with the board to establish a site outside the central part of the Pueblo for a more permanent museum structure. He explained later that "we didn't want to be in a location that would be disruptive to the people around it. The tourists who were visiting the museum [were] independent to our lack of promotion about activity. We didn't want people to disturb people around us. So we wanted to be out of town a little bit."[21] A site-selection process was initiated, and a number of locations were assessed. The land eventually chosen was situ-

ated in Blackrock, a few miles outside of the central part of the Pueblo—
an area that was also seen to provide the museum board with the opportunity to build an ecologically appropriate building, which was part of
their interest in following the ecomuseum approach. By 1995, however,
the plan had been delayed by difficulties in finding the funds needed to
develop and operate a new facility. Current staff also voiced concern
about relocating the museum away from the center of the Pueblo because it would exclude easy access by the younger members of the tribe
without their own transport.

The problems the museum faces are extremely difficult to resolve—
not only because the issues cut to the core of the Zuni system of knowledge, but because the process is about a culture negotiating its identity,
which is a sensitive process if taken out of context. If the museum is
concerned with affirming Zuni identity and reconciling different expectations about traditional knowledge, it is also faced with finding ways for
achieving these goals within a nontraditional setting and alongside competing interests, such as tourism. As of 2006, the museum board and staff
members were working toward establishing an environment that privileges the insider's view of Zuni culture but at the same time educates the
misinformed outsider. Community members' trust is crucial for the
stability of the museum, and at times tensions have appeared regarding
the presence of outsiders, who threaten the development of an intimate
and private space of self-discovery.

Visualizing Knowledges

During the time of my research at the museum, a mural project on the
origins of Zuni clans and how they came to the Middle Place resolved
many of the issues addressed here. In 1997, a collaborative project was
formed between the artist Alex Seowtewa, apprentices from the JTPA,
and the museum staff. Seowtewa's narrative of the migration to the
Middle Place provided the structure for the mural, and the artists Ronnie
Cachini, Raelyn Cachini, and Vernon Quam carried out extensive research in order to re-create a visual representation of the origin stories,
using petroglyphs and clan symbols.[22] Important landmarks that figure
in the story were created, where possible, from memory or depicted
through reference to photographs.

As discussed previously, clan histories are usually separately owned
and controlled by each clan. To portray these stories accurately together

Mural artist Ronnie Cachini giving a tour of the migration mural to museum visitors Rose S. Peywa and her granddaughter, Lou Ann Johnson, Pueblo of Zuni, 1998.

as one narrative and to complete the narrative to the satisfaction of religious practitioners was challenging and in many ways a new performance of the knowledge. The end result, however, was a mural that contained a vast amount of local knowledge about the origin stories and Zuni cultural geography. The museum staff felt that combining the clan histories allowed for the most comprehensive account of the creation of all the clans, and in this manner the mural helped provide a structure within which an individual could interpret his or her clan identity and the communal interrelationship of clans within Zuni society.

Community members who visited the museum during the mural's construction were talked through the five panels, and soon it became practice that the stories were told alongside the tour of the mural. Although this practice may not have been the mural's original purpose, the images now served as an iconographic aid to traditional storytelling. Many of the landmarks and features were illuminated to younger Zunis who did not know the links or significance between place-names and the creation stories. In addition, non-Zuni visitors would most likely not understand the various details unless they were explained, so the mural became a secure way of recording the knowledge within the museum without opening esoteric areas to non-Zunis. Tourists would not know the Zuni terms for the places and clan symbols, and the crucial mapping or detailed knowledge would be hidden from them.

A parallel can be drawn between the way in which the Zuni mural operated as a graphic and symbolic presentation of clan history and what Dussart (1997) identifies as the multifaceted nature of Yolngu paintings from northern Arnhem Land in Australia. Dussart argues that although elders were concerned about allowing these paintings to be displayed in a public space, they soon discovered that non-Aboriginal collectors or tourists who purchased them did not understand the iconography that depicted esoteric clan histories or ancestral landmarks. As argued previously in regard to the Yolngu use of secrecy as a pedagogical device, the internal hierarchy that layers knowledge according to clan or moiety membership determines who has access to the skills of interpretation. According to Dussart, this control of interpretative knowledge does in fact exclude outsiders from obtaining inside knowledge from the paintings. The knowledge remains "closed" even during the paintings' engagement in international "public" art markets.

The artist Alex Seowtewa, who helped develop the museum mural project, is well known for his painting of a complex and ornate frieze within Nuestra Señora de Guadalupe, the Spanish mission church in the Middle Village. The frieze depicts a line of kokkos, ancestral gods, that progress around the interior walls of the church, thereby representing the Zuni calendar and the continual cycle of religious ceremonies. Tourists to the Pueblo could formerly visit the church and arrange to have Seowtewa talk about these murals.[23] In his guided tour, he often remarked on the criticism from particular community members uncomfortable with his replication of an entire calendrical formation of kokkos—an act of ritual mimicry that could be considered taboo. Concern is still expressed that the kokkos have been placed inside a Catholic church. Yet Seowtewa argues that because some of the knowledge associated with the kokkos has been lost, his work is about celebrating and maintaining the Zuni religion through painting. When he visited the Smithsonian, he found nineteenth-century photographs of the church interior taken by Matilda Coxe Stevenson, revealing earlier murals that used Zuni religious iconography.[24] When the mission was renovated in the 1980s, he wanted the people of Zuni to remember the tradition and history of bringing Zuni symbolism into the interior of the church. Although some community members and religious practitioners have criticized his depiction of the kokkos, the paintings have endured so far, and Seowtewa has received national attention and financial support from external funding agencies.

In similar situations, concerns have led to the removal of images of kokkos. During the development of the Indian Pueblo Cultural Center, a combined Pueblo-operated visitor center and museum in Albuquerque, the Zuni artist Phil Hughte was commissioned to paint a mural on one of the courtyard walls. In Oxendine's research on the Pueblo Cultural Center, she includes comments from the center's curator regarding the decision to remove murals that showed culturally sensitive material:

> As with the museum, the need for tribal control is evident in the choice of subject matter for public display. After the initial murals project was completed, one of the murals on the exterior wall of the Center, the "Shalako Mural," by Philbert Hughte, had to be painted over and replaced with another mural, "Eagle Dancer," by Hughte. The reason given by the curator was that the Shalako [sic] are the mightiest of the kachinas which visit the Zuni Pueblo yearly. . . . Although the Shalako mural was originally approved by the IPCC board, a later group decided that because the painting revealed too much of the Shalakos for public display it had to be covered up with another painting. (1992:80)

It is difficult to state exactly why Hughte's mural was painted over, but Seowtewa's mural was not. As previously illustrated, the creation and migration stories are allowed to be told only at a certain time of year. It is possible to suggest that Hughte's painting represented a god that appears only during the winter solstice and therefore should not be established permanently within a public space. Moreover, unlike the mission church in Zuni, the Pueblo Cultural Center is a public venue that caters specifically to tourists.

Further research on how the iconography of the A:shiwi A:wan Museum clan mural is read by insiders or outsiders would be worthwhile. Throughout its construction and as knowledgeable elder Zunis and the artists discussed the symbolism with younger Zunis, the mural did appear to encourage the use of oral tradition. Thus, as Fuller and Fabricius point out, "the museum becomes a facilitator for, but not a replacement of, the traditional family or clan system" (1993:236). The mural provides

The Cultural Ambassadors exhibit, spotlighting former Miss Zuni pageant winners, A:shiwi A:wan Museum and Heritage Center, 1997.

an example of a museum project that allows the staff to involve younger generations in the Zuni pedagogical system. It brings together the Zuni way of doing things with the museum's desire to facilitate the education of the younger generation. It also facilitates Zuni traditional control mechanisms because oral accounts exclusively maintain the central core of this knowledge, in this way restricting outsiders' access to the knowledge. Only a knowledgeable practitioner can guide someone through the mural, so he or she can control the amount of information and the context in which it is transmitted.

At a fundamental level, therefore, the elements of Zuni culture that the staff identified early on as suitable for the museum environment were those that originated from what can be termed the familial sphere of knowledge. These elements consist of generally accepted methods for preparing foods, the identification of clan affiliation, and the technical knowledge used for producing adobe bricks and maintaining waffle gardens. Another example in this arena is the Cultural Ambassadors exhibit designed by Vernon Quam, which displayed the images of past winners of the Miss Zuni pageant. The exhibit also served to recognize the history of design for the Miss Zuni crown. The staff members were continually called upon to utilize knowledge that was accepted as available to all members of the community, regardless of status within religious hierarchy or clan. Staff at the museum frequently entered into discussions about the level of details that could be included in each exhibit, article, or game produced for the Zuni public. Certain programs were also reorganized after concern was expressed about the use of certain knowledge within the museum environment. For example, Quam had also initiated a project to teach the youth about the traditional plants used for food and medicine. After careful consideration, however, he chose not to pursue the program because it would overlap with the specific duties of priests and members of the medicine lodges, who were responsible for controlling the knowledge associated with the majority of these plants.

During its initial stages of development, the museum became an arena where expectations about traditional Anglo-American museums and traditional Zuni philosophy were negotiated. My use of the term *traditional* to describe both conventional Anglo-American and Zuni approaches is not coincidental because it serves to illustrate how the museum developed as a space in which Zuni culture was explored in a manner that could be seen as both conventional and innovative according to both Anglo-American and Zuni expectations about the transmission of knowledge. This line of argument helps to highlight how the museum in Zuni was designed to occupy a middle ground—a position crucial in allowing people to balance expectations about the preexisting system for the transfer of knowledge with any changes taking place in the Pueblo. These changes have created additional hierarchies of knowledge and forced those Zuni educated within the Anglo-American system to look for new institutions for the enhancement of Zuni identity, institutions that could bridge both the conventional and innovative approaches to knowledge.

6

Living with Contradictions
Ambiguity as a Means for Reconciliation

In October 1997, I was fortunate enough to accompany the museum elder Rita Edaakie on an outing to Acoma Pueblo, which lies some fifty miles east of Zuni. We had been invited by a tribal official, who offered to take us to visit Sky City, and while we were waiting for our escort to accompany us to the Pueblo, we wandered around the Acoma Visitors Center, which lies in the valley below the mesa and acts as a gateway for visitors.[1] On observing the wide range of historic Acoma pottery exhibited in the Visitors Center museum, Edaakie commented on how she would like to see a similar display of Zuni pottery at the A:shiwi A:wan Museum because it would provide an opportunity for people to appreciate the knowledge and skill of the Zuni potters of the past. For Edaakie, the Zuni pottery represented an inheritance from her ancestors worthy of recognition within a public institution.

What stayed in my mind following the conversation with Edaakie was that she was reflecting on the issues integral to the Zuni museum's position on collecting and displaying objects. More important, her view countered the current ethos of the museum, which had been formulated as a "living" museum, an ecomuseum, in which historic collections were problematic vestiges of Anglo-American museum ideology. A number of other individuals from the community had also made comments to me on separate occasions about how they would like to see some of the historic material or, more generally, the material culture of Zuni displayed at the museum. Edaakie's viewpoint demonstrates the problems of an oversimplistic reading of what community members or, for that matter, museum staff want or do not want from their museum. On the one hand, Edaakie's interpretation of her role in the museum as a Tradition Bearer supported the ecomuseum concept of teaching through the current practice of living traditions. On the other hand, Edaakie saw something in the Acoma display that appealed to her and that affected how she viewed the purpose of museums.

I am using this encounter to illustrate the intricate and conflicting

Jessica Chimoni preparing scorched corn for a family night at the A:shiwi A:wan Museum and Heritage Center, 1997.

nature of the perspectives on the museum's manifestation of Zuni history and culture. If we step back momentarily from my analysis of the various viewpoints and seek a wider interpretation of the issues involved, two areas come into focus. First, we must consider the diversity presented by the community—more specifically, the differences between generations (i.e., different approaches to language and expectations about learning or teaching traditional knowledge)—together with the differences established by the religious and social structure that locates practitioners and participants within various levels of knowledge. Second, it is apparent that these diverse perspectives can actually overlap or be linked by individual approaches, as in the case of Edaakie's view, which combined her appreciation of the display of historic objects with her appreciation of an ecomuseum concept that downplays the role of objects. This area of overlap is associated with the negotiations of tensions and the purposeful uses of ambiguity; it is the middle ground and the natural product of individuals' cross-referencing between different philosophies. Here, individual Zunis must make sense of teaching traditional concepts out of context and within a nontraditional setting. The tensions that arise from this process can be both divisive and dynamic; in the case of the Zuni museum, they force people to question both the original context or meaning of concepts and the processes that either facilitate or prevent the circulation of meaning.

As a social institution that seeks inclusion within the heart of the community, the A:shiwi A:wan Museum is inevitably entangled in the negotiation of the differences between religious and secular authority, as well as in the challenges posed to oral tradition by the increased emphasis on literacy. It is also engaged in the ongoing debates about the tensions between tourists and locals, between outsiders and insiders. As discussed previously, board members have acknowledged that some members of the younger generation may not be receiving primary elements of their cultural heritage, such as knowledge about their clan lineage. The board's response to this problem was to develop the museum as a new forum in which to teach Zuni history and culture. The methods used within the museum, however, introduced new ways to transmit traditional knowledge, which placed the museum in a paradoxical position wherein it relocated Zuni traditions in a nontraditional setting and within a public institution.

In this analysis of the museum, the community, and Anglo-American interests in Zuni history and culture, specific tensions between different approaches to knowledge have been highlighted. The purpose of this chapter is to look at the different and overlapping expectations regarding the museum held by staff, community members, and non-Zunis and to see how these differences have been negotiated thus far.

In the spring of 1998, I met with Nancy Fuller, the research program manager at the Smithsonian Center for Education and Museum Studies. Her role as a consultant for tribal museums had provided her with a close understanding of the questions raised by Native Americans while developing community museums, and her published work on tribal museums certainly proved to be the most applicable literature in regard to the questions I was asking of my own research results from Zuni. I had presented to Fuller the issues raised by my fieldwork, as well as my thoughts on the institutionalizing of traditional knowledge, and I was intrigued to find that she had encountered similar issues during her work as a consultant. Although it could be suggested that a conversation with Fuller would have been more useful preceding my time in Zuni, the fact that these specific issues were raised independently as a result of fieldwork confirmed that they were considered central by both the Zuni museum and the Zuni community, rather than being topics determined or driven by my own interests.

A closer look at how the literature has explored the process of institutionalizing traditional knowledge is apropos here. In "Native American Museums and Cultural Centers," Fuller and Fabricius attribute some of the problems that arise in tribal museums to the institutionalization of traditions within a nontraditional environment: "Given the fact that museum operations differ radically from the centuries-old family or clan systems of transmitting culture, it is not surprising that obstacles arise when a community attempts to institutionalize the process of preserving and transmitting cultural heritage" (1993:232).

Although Fuller and Fabricius structure their conclusions through an identification of the different approaches to material culture, the issues they raise are centered on how meanings are defined by their original context and by different approaches to knowledge. In providing an example of the processes involved in accessioning material culture within a tribal museum, they illustrate how the object not only takes on new meanings but also presents problems for the preexisting system in the transmission of knowledge: "The process (a) changes the meaning and value of the object from one that is subjective (determined by association with an individual owner) to one whose meaning is relative and whose value resides in the object (determined by generic classification schemes); and (b) makes the object and the knowledge it possesses accessible to the public" (1993:232–33). Fuller and Fabricius conclude by saying that "the transformation of value, and the loss of the intellectual ownership of knowledge" create "the core differences in approach to organizational systems between tribes and institutions" (1993:232–33).

In order to explore further the issues raised by Fuller and my fieldwork experiences, I chose to look more closely at perspectives on the institutionalization of traditional knowledge and to investigate the links that appeared to tie together different approaches to knowledge. Yet in reflecting on my experiences in Zuni and on my postfieldwork analysis, I was faced with the problem of how to interpret the seemingly contradictory nature of the interview narratives I had transcribed. While I was conducting a number of interviews with individuals from the museum and the community, I was at times left perplexed by each person's insistence on giving an equivocal interpretation of the events or subjects discussed. They often discussed both sides of any issues raised or presented within the interview.

Over time, however, these interviews provided me with insight into the Zuni perception that the art of conversation or oration requires people to be fair and balanced in their views. An emphasis is placed on understanding the alternative perspectives that oppose one's own viewpoint and at the same time on not taking an absolute stand on any issue to the detriment of reaching a consensus. Equally, an orator cannot assume that he or she has the right to speak for others. Similarly, my observation of group discussions revealed that to achieve the status of an accomplished speaker, an individual must facilitate the group in reaching an understanding of the issue at hand without actually being the perpetrator of a decision. In this perspective, a skilled orator is a guide, not a preacher. Nevertheless, according to my inexperienced ear, the interviews presented a blurring of viewpoints wherein each individual appeared to take the middle ground by combining a range of viewpoints into one perspective. This blurring posed problems in my analysis of the interviews and highlighted the need for a framework that not only acknowledges how people mediate different perspectives but also allows for an analysis of how individuals separate out or value specific elements and how Zunis at times purposefully employ ambiguity as a means for reconciling differences.

Ambiguity between disparate elements or factions is a familiar device used by Zunis to negotiate dissimilar concepts or spheres of influence. For example, as Holman argues, Cushing's "initiation" into the Priesthood of the Bow may have been strategically designed to be uncertain enough to serve both Cushing's needs and the religious leaders' and government officials' needs.[2] In a more recent example, the level of enforcement within the ban of non-Zunis at Sha'lak'o in 1996 was in many ways imprecise, allowing numerous parties to determine what they viewed as appropriate protocol. Through an exploration of these subtle, yet purposefully structured ambiguities, a more nuanced view of informal or vernacular approaches to mediating knowledges can be provided.

In establishing a museum, the board, staff, and community members were faced with issues such as the relationship between oral tradition and literacy, which were also being discussed in a variety of contexts within the community itself. I needed to explore how the museum encapsulated some of these debates but also to examine the museum as an institution made up of individuals, all of whom were engaged in these issues as community members. In the previous chapters I have explored the processes involved in the development of the Zuni museum through an examination of three broadly defined perspectives: (1) Zunis' perceptions about the preexisting methods used for the transmission of cultural knowledge; (2) Anglo-American assumptions about anthropology and museum practices; and (3) Zunis' perspectives on Anglo-American museum methodology and its application to the Zuni museum. Following a secondary analysis, the interviews with museum staff or community members revealed that individuals may adhere to an ideology from all of the perspectives or from two out of three of them, thus resulting in viewpoints that adjudicate or represent a combination of elements. This pattern was revealed in the discussion of the issues relating to the ban on non-Zunis attending the Sha'lak'o festivals, where factions or groups may separate on the issue of banning tourists altogether, but *all* members of the Zuni tribe agree with the decision to restrict photography. It is therefore important to point out that on the ground it is difficult to separate out or attribute an individual's perspective to any particular faction because an individual's viewpoint often combines or overlaps with the views of other groups. Nowhere is this more important to acknowledge than within the study of how an institution, such as the A:shiwi A:wan Museum, negotiates knowledge systems and encourages the synthesis of ideas.

During my first attempt to determine an appropriate structure for the analysis of the museum as a space that privileged the process of mediation, I used various topics, such as tourism, to illustrate how the museum staff has explored various opposing positions on the use or representation of Zuni culture. Yet this approach implied that "the community" and "the museum" were homogeneous but separate entities and that people adhered to a point of view particular to their "group." The danger with this approach was that it relegated to the shadows the complexities and ambiguities of the issues involved. Of equal importance was the fact that fieldwork had provided me with an opportunity to utilize primary sources and the viewpoints of specific individuals. To limit these viewpoints to a single category or to ignore the links or crosshatching of ideology would result in a decidedly two-dimensional ethnography.

Following my fieldwork and during many revisitations of the data and structure of analysis, I chose to look more closely at the range of perspectives represented and to open up a discussion of how views differed. I also looked at the views shared by different groups and identified where people combined ideologies that stemmed from different perspectives. Consequently, I have structured this particular analysis through an examination of the perspectives revealed by interviews with museum board and staff members, community members, and, finally, external consultants and non-Zunis. Following a discussion of these three groups, I return to the topics that illustrate the areas where viewpoints interacted and overlapped: new technology designed for educational purposes; tourism; and the museum mural project. This approach allows me to explore the divisions in ideology concerning the institutionalization of traditional knowledge and at the same time to look at the overlap or ambiguity in perspectives—an area in which many Zuni seemed at home or actively sought to create.

Looking at the Museum from the Inside

The Zuni museum forms an intimate and interactive environment where all board and staff members are involved in its development and direction. The advantages of a small institution are revealed in the A:shiwi A:wan Museum, where all employees share a communal work space and collaborate with each other on developing and facilitating public programs.

The central issues that concerned board members during my time at the museum included the museum's financial stability and its organizational accountability (e.g., appropriate programming for the community, staff employment and management, and accreditation with national museum associations). It is worth noting that the majority of board members viewed their role in the museum as a form of community service. Georgia Epaloose shared this perspective about her role as a board member: "I've always been service oriented . . . that's just from our upbringing. My great-grandmother, who was very service oriented . . . she always emphasized the whole philosophy of service—to do service, to do whatever you envision . . . as personal gain, but to also put it on the back burner, if there was something you could do to help."[3] Another board member suggested that it had always been one of his goals "to do a lot of public service because . . . sometimes you need to look at what's the best option, to really elevate the quality of the lifestyle of the Zuni community."[4] The board members of the A:shiwi A:wan Museum were also chosen because of their experience in the public-service sector, such as in the hospital or the school district. Yet I was aware that the board found defining the museum's public role an extremely challenging process, in part because it was a new institution but largely because it was also faced with defining the trajectory of "public" history and all the weighty responsibilities attached to this concept.

Although the board was part of the museum oversight mechanism, the staff were in effect in the front lines in determining how public history and culture were to be defined. In their active role working alongside community members, they were given direct experience of the challenges involved in institutionalizing traditional knowledge. They were responsible for the majority of the interactions with the community, and this proximal locality provided them with insight into how community members responded to the museum. The tribal archivist, Wendy Fontenelle, explained that her job at the museum required her not only to look at the most feasible routes to institute archives within Zuni but also to communicate to community members her role and the rationale behind archives as a resource:

> To explain to an elder is somewhat difficult for me to do because—I think the elders should be telling us things, which they do—but it is not in the white man's concept of the word *archives*. If you sit down with an elder and you explain to them what an archive is, they go "Hay eh, hay uhs'ona'shi." Meaning, "Oh, that is what that means. I have always heard the word, but I never knew what it meant." So just explaining to her [one of the elders] about the building that we are renovating . . . and working with all these documents pertaining to Zuni tribal administration, different departments and for the museum . . . and everything that has been collected here in Zuni. One thing that I thought was funny was that she went and thanked me for telling her and explaining to her what the archives were. So I think that this is something that really needs to be stressed.[5]

Vernon Quam, in discussing how he saw his role in the museum, suggested that for staff the day-to-day involvement with community members raised certain issues about the sharing of traditional knowledge within the museum environment:

> My role varies from working at an administrative level or working with the youth of all ages. The other part that I play is working with our elder mentor, Rita Edaakie ... going out into the community and locating elders for knowledge sharing because they are the bearers of our Zuni traditions, and we try and focus in on the senior citizens group. ... It is hectic because some of the senior citizens don't want to come to the center [museum]. I don't know why, but some of them are very reluctant to come and share their knowledge. I don't know why, because we have gone there several times, and we have told them that they shouldn't be keeping what they know. ... But then again, working with the leaders and working with the museum, it is something I really enjoy. It should be working that way because I think museums are a place for sharing traditions, especially us, being an ecomuseum—a community museum.[6]

Quam's perspective touches on the dilemma faced by staff who have to understand both sides of the terrain inhabited by the museum: first, the museum's aim to facilitate the documentation of Zuni traditions and history, and, second, the areas where suspicion has been aroused within the community as to how this knowledge will be used.

The appropriate use of Zuni knowledge was a subject frequently discussed by staff, particularly when they felt they needed to respond to a situation that required careful consideration, such as incorporating traditional knowledge within the museum's programs or exhibits. Quam suggested that this process was difficult because not all community members shared the same views about what was and what was not sensitive knowledge:

> The museum can play a role in teaching history and culture, but only at a certain level ... because there are certain teachings you can do at a certain level, but our religious teaching, that is something we have to stay away from, because that is not what we are there for. We don't want to be a part of that role. ... The museum can do a lot for the community—you just have to be aware of what's sensitive and what's not sensitive—to be shared among Zuni people and the visitors to Zuni. You will have to look at it from different angles, and you will have to be careful because ... some people might think [something] is

not too sensitive and the other person might think it is. When that happens, you have to look at two different points and weigh them down to see if it is really sensitive or not.[7]

Quam's viewpoint suggests that staff were sensitive to the diversity of perspectives within the community and to how the museum needed to balance these views.

In re-reading and reflecting on the interview transcripts, I noted that an individual's consideration of opposing elements was most apparent in discussions about the museum's role in regard to use of and access to traditional knowledge. Staff members did not merely discuss the issues; they also pointed out the various ways they felt that these issues existed within a much broader and all-encompassing Zuni narrative about the challenges presented by external influences and their effects on Zuni traditions. The staff thus spoke from their perspective as members of the Zuni community and as the facilitators of outreach programs, using both perspectives to reach a closer understanding of the often ambiguous relationships between the public and private spheres of knowledge.

It is apparent from the discussion in chapters 2 and 3 that a number of the issues raised by the institutionalization of traditional knowledge in Zuni had surfaced prior to the establishment of the museum. The same is true for how Zunis have continually looked at the relationship between oral tradition and literacy, an issue discussed with regard to the establishing of government schools and in debates about the teaching of the Zuni language within schools. Since the 1970s, the Pueblo of Zuni has supported a bilingual program that has been devoted to determining which specific contexts will permit written Zuni without endangering the control of esoteric knowledge.

The museum environment, not unexpectedly, has proved to be an important and applicable terrain for this debate. For example, one of the museum administrators stated that she preferred the oral transmission of traditional knowledge but that at the same time she could understand the benefits of having written documentation: "I would rather have somebody tell me . . . [to] pass it down to me orally, than to have to see it written. But on the other hand . . . there are some other stories others know about and others don't, and it would be best to write it down and someday, someone would discover it and be totally impressed by what they told a long time ago."[8] Similarly, Quam suggested that the museum does not replace the Zuni ways of transmitting information; rather, it should be seen as an additional resource: "Zunis carry their traditional learning methods in a different manner to outside people. . . . Some people use museums as learning tools. As to us, we use both our traditional methods and our tribal museum as a learning method—so we have at least two different ways we can learn our history and our culture."[9] From this perspective, oral tradition can exist alongside alternative methods for transferring knowledge. Although it is possible to theorize how combining these two approaches may work, in practice the combination involves areas of ambiguity that are affected continually by the changing juxtaposition of external and internal influences. There is tension, therefore, between stabilizing and controlling the context of knowledge, on the one hand, and transforming preexisting systems to incorporate new approaches to the transmission of knowledge, on the other.

These oppositional forces can be understood fully only when the nature of the relationship between literate-based learning and the use of oral traditions is examined. In the past, the application of anthropological models to the changing relationship between oral tradition and literacy focused on cognitive frameworks that attributed different "mentalities" to oral or written modes of transmission (Ong 1982) and on developmental frameworks that have looked at how writing has influenced society (Goody 1987). It is important to point out that the reproduction of culture and tradition, on the one hand, and the specific dynamics of each mode of transmission, on the other, are mutually dependent. My exploration of the perspectives on the relationship between orality and literacy in the Zuni museum brought to the surface how individuals believed these modes should operate. Hence, I have analyzed the *expectations* regarding oral tradition and literacy rather than how the two actually operate as different cognitive approaches to the transmission of knowledge.

Tom Kennedy, the museum director at the time I was doing my research, suggested that things were changing in Zuni but that community members' misgivings about the written documentation of oral traditions were still prevalent. His viewpoint also operated as a commentary on the response by some community members to the development of repositories such as archives and on the questions these institutions pose about the control of knowledge:

> Increasingly, you will find Zunis who feel the need to document their own cultural history and cultural traditions. I don't see that actively done right now, in fact there continues to be great suspicion about

that. . . . There are still individuals in the community who feel that it is somehow inappropriate to be documented. . . . What we are seeing is the vestiges of the old, more conservative sense that certain kinds of knowledge are the property of certain individuals—there is a certain time that it can be transmitted in a certain place and context, etc. All that is very important. But at the same time, there is a dawning awareness that "gee—we really need to do something about this." All this has happened simultaneously, so nothing has quite been figured out. You will have people who are very progressive and [who] say, "Sure, let's record it and put it in the archives," and others that are saying, "If it is recorded, what do we do with it? Do we share it? Do we keep it under lock and key? We don't know yet."[10]

In the same way that museum staff members had to counterpoise different perspectives stemming from Zuni and Anglo-American constructs of knowledge, Kennedy was also presented with the challenge of learning how things operated in Zuni and then exploring which elements from Anglo-American philosophy were compatible or incompatible with Zuni concepts within the museum environment. He suggested that the museum was, in fact, an appropriate venue for the exploration of the relationship between oral traditions and writing to take place because documentation was the natural function of a museum:

I think that the culture has not yet come to terms . . . with writing as a valid tool for preserving and perpetuating cultural knowledge. . . . The museum can serve as the forum, as the conduit to help preserve this knowledge because museums are . . . literate based . . . so we are talking about written knowledge, captured knowledge. . . . Is the museum the proper place for knowledge to be shared? I would pose that it needs to be culturally redefined as the appropriate place. . . . We can serve as the storehouse for much of this cultural information. We have the means and the wherewithal because that is the business that we are in—in the larger sense of museums collecting and preserving.[11]

Although the non-Zunis, myself included, who participated in the programs at the A:shiwi A:wan Museum openly supported the decision to establish the museum according to Zuni philosophy, our role is a difficult one to decipher within the context of exploring oral tradition and literacy. Through our involvement in the museum, we took on specific museum-related responsibilities. However, these duties did not place us within the traditional network of responsibilities defined by religious societies and the clan system. We were therefore excluded from learning the responsibility attached to the transmission of religious or familial spheres of knowledge. I would argue that the consequences of our involvement in the decision making of the museum were profound. We often introduced Anglo-American ideology without realizing that it might compete with areas of Zuni culture.

Kennedy also envisioned the museum as providing a service to the community by being *the place* designated specifically for the purpose of exploring the different cultural practices at play within Zuni. His idea of the museum's future was that it would be "a forum for neutral discussion" because "there is nowhere else where this forum exists, where there can be an exchange of ideas."[12] Although postmodern scholarship eschews notions of the museum as a "neutral" space, this viewpoint does not take into account the museum directors who aspire to or are expected to maintain a "neutral" position, especially in regard to politics. As can be gleaned from the debates that surfaced during the *Enola Gay* exhibit in Washington, D.C., a sector of the public argued that there is merit to presenting a balanced view on history and politics, and therefore that museums should not be seen to be taking sides (Gieryn 1998). In Kennedy's case, he was choosing to identify the museum as an institution that should be a "neutral forum." He also suggested that the museum might operate as an intermediary environment in which external influences can be examined and redefined according to Zuni ideology:

> The other area that we serve—is as a bridge . . . a neutral zone where a traditional community, [a] minority within this dominant United States of America cultural structure, can redefine, as it were, certain aspects of dominant culture, but in the context of Zuni culture. . . . Individuals play that out in their own lives. . . . What I think most Zunis do . . . is to adopt a parallel culture, with one foot firmly planted in each of those cultures. . . . I am proposing that the ecomuseum would serve as a place where a community would gather and start to come to understand its roots and then start to look at those elements from the outside world that are coming in, that are ever present . . . and redefine those in culturally appropriate terms. Again—it is a neutral zone, it is a forum for playing this out . . . at least people will have a more conscious choice in that, it is cultural empowerment to make these choices, to set an agenda for the future.[13]

His comments imply that the "neutralization" of Anglo-American practices can take place in the Zuni museum, as opposed to the development of a balanced forum, which is a slightly different concept. As this excerpt also reveals, the idea of the museum as a forum for exploring identity was also examined simultaneously from non-Zuni perspectives.

There is also the expectation among board and staff members that the museum should provide a place to teach Zuni culture to those individuals from the community who are not in a position to gain this knowledge from within the preexisting system. From this perspective, it is understood that many younger children are located at the junction between the two approaches to knowledge. Like the museum staff, the community also has different perspectives, many of which stem from the generation gap between elders and youngsters.

The Museum from the Outside Looking In

At one point during the second summer I spent in Zuni, a group of Zuni High School students sat in a circle in the museum gallery and gave me their candid views on the museum. They were interns at the museum as part of the tribe's JTPA, and the museum was a relatively new experience for them. They argued that because they saw tourists in the museum more often than members of the community, they considered it a visitor center. I took away from this interview the sense that many community members did not feel at home in the museum and assumed it was an institution developed and operated for visitors. I then set out to look at community members' perception of the museum and the cause of some of the distance that had developed between the museum and its intended audience.

Some community members feared that reliance on an institutional repository would deprive them of their right to perform or to teach traditional knowledge. In particular, the cautious distance that some elders have placed between themselves and the museum suggests that they view the museum's practice of linking traditional knowledge and new technology as an approach that does not subscribe to their expectations of the preexisting system for the transfer of knowledge.

By suggesting that two approaches to knowledge are mediated through the museum, I have located public programs for dissemination at one extreme and the control of knowledge through oral tradition at the other. As previously mentioned, however, a large proportion of people who were interviewed supported or attempted to present both approaches to knowledge from a balanced viewpoint. Furthermore, in the same way that the board and staff were divided through a differentiation between ideology and practice, the community was also divided. We should, therefore, make a distinction between expectations regarding and actual practices in the oral tradition. For example, in response to the question "How do Zunis learn their history?" one young Zuni woman stated that it was through stories and oral tradition, but "that is how I see others teaching them. I have never been taught, but that is how I see it."[14]

Following my fieldwork in Zuni, I searched for case studies that would assist with the interpretation of the relationship between oral tradition and literacy within the context of a widening gap between elder and younger generations. The most relevant study came from a farming community approximately a hundred miles north of Zuni. In *Competence in Performance* (1988), Charles Briggs examines the discursive techniques used in oral tradition within the Hispanic community of Cordova, New Mexico, and identifies the specific contexts of performance that structure Cordovan oral tradition. In discussing the particular nature of this educational genre, Briggs suggests that "the basic goal of pedagogical discourse . . . is to teach the young how to undertake this dialectical and interpretative process themselves" (1988:94). His framework shows the performance of oral tradition as a process that is tantamount to instructing younger generations how to interpret stories:

> [Performance] entails co-ordination of a number of distinct types of communicative resources. This is not a mechanical process, but an active interpretative one that extends principally in two directions simultaneously. Individuals gain the right to perform by mastering one or more genres of the talk of the elders of bygone days. This involves learning how to interpret the beliefs and practices of the elders of bygone days as well as the formal devices that are used to convey them. (1988:20)

If we look at how this situation relates to the oral tradition in Zuni, we can see that those who rely on traditional oral transmission are concerned with issues of interaction and responsibility between performer and audience. Interaction is required to transmit responsibility effectively, thus cementing particular relationships.

From a Zuni elder's point of view, it is crucial for students to learn the nature of the discursive framework in which the oral tradition is performed because it is the structure within which knowledge is embedded and given meaning. For these particular members of the community, oral tradition is not merely about the content of the stories and prayers but also about stories and prayers' performance at a metaphorical level, in which the instructive framework conveys social protocols that are rendered by the stories.[15] The performative processes inherent in Zuni oral tradition also ensure that students are participating and interacting with their instructors. At the complex esoteric levels, however, the use of this knowledge is also understood to have a physical impact—as seen in the responsibilities that the priests have in being able to control the elements. Oral tradition is a communicative network that instructs and structures a wide range of relationships and is viewed as a causal factor in social relationships. As Briggs suggests, "Language is not a passive instrument for describing a world that is independently constituted. Through its performative force, language can effect action, whether it is the baptism of a baby or the delivery of a command. In performance, an individual assumes responsibility for invoking the tradition itself, not just pointing to its existence" (1988:8).

In the late 1990s, elders in Zuni appeared to be questioning the museum's educational environment and were concerned with how it was going to teach the younger generations according to the Zuni system of values when responsibility is not attached to knowledge transmitted by tapes or texts. An archival repository makes the contents of oral traditions more readily available, but it does not guarantee the students' comprehension of the meaning or the discursive framework of the knowledge—or their understanding of its appropriate use and subsequently of the responsibility of maintaining its meaning for future generations. This viewpoint is also prevalent in William Schneider's exploration of the implications of recording Alaskan oral tradition. He argues that "when oral traditions are recorded, the recordings take on their own life, independent of the interactions between tellers and audience, the setting, and the original reasons a story was told. They function as a created record that is widely accessible and outside the control of the narrator and his or her folk group" (1995:196).

In Zuni, some members of the community who maintain oral history also fear that their stories and prayers, once recorded, can be mimicked even though only they have earned the right to perform them. The recording circumvents the preexisting system used to accord status to those who prove their competence in the performance of oral traditions.

Maurice Bloch's ethnography of the Zafimaniry education system in Madagascar also looks at this relationship between the transmission of knowledge and the construction of status. He examines the villagers' ambivalent attitudes toward schoolteachers and suggests that "[s]chool knowledge cannot in every way be that simply assimilated into the pre-existing system. This is because Zafimaniry theories of knowledge assume a homogeneity between the type of knowledge and the kind of person who professes it. If school knowledge is a form of 'wisdom' it is being transmitted by the wrong kind of people to the wrong kind of people, since it is taught by the young to the very young" (1993:101).

The Anglo-American concept of equal access to archives and museum collections is part of a move to "democratize" public institutions (Ames 1992). Yet, as Briggs points out, specific relationships presented by performer and audience exist within a social hierarchy: "All members of social groups do not have equal access to particular traditions. Such factors of age, gender, occupation, ethnicity, and political or religious status often define the range of possible performers for a given genre. . . . In many cases, however, not all individuals of the appropriate age, gender, or status will be accorded the right to perform" (1988:8).

This specific aspect of the "right to perform" raises issues about the ownership of and the criteria used to determine an authoritative source for each genre or story within an oral tradition. As seen from previous discussions about the interaction involved in the transmission of knowledge among the Zuni, an authoritative performer is one who has earned respect for his or her experiential knowledge of the meanings embedded in the stories. Although Zuni museum staff may be able to determine who has the right to perform a particular story, some community members fear that once a story has been recorded, the recording allows others to listen to it without interacting with the authoritative source of this knowledge. In Zuni terms, the museum represents an area of exposure within the system and acts as a competitor for the control of knowledge and therefore for the position of authority.

When the nature of the generation gap is examined, it also becomes clear that a large portion of the responsibility for contextually appropriate use of knowledge falls on the instructors, who need to perform their stories so that they are relevant to contemporary life. Briggs suggests in his analysis of the generation gap in Cordova that relevancy is integral to the interactive nature of the pedagogical discourse:

The difficulty lies in the fact that the young lack a common basis of experience with the elders of bygone days. By the time Cordovans under the age of forty were born, the *viejitos de antes* were dead, the uplands had been lost, the agriculture was no longer the major means of subsistence. In order to comprehend this talk, the young must cross an experiential chasm that separates them from the world of bygone days. The present *viejitos* could simply *describe* what transpired in the past, but this would fail to show the young why it is important to learn about bygone days. They would also fail to grasp the *sentido* of what was being said. If the younger generations miss the deeper significance of the talk, the elders will be unable to realize their basic goal—helping people to see the meaning of the past for the present. (1988:88, original emphasis)[16]

Performers need to link their stories constantly to the modern world, and in this manner the elders are also students within the interactive process of oral tradition. In his account of pedagogical discourses, Briggs notes that the *sentido*, or significance, of the oral tradition must be approachable by a contemporary understanding of the world: "performers will not be able to convey *el sentido*, however, unless they are astute students of unique, ongoing social encounters" (1988:88).

The individuals in support of the Zuni museum imagine that it is one of the most likely environments for this kind of interaction to take place—both the teaching of traditions and the exchange of views, so that the elders are also participating in the things that are changing the lives of the younger generations.

Younger members of the community acknowledged to me the need for this exchange of experiences. In particular, many of them saw a role for the museum in their cultural education—particularly if it was also geared toward educating parents. During an interview, a high school student suggested that a few of her peers did not grow up with parents who were teaching them about their religion or history: "Some of them that I know, they have forgotten about everything, and they are not really into their religion anymore. But the museum could encourage the parents to keep telling their kids, so they don't forget what they have to do on certain days and stuff like that on a religious holiday."[17] The emphasis was not only on the information that would be provided for children but also on the fact that it would also be provided for parents as well, who would then be able to teach their children. Younger members of the community also voiced their disappointment in the elders' resistance to sharing knowledge. Some felt that the elders had erected these boundaries and therefore that it was the elders' responsibility to bring down these barriers.

But was there any common ground in community perspectives on the museum? The majority of community members I interviewed presented a clear argument that any knowledge shared should be between Zunis. There were also indications that to Zunis the presence of non-Zunis at the museum implied that the museum was geared more toward tourism and therefore created the problem of the noncontainment of knowledge. A Zuni artist discussed a number of these issues in an interview. The artist declared the need for a place where the younger generation can learn more about their culture and argued that it should be an environment that specifically passes knowledge from one Zuni to another:

> ARTIST: The oldest elder in our family is my grandmother, but things, when you ask her, she can't remember. So I think in that way the museum could help with the history.
> INTERVIEWER: Do you think the museum is the right place for that to take place?
> ARTIST: If it is coming from a Zuni person instead of [indicates the interviewer], no offence. I think it's only right. I think that is what's going to make it a fully Zuni museum, if they have a lot more of the Zuni members working there. You know, like I said about the elders, get them involved, and then I think you can call it an A:shiwi A:wan Museum.[18]

During an interview I conducted with a high school student, she also emphasized the importance of elders as the central resource for traditional knowledge: "The museum should have more elders so that youth can come in and ask questions . . . and the elders would tell our youth the culture and history of Zuni."[19]

Two points need to be summarized here. First, Zunis shared perspectives on the ideal approaches to the transmission of knowledge, but some members of the younger generation felt that they had not participated in this form of traditional education to the extent that they had hoped. Second, if we highlight the diversity represented in the Zuni community, we can see, on the one hand, that elders considered that the museum aimed to retrieve and disseminate knowledge and so were concerned about their right to perform or maintain traditional knowledge. On the other hand, the younger members of the tribe found the idea of a museum that would rely on elders to be an appropriate solution for educating the younger generations. Overall, community members' shared perspective was that knowledge, if kept in the traditional social network, can be controlled and maintained appropriately. In this manner, community members found common ground in their agreement that the museum should be for and by Zunis, but that it had to prove to the community that it operated this way.

Community Outsiders as Museum Insiders

Non-Zunis' involvement within the development and organization of the A:shiwi A:wan Museum has obviously added another perspective to the debate. Two non-Zuni directors have managed the museum programs between 1990 and 2006. The presence and influence of a non-Zuni director cannot be disregarded, particularly when discussing the practices subscribed to or explored by the museum. Between 1995 and 1998, four non-Zunis were involved with programs at the museum: Tom Kennedy, director of the A:shiwi A:wan Museum and Heritage Center; Anne Beckett, director of the A:shiwi Publishing Company; Nathaniel Stone, coordinator for the *Shiwi Messenger*, the local newspaper that was housed in the same building as the museum; and myself, an assistant for the Zuni Tribal Archives Project. All of us were directly involved in work that relied heavily on projects based on written knowledge: e.g., documentation, publishing, journalism, and archives. We undoubtedly adhered to assumptions or had expectations about literacy as a tool that facilitated the sharing of knowledge.

I was surprised when initially faced with the number of non-Zunis who were residents of the Pueblo of Zuni. I had to question continually my view of myself as the "outsider" when a large number of schoolteachers were non-Zunis and the hospital was also populated by non-Zuni doctors. Similarly, one of the supermarkets was run by a non-Zuni, as was the hardware store and one of the garages. My day-to-day encounters included exchanges with people from a vast array of backgrounds, from across the United States and from across the globe.

An examination of the historical representation of non-Zunis in the anthropological literature reveals that, for the most part, they are excluded from the ethnographic depiction of Zuni life and politics. The few exceptions to this general rule include the research carried out by Triloki Nath Pandey (1967), who explored factionalism in Zuni and the involvement of non-Zunis in the religious and political history of Zuni, and the research by Evon Vogt and Ethel Albert (1967), who looked at the intercultural relationships between Zunis, Navajos, and Mormons in the Rimrock area. Similar issues are also raised in Pandey's article "Anthropologists at Zuni" (1972), which exposes Zuni perceptions of ethnographers' involvement in Pueblo life and Zuni attitudes toward being the subjects of research. On the whole, however, non-Zunis who acted as informants have rarely been cited or positioned in the ethnography as such.[20] Furthermore, I have not encountered an ethnography that appears to have openly incorporated non-Zunis as part of the ethnographic subjects or included them within the actual process of fieldwork—that is, by means of interviews with them or direct citations of their views.

In the context of my research, however, it was critical to explore non-Zunis' role in the development of the museum and in environments similar to the museum, such as schools, in order to understand their views on instituting Anglo-American concepts in the Pueblo and to investigate different approaches to transmitting knowledge. Of equal importance was how they perceived or contributed to the processes involved in the institutionalization of Zuni traditional history and culture. At the heart of this ethnography lies the exploration of the different approaches to knowledge presented by Anglo-American ideology and by Zuni traditional methods for retaining and transmitting knowledge. Up to this point, I have been concerned largely with Zunis' viewpoints regarding the A:shiwi A:wan Museum and the institutionalization of traditional knowledge. This ethnography, however, would not be complete without looking at the direct involvement of non-Zunis in the development of the museum.

The subtext of this chapter is also the range of perspectives presented by the population that forms the Pueblo of Zuni; non-Zunis are crucial to understanding this diversity. Interviews I carried out with non-Zunis reveal a variety of viewpoints on themselves as outsiders and their views on the degree to which they have influenced the institutionalization of Anglo-American or Zuni practices. Although all non-Zunis commented on a range of subjects, a number of individuals were diffident about being cited when discussing issues that involved Zuni religion or some of the changes occurring in the Pueblo. In these particular cases, the interviewees were most likely to intimate that they, as non-Zunis or outsiders, could speak only from their own perspective and therefore did not want to be seen as an authoritative source on the specific processes in which they had no part. In one example, a high school teacher reflected on her background and how this affected her expectations of her role in Zuni:

> I hope that whatever you do with this, that you say that it is just one person's uninformed egocentric viewpoint. Zunis are expected to speak for all Zunis, and Anglos are expected to speak for the experience of all Anglos in Zuni. It is very much filtered [through] your own view. I grew up in a small town, and I hated it and what it did to people. I said that I would never go back to it. . . . The insider/outsider thing is your chronic situation here. It gives me some protection against some of the small town ugliness—being the outsider. So I can be my own person, but still be in a small town.[21]

The implication here is that she can engage as an individual at some level with the community, but she prefers not to be wholly inducted into the Zuni structure of society. Another teacher discussed how his background specifically affected his role within the schools. He emphasized that his position within Zuni required him not to be engaged too closely and that he should not interfere with the traditional system of belief: "Part of what I am teaching is who I am, and what I believe and what my values are. I cannot escape that. That certainly permeates my lessons, and there is no denying that. You can't help but do that. But you need to do it in a responsible way and to show deference and respect to their beliefs."[22]

Anglo-American scholars have had an ongoing investment in Zuni history and therefore in the development of repositories for further research. During the previous three decades, numerous consultants and researchers have been a part of the evolution of the museum. Non-Zunis I talked to, however, held an extremely wide range of perspectives on what the museum could or should be. Holman suggested that this diversity had a particular impact on the development of the museum: "I think the hallmark of this history is that everyone that has been involved has had a different image [of the museum] . . . so that there has been [the creation of] a corporate identity."[23] He also noted the high number of consultants involved in the development of the museum, suggesting that although they may not have agreed on the final form or structure that the museum was taking, their role was to help bring the staff to a position of self-sufficiency:

The whole point about the ANA [Administration for Native Americans] grant was that the museum was to be run by tribal members, who would get the training they needed to run the museum during the course of the grant, and when the grant ended, the staff would be self-sufficient, and the museum would be self-sufficient. . . . But there would be a series of consultants who [would] shadow the work of each of the staff members and provide ongoing practical training and advice. There was an archive consultant and a museum consultant . . . a whole series of them.[24]

The photographic collections also presented a number of challenges to non-Zunis. First, when duplicates were transferred from the Smithsonian in 1992, they were arranged in the same manner that they had been found at the Smithsonian, so that collections were organized by the photographers who had taken the images. This organization presented a number of problems for Holman, the first of which was how to rearrange the collection in a way more suited to members of the Zuni community, the majority of whom were more familiar with the subjects presented in the photographs than were visitors to the Smithsonian:

The impression I had was that the Smithsonian documentation . . . was useful to note, but it wasn't the kind of stuff that was of great value to the community members looking at the photographs. In other words, it didn't really matter if the Smithsonian catalog said: "Taken in 1904 by A. C. Vroman" and "it is a photograph of the church." . . . They didn't care if it was taken by Vroman or Stevenson or anything like that . . . they knew it was a picture of the church, because they knew the church. . . . For all intents and purposes, the kind of information that was of tantamount value to the Smithsonian was not a lot of value in Zuni.[25]

As a non-Zuni, Holman was positioned between two different ways of perceiving the use of collections. This position challenged him not only to find an appropriate solution for a museum for Zunis, but also to question to what extent he could compromise conventional—or, in the terminology used here, Anglo-American—museum practices. According to Holman, nowhere was this question more crucial than with regard to the photographic collection that mixed together sacred and secular subjects: "When I arrived, the museum's main resources were the photographs. My goal was to get the photographs used as much as possible. It was one of these situations where you have to try and develop some sort of compromise between what is good museum practice and what is good practice in Zuni. This is perhaps the best example of how I tried to resolve this. I know what I did was not to the liking of the folks at the Smithsonian."[26]

Holman labeled himself as the protagonist within the processes that led to the separation of the sensitive images. In the context of discussing non-Zunis' role in the development of the museum, he implied that other non-Zunis connected to the museum provided explicit information about the problems presented by housing sacred subjects in the collections:

> It became increasingly obvious to me that the photographs could never be used properly while there was this growing concern about the nature of the sensitive images. That ties to all sorts of other things happening in the community at the time—concern with public access to the ceremonials—concern about intellectual property. Certainly, I didn't want the museum to become a repository for religious information—that was something that was made very clear to me very early on, or at least became clear to me. Nothing was said very explicitly, and if it was, it was said by Roger [Anyon], rather than by people on the board. . . . I didn't want the presence of the sensitive images to lower the use of the nonsensitive images. . . . I was the protagonist for getting all that done—in terms of separating the images, the documentation project, and things like that. But it was not as though I was doing it because I wanted to do it and nobody else wanted to do it. It was clearly the thing that the advisory team [ZCRAT] wanted to do. It was the thing Roger felt was advisable—it was the thing the tribal council was in favor of, and the board. Everyone knew it was the right thing to do, and to a certain extent I made it one of the things that I worked toward.

Holman's approach also reflects how he viewed his position as an intermediary between traditional museum practices and the processes involved in institutionalizing traditional knowledge.

> I wanted to make the point to everybody in the community that "these are historical resources, and you have to treat them like that,

and if we are going to separate them out, you have to carry on using them in an appropriate way, and you have got to perpetuate the information that is contained in the photographs by having the documentation project, by [having] the advisory team, who are the descendants of the people who were participating in the religious activities at the turn of the century." It was this notion of wanting to create a compromise between simply having a conventional museum where everything would be documented and everything would be open, and not wanting to say, "They are sensitive, the religious leaders can have them, and we don't care what happens to them after that." . . . It was also a project that gave the museum some respect in the eyes of the religious leaders. I was clearly interested in helping the museum to develop an identity within the community and an identity that was nonthreatening, so people, if you mentioned the museum to them, they would think about the museum in a good light. They would perhaps think about an exhibit they saw that they liked and also they would remember that they had done the right thing with the sensitive images, that they tried to do the right thing for the religious leaders, [that] they respected the religious leaders.[27]

Each non-Zuni concerned with the development of the museum has held different views on the interpretation and treatment of religious knowledge. For example, according to Kennedy, the museum should recognize that in Zuni philosophy there is not a division between what is sacred and what is secular. He suggested that for the museum to be considered a true member of the community, it should be blessed by the Mudheads, or Koyemshi—the sacred clowns that are part of the kokko priesthood—in the same manner that the houses built at Sha'lak'o are blessed:

We have not made the transition into the core or been adopted by the community yet. I was talking with one of the board members, a non-Zuni, but someone who is a longtime resident here, that an indication to me that we will have arrived is when the Mudheads visit us to bless us. . . . I think that is absolutely right. That is the recognition within the community that your structure, your house, your entity is part of the community. I live in the community in a house that is owned by a Zuni, but the Mudheads don't visit me. They know that Melikas live in that house, and they pass us by, and they go to the neighbors. That is recognition to me that we are not recognized as being integral to the community; until that happens for here, I think we will always be marginalized to some extent. We try and we make inroads, but we have not been totally accepted in.[28]

We can also learn a great deal about non-Zunis' perspectives from their involvement in the decision to establish the museum as an institution separate from tribal government. Their role in this decision is difficult to gauge, but, like so many of the processes in the development of the museum, a number of outcomes were the result of collaboration. Yet non-Zunis' perspectives of the purpose for the museum's independence present an ironic epilogue to the history of non-Zuni involvement in tribal affairs. At least three of the non-Zunis I interviewed suggested that they had supported the decision for the museum to seek independence because they had been concerned that it would be vulnerable to factionalism if it were to remain under tribal administration. Factionalism has historically been seen to be the complex product of non-Zuni/Zuni interactions within local government—a process in which both Zunis and non-Zunis have used contrasting ideologies as a device to divide and weaken certain groups (Pandey 1967). During an interview in 1997, Holman explained his awareness of factionalism in Zuni: "this whole notion of the factionalism of Zuni . . . that is obviously, in the anthropological literature, very well documented. If anyone spends any time in Zuni, they understand it, at least at some level."[29] He supported the idea of removing the museum from these divisive processes: "the idea was to take the museum outside of the factionalism. I still think this was an excellent idea."[30]

The history of anthropological involvement in the Pueblo of Zuni has introduced to both Zunis and non-Zunis different ways of looking at Zuni culture, but because this involvement has not been passive, there is now a continual process of feedback between anthropologists' perception of Zuni culture and Zunis' perception. The museum is a product of this history—the history of factionalism, the history of non-Zuni intervention, and the history of adherence to or transformation of traditional practices in new contexts. If non-Zunis' involvement within the museum is not teased out, however, the more sensitive conflicts between Zunis and non-Zunis that have marked the history of Zuni will be lost. The methods by which this history is recorded or transmitted are where the lines are drawn between the two cultures.

How does a public institution represent the diversity of community perspectives, many of which are structured through the contexts of gender-related or esoteric knowledge or both? Many of these contexts are seen as immutable and reflective of the social ordering of the Zuni world, and, as a result, the community's diversity is highlighted or aggravated through the introduction of Anglo-American practices. Kennedy suggested that the museum is associated with Anglo-American influences and is therefore held at the periphery of the community: "For the majority of the community, we exist in the fringe institutions and organizations that are here. . . . I think we are on par with organizations that are noncentral to the core of the community and culture, [such] as the school, the church, some of the missions . . . tribal government, the BIA, the hospital. We are in the Melika world."[31] On the one hand, there are expectations about the need for creating a subjective intimacy in the museum that will foster internal cultural awareness, and, on the other hand, there are expectations about the objective distance required to investigate Zuni history and present this knowledge to non-Zuni visitors.

As I have outlined previously, the majority of literature on tribal museums does not interrogate the diversity of perspectives present in each tribal community. Similarly, when discussing the political sphere in which these museums operate, scholars have located the museums only within the national arena. They see such museums as symbols of political empowerment and the renegotiation of postcolonial relations. Yet, as my analysis demonstrates, the values ascribed to the politics of representation differ radically in tribal institutions and nontribal institutions. In each cultural context, status is entrusted to individuals according to a very different set of criteria. If we isolate tribal museums from their immediate political sphere and view them only in relation to national politics or the chronological history utilized in the Anglo-American model of museums, we are prevented from understanding the particular nature of the relationships developed between local museums and the communities they represent. The discursive techniques used to maintain and transmit knowledge—including the negotiation of meanings created through the intersection between different philosophies or through the purposeful use of ambiguity—can give us insight into how historical and cultural narratives are socially structured, controlled, and politicized.

7
Conclusions
October 2006

A period of absence from a place always heightens awareness to change. On returning to Zuni in the summer of 2005, I found that the museum had moved to the Hebadina Building, a former trading post at one of the major crossroads near the Middle Village. A new exhibit, Hawikku: Echoes from Our Ancestors, was the collaborative offspring between the A:shiwi A:wan Museum and the National Museum of the American Indian. Not only had the physical landscape of the museum changed, but there was also a new director and staff.[1] The institution I had studiously documented over the years had, on the surface, changed into a very different entity from the one I had first encountered in 1997.

My return visit alerted me to transformations that had taken place not just with the Pueblo but also in my own life. After many years as a graduate student, I had recently accepted a teaching position at Arizona State University. As I prepared to leave England for Arizona, my professors bluntly stated that I would learn more in the next year than I had in the past seven years of graduate studies. It is worth asking why this transition from student to professor is so challenging. As a graduate student, I was trained to interpret and write about information concerning the world around me. Although I was provided analytical tools, I was not instructed on the responsibilities that came with this acquisition of knowledge. On my arrival in Arizona, I discovered that this passage from student to professor was immensely difficult, not because it was harder or involved more work, but because for the first time I was wholly accountable for the knowledge I acquired and transmitted.

My new situation brought into sharp focus the delicate balance that exists between responsibility attached to and power gained from knowledge. With all this in mind, I was impelled to situate my earlier findings about the Zuni museum within the context of the politics of the control of knowledge. I therefore am devoting this conclusion to an explanation of these specific interrelationships involving power and influence not only within the Zuni system but also in the areas where the Zuni system overlaps with Anglo-American systems, in particular the academic arena that shapes how specialist knowledge of Zuni is disseminated. Much has been written about the relationship between knowledge and power (Fardon 1985) and about the hierarchies of control (Foucault 1970), but I am specifically interested here in detailing the vernacular practices that accompany knowledge transmission and control. It is largely during everyday negotiations over access to and use of knowledge that our expectations are shaped about our inclusion within or exclusion from social arenas. This approach also leads us to identify paradigmatic shifts that are taking place in both Zuni and the discipline of anthropology, calling for an open discussion of the political agenda attached to the distribution and use of knowledge in Zuni and the academic community.

Politics and the Control of Knowledge in Zuni

As the site of first contact between Europeans and the indigenous inhabitants of North America, the Zuni ancestral village Hawikku plays a key role in both Zuni and U.S. history. To Zunis, it embodies the introduction of European ideology and the subsequent challenges that accompanied colonization. To anthropologists and historians, it signifies the beginning of the historic era and rapid cultural change in the New World. In 1995, in recognition of this resonant history, a collaborative research team made up of individuals from ZAP and the Museum of the American Indian in New York successfully obtained funding from the National Endowment for the Humanities for an exhibit to be developed to explore "the 450 year-old relationship between Zuni and European and Euro-American cultures."[2] The strategy was to bring together a research team of tribal members and humanities scholars, combining anthropological, archaeological, and historical approaches with Zuni perspectives in order to develop new insights into the shared histories of Hawikku. As one of the authors of the grant and in line with many of his previous museum initiatives, Nigel Holman argued that Zuni values would be used to develop the exhibit, and this process would also help develop protocols that would provide a workable model for other collaborations between tribal and national museums, thus asserting cross-cultural relevance to the research.

For many years, anthropologists have been eager to uncover the history of Hawikku through scientific inquiry. From 1917 to 1923, the Hendricks-Hodge Expedition, under the auspices of the New York

Museum of the American Indian (now known as the National Museum of the American Indian in Washington, D.C.), conducted excavations at Hawikku. As noted previously, the expedition was led by former BAE director Frederick Webb Hodge and "was one of the most extensive archaeological excavations ever conducted in the Southwest."[3] The exhibit proposed in 1995 would consider some of the cultural conflicts that arose between the Zuni and Spanish colonizers, as well as between Zuni and the anthropological community. The Hodge Expedition provided one example of such conflicts. Although Hodge had gained permission from Zuni leaders to film the Sha'lak'o rituals in 1923, an acrimonious dispute regarding this decision ensued within the community. Holman has identified this confrontation as the beginning of the official ban on photography at religious ceremonies.

The site of Hawikku now presents a stratified history not only of first contact but also of the conflicting ideologies concerning the excavation of the village and the dissemination of Zuni knowledge. With Europeans, Anglo-Americans, and Zunis claiming Hawikku as a central part of their history, and with disagreements over its excavation and over the eventual decision to ban photography of sacred ceremonies, it provides a good starting point to reexamine the political agendas that underpin the themes of this book.

There should be no surprise in the fact that the Hawikku exhibition was largely initiated by archaeologists working in Zuni, many of whom were the most aware of the extent of the Hawikku collections held at the National Museum of the American Indian and who wanted to see the community have the opportunity to reengage with these objects. These scholars had also helped design other collaborative projects in Zuni, so the exhibit was a natural next step. What is intriguing, however, is the manner in which the project transformed over the next seven years (1995–2002). At first there was resistance from Zunis to opening up the tragic history of particular events at Hawikku, and later there was the decision to exclude non-Zuni consultants from the planning phase of the project.

The funded portion of the National Endowment for the Humanities project was initiated during the time I was working at the museum. Under the guidance of the new director, Tom Kennedy, a group of tribal historians and museum staff were organized to provide Zuni perspectives on Hawikku. Looking back at these meetings, I have come to see them as a turning point in how I perceived Zuni perspectives on the nature of history itself. At one point, an elder spoke dramatically of stories that portrayed acts of cannibalism at Hawikku. They were awful signifiers of the Pueblo peoples' starvation and immeasurable suffering during colonization. It was made very clear that these stories should not be allowed to encourage voyeurism because their importance lay in their lessons of ancestral survival and resilience. In response, another elder added that telling the stories of Zuni deprivations under Spanish colonization should be avoided altogether; in fact, many of these topics were considered taboo subjects. It became clear that Hawikku held an ambiguous role within Zuni oral traditions. Although the stories might teach younger generations of their ancestors' persistence in maintaining their religion despite colonial rule, questions about this history were met with silence more often than not. If pressed, elders mentioned the brutality of the Spanish only in hushed tones. It was better to revere and respect the longevity of one's ancestors than to stir up the ghosts of those who suffered in the past. It was best to leave them in peace.

The southwestern Pueblos have a long history of resisting the excavation of ancestral villages. Accompanying this resistance is the belief that these physical embodiments of the past are ongoing sources of power and knowledge and therefore should be left alone. As such, they are represented as not "the past," but as sacred places that play an active role in present-day ritual practices. This representation should also alert us to the fact that "heritage" is neither a cross-cultural category nor a collection of common ideas of the past, and that the elements that Anglo-Americans see as the manifestations of heritage, such as archaeological sites, often exist as different concepts in other cultures.

During my time at the museum, there were also frank discussions about intentionally excluding external scholars, especially anthropologists, on the grounds that they had already dominated the study of Zuni history and it was time for Zunis to reclaim their past. Yet, contrary to what many would assume, this argument was initiated not by Zunis but by non-Zunis involved with the museum. At times, in very polite terms, Zunis involved in the project agreed with these sentiments, but at no time did they actively pursue or initiate decisions that would prevent external scholars from participating in the project. In hindsight, it is possible to suggest that if some of the Zuni team members had wanted more external collaboration, they may have felt it discourteous to contradict those who had argued to exclude these individuals. The non-Zunis expressed their opinion in very strong terms, so, as is general practice in Zuni, few Zunis were comfortable with challenging it or with belaboring sensitive discussions about Anglo-American/Zuni relations. Although consultants were invited to a meeting at the final stages of the project, they were not included in the previous five years of research and planning.

Ultimately, the elders graciously declined to talk about Spanish colonization of Hawikku, and external scholars were for the most part excluded from the project. The imagined collaboration between local and external historians and experts was deferred. A new group made up of a number of Zuni artists who had previously worked with the museum was eventually formed to collect Zuni perspectives on Hawikku. Some had participated in prior programs, encouraging younger Zunis to take an interest in Zuni traditional arts, and others joined with an interest in learning more from the museum about archaic pottery designs from ancestral villages. Over the first four years of the project, the research team gradually shifted from the collaborative team conceived by the original authors of the grant into a group composed of artists interested in learning more about their history and links to Hawikku. What resulted was an exhibit with an extremely vivid visual portrayal of Zuni perspectives on the history of Hawikku.

At the start of this book, I introduced the museum with a tour of the galleries as they were in 1997. The Hawikku exhibit and the new museum location near the Middle Village create another illuminating view.

You enter the Hebadina Building through a simple shop front of white-washed adobe walls and sky blue awnings. A nondescript building with a colorful past, it is the site of the house of the infamous anthropologist Frank Hamilton Cushing and subsequently the location of Kelsey's trading post. To your right is the introduction to the Hawikku exhibit—a dark tunnel-like corridor with moss green walls and a dappled shade-covered ceiling. This corridor represents the *shiba:bulima*, the point at which the Zuni, or A:shiwi, emerged into this world and began their journey to find Halona:wa Idiwana'a, the Middle Place. The tunnel shadows lead into a bright circular opening with a panoramic view of the Zuni Valley. It is within this room that you encounter your first glimpses of Hawikku—a complex array of pottery from the Zuni and Mogollon cultures as well as Gila and Roosevelt wares. They are accompanied by a macaw skeleton, illustrating the elaborate trade routes connecting Hawikku to cultures farther south in Mexico. The circular room is broken on the right-hand side by a narrow exit with a mural portraying

Bread oven in front of the Nuestra Señora de Guadalupe Mission, Middle Village, Pueblo of Zuni, 1997.

the arrival of the conquistadors. You are brought into the transitional worlds of the Spanish and Zuni during the colonization of the Southwest. Through Romanesque arches you reach a square space representing the Catholic mission church at Hawikku. To pass through this room you must walk over a black silhouette of a kiva painted on the floor, indicating how Zuni religious practices were forced underground in order to survive Spanish rule.[4]

The last part of the exhibit provides stories of how, following the Mexicans and subsequently the U.S. government, anthropologists arrived in Zuni. Although Zunis learned to become more cautious of these observers, one such story details how Frank Hamilton Cushing betrayed his Zuni teachers by publishing esoteric knowledge. Similarly, in discussing the excavation of Hawikku and removal of objects to the East Coast, a firsthand account is given by a ninety-two-year-old elder who as a child watched large crates being loaded up on wagons and driven out of the Pueblo. He always wondered where they were going and what they contained.

The exhibit's underlying message is that the Zunis' artistic and cultural inheritance has survived colonialism and flourished in recent times. This message is portrayed directly through texts that outline the arts and industries of precontact A:shiwi and through the display of turquoise inlay combs, earrings, and the intricate array of pottery from Hawikku. The celebration of the Zuni arts is also communicated through the colorful murals that dominate the gallery space, encouraging visitors to interpret Zuni history through visual means.

Two commonly recognized narrative genres that incorporate oral and visual means for transmission are used to communicate past events. First, the origin and migration genre of narratives speak of the A:shiwi emergence through the four worlds and their search to find Halona:wa Idiwana'a. Because these narratives hold powerful performative knowledge from the ancestors that is still used today, they are largely ritualized and restricted in their telling. Zunis admit to a plurality and heterogeneity in their narrations of the past. Each clan holds a different version of the origin and migration narratives.

Second, stories of the ancestors encompass a more fluid and innovative category of narratives, including those passed down from Hawikku. These stories are not individually owned, but because they concern the ancestors, they are treated with caution. As the elder consultants for the Hawikku project pointed out, there must be a controlled context for the narration of these ancestral stories because intricate responsibilities are attached to their telling. The restrictions on stories of the ancestors, such as the Hawikku accounts, involve self-censorship or vernacular controls, wherein individuals err on the side of caution if unsure about the consequences of sharing this knowledge.

Because museum staff were actively engaged in transmitting traditions in this exhibit, we must consider the politics involved in finding a common and public form that could be presented within the museum space. In considering whether the staff actively constructed Zuni history, I would suggest that they created a public display of Zuni traditions that branched away from the preexisting Zuni system for the transmission of knowledge, largely by marking out more profoundly what public history is in Zuni terms. However, although this line of investigation is useful, we have to consider the different cultural concepts of history when we apply it to Zuni. The people of Zuni are continually exploring the difference between what they view as history (i.e., what current responsibilities come from clan origins and define an individual's role or identity within Zuni) and what Anglo-Americans define as history (i.e., in this context, what has been uncovered through the interrogation and reinterpretation of archaeological sites and historic documents). In this way, Zunis are not simply constructing narratives of their past but are also involved in a process that defines their relationship to Anglo-American and Zuni concepts of history, as well as how they view their origins and how these origins are interpreted by outsiders. In the case of the Hawikku exhibit, Zunis sought to dispel what they saw as the Anglo-American mode of reading their past. As a consequence, staff members learned to mediate external influences and their implications for both Zunis and outsiders, thereby forging a cross-cultural definition of Zuni public history. The staff also largely employed visual and oral means for transmitting this history, bringing together both familiar and specialized knowledge and therefore introducing a level of ambiguity about access that diffused community sensitivity regarding the new institutional context in which this history was being displayed.

The most intriguing element in this construction of a public past is the politics behind it. In developing this specific form of telling history, Zunis have added a third cross-cultural narrative genre to the two preexisting genres. They have the origin narratives, the ancestral stories, and now public history developed from the negotiation of esoteric and familial knowledge. This particular performance also incorporates the negotiation between Zuni and Anglo-American perspectives on the Zuni past. It would appear Zunis have actively sought, through the museum, to create community narratives that differentiate between privileged and familial knowledge in order to render exhibits suitable for all Zuni audiences. This process is also now used to create narratives for non-Zunis that follow the Anglo-American constructs for telling history. Internally, especially in the museum, there is also the interaction between the impetus for the inclusion of public history and the circumstances that have created a gap between the generations. The aim is to close this disparity by teaching tradition to the younger generation and by creating an arena in which these changes can be explored.

At present (2006–2007), the new director and former board member, Jim Enote, is planning exhibits on war veterans, firefighting crews, Zuni musicians, and Zuni home building. A new program, Pathways to Zuni Wisdom, funded by the National Science Foundation, brings together sixth- to eighth-grade students and experienced Zuni cultural specialists to explore Zuni philosophy; it also attempts to find ways to link this type of learning situation with informal science learning. Not only do these recent projects stay away from esoteric knowledge, but they can be used to develop a more socially cohesive idea of contemporary Zuni identity that does not divide by means of access or nonaccess to ritual knowledge. This approach has also become politically advantageous to the younger generations otherwise disempowered within the traditional religious and ritually hierarchical system. A particularly strong example of the current programming that explores this avenue is the A:shiwi Map Art Project, in which three Zuni artists are creating paintings of areas of cultural interest in the Zuni region. According to Enote, "the art will then be labeled with Zuni place-names to replace Spanish and English names."[5] An advisory committee made up of community members has been formed to facilitate the process of determining, through current knowledge restrictions, what should and should not be included on the maps. The members of this group "understand that at the front of place-name mapping is what *not* to map" and that "only general place-names that the group feel should be known by all Zunis will be included."[6]

The layer of instruction added by the museum to the Zuni knowledge system clearly has the potential for creating tensions between this new institution and the preexisting system run by the religious leaders. We have already seen how tensions have arisen between traditional methods for teaching knowledge on a need-to-know basis and the museum's approach, which requires a more public and accessible view of the transfer of knowledge. Although the museum has implemented programs that privilege younger age groups, it has relied on participating elders to provide this knowledge. Consequently, the museum has been located in a position where it needs to reconcile between the preexisting system for the transmission of knowledge and the younger generation's changing expectations regarding how they are taught and learn. Current programs at the museum illustrate how staff continue to explore innovative ways to alleviate these tensions and negotiate a public and, at the same time, traditionally informed educational forum for Zuni youth.

If we revisit the statement that tribal museums are vehicles for self-empowerment, we must also go back to our original question, Who empowers whom in these institutions and in their interactions with the communities in which they are located? Regarding the A:shiwi A:wan Museum and Heritage Center, the younger generation has become privileged within a public institution that recognizes the changes taking place in Zuni. The museum also provides a space for members of the community who have little influence in the traditional system for the control of knowledge. It empowers a very specific group that is disenfranchised within the larger group. At the same time, however, we must consider how the museum has been seen by the elder generations who rely on the more familial system for the transfer of knowledge and who therefore share concern about intrusions into the way they are comfortable with doing things. Although it would be simplistic to argue that the museum reduces the elder generation's influence in teaching tradition, it is possible to suggest that the elders are fearful of this very result. Moreover, when the issue is considered from a broader perspective, it is clear that they are concerned not only about the museum, but also about the total network of schools, missions, *and* the museum, all of which they see as an indication that education is being taken out of their hands. This process of institutionalizing traditional knowledge has alerted the elder generation to the way in which public institutions may absolve the youth from the responsibilities that accompany the transfer of traditional knowledge.

Zuni is stratified according to families that hold powerful ritual knowledge and paraphernalia, on the one hand, and, as Bunzel points out, those that are ritually "poor" (1992:617). Tribal government forms a secondary hierarchy of power that provides political influence alongside religious leadership. Government decisions are often made in consultation with religious leadership. Authority is also given to elders who have the benefit of experience and a deeper knowledge of Zuni history, language, and ritual ceremonies. Zunis who have grown up in marginalized or fractured families feel detached from the processes through which knowledge is passed down. The majority of high school students I worked with in Zuni spoke of their desire to learn more about "being Zuni" and of their frustrations at being excluded from some of the influential and traditional groups within the community. They often presented their plight as one determined by barriers put up by elders, who exclude them from the passing down of traditional knowledge.

Similarly, individuals who were educated in schools and universities outside of Zuni felt that when they returned, they, too, faced barriers designed to exclude "outsiders."

It is to be expected that in a context with this level of exclusivity, the younger generations and the educated professionals became the leaders and founders of the museum. By working to bridge the gaps between generations and the practices that may bar individuals from religious societies, a new "family" formed that recognized its own need to belong to the Zuni community. This new group not only recognizes itself as made up of like-minded individuals but also is aware of its political power through its numbers. The museum has not only created a space for these people but also presents opportunities to increase their confidence, resulting in another layer of influence to the strata of power. This form of power is vernacular: it is neither judicial nor theocratic, but built on people's perceptions and renegotiations of their own social values within the larger group. In this manner, the museum has helped give influence and stability to a cohort otherwise disenfranchised from the community as a whole.

Thus, the museum has used the negotiation between Anglo-American and Zuni knowledge as a way to build a new theoretical and political arena in Zuni. It has empowered by giving a deeper understanding of the relational hierarchies attached to knowledge transmission in the Pueblo and of the relationship between these hierarchies and Anglo-American practices. This negotiation process does not involve the simple addition of "Western" philosophy to Zuni philosophy. The museum has no choice but to negotiate these different knowledge systems carefully and to carve out a new territory, but the museum itself is only a part of readdressing power structures within the Pueblo.

By viewing the museum staff and community members as active agents in the conceptualization and construction of the museum, I have introduced the theme that the staff have served as intermediaries who negotiate the use of traditional knowledge according to the current internal expectations about the pedagogical system and the external expectations about the right to access knowledge. Although tensions arise over teaching within a public institution, it is clear that the museum provides a space that privileges the process of mediation between public and private knowledge and between elder and younger generations. As such, it is more likely to engage with the processes that link the two generations together.

Anglo-American Politics and Pueblo Knowledge Systems

Colonial regimes have transposed Anglo-American structures of authority and their related knowledge systems onto the Zuni system of government and education. This has not, however, been a one-way process.
Anglo-Americans have also used the Zuni knowledge system as a way to
adjust the power structure within their own culturally familiar arenas,
such as academia. The type of anthropology that dominated Zuni during my fieldwork centered around negotiations between Zuni and the
Anglo-American governments, with many scholars becoming intermediaries who collaborated with Zunis who were employing the Anglo-
American legal and political system to achieve Zuni goals, such as land
claims (Hart 1995). As a result, they became interpreters for both Zunis
and Anglo-Americans, and many of them formed relationships built on
the cross-cultural exchange of knowledge. By the 1970s and 1980s, Zuni
had gained a reputation as an attractive research site for scholars who
were interested in collaborative anthropology, represented largely by
field schools that trained Pueblo youths in archaeological techniques.
That the Pueblo of Zuni became one of the first tribes to repatriate
objects from museums prior to the passing of the Native American
Graves Protection and Repatriation Act in 1990 and to be at the forefront
of the design of models used within the process of repatriation should
also be seen as catalyst for and a product of these cross-cultural exchanges and of the successful growth of historic preservation projects
under Governor Lewis. Some of the architects of the act, such as Keith
Kintigh, worked at Zuni, as did T. J. Ferguson and Roger Anyon, who
supported the religious leaders in the first repatriation cases for Zuni
(Merrill, Ladd, and Ferguson 1993; Ferguson, Anyon, and Ladd 2000).

Anthropologists' mediational roles, however, have had secondary un-
anticipated effects. Cultural resource management, repatriation, and the
politics of anthropology have become subjects in the academy in their
own right (Gulliford 2000; Mihesuah 2000; Bray 2001; Fine-Dare 2002;
Fforde 2002; Jaarsma 2002; Tweedie 2002; Turner 2005). Because these
areas deal directly with the mediation of Native Americans and Anglo-
American ideology, scholars have developed theories about the concilia-
tion of different beliefs, leading to the creation of a new area of anthropology focusing on the resolution of divisions between scientifically and
subjectively determined theories. For example, Nancy Mithlo uses the
term *the third space* to refer to this "new conceptual terrain," which

should be established outside of the existing and oversimplified dichotomy between scientific and indigenous knowledge (2004:760).

Repatriation is commonly looked upon as the process that adjusted the balance of power between Native Americans and Anglo-Americans. It was also used, however, by anthropologists who sought ways to readdress the power struggles between "scientists" and "postmodernists" within the academy. There was (and possibly still is) a divide between two theoretical schools within the larger ideological construct of anthropology, which supplements my analysis of the effects of repatriation on the academy. A number of science-based scholars viewed anthropology as made up of empirical methods that contribute to a singular and cumulative body of objective knowledge (this group was represented largely by physical anthropology and areas in archaeology). Postcolonial and postmodern scholars questioned this objectivity, arguing for the plurality of knowledges and pointing out their concern over how culturally situated knowledges lose their original significance if recontextualized within scientific paradigms. Although often presented as in stark opposition to each other, with the debates labeled as the "crises in anthropology," postmodernist and scientistic stances have now coexisted for at least half a century, resulting in indistinct boundaries between them. The desire to introduce the process of repatriation as a form of mediation between knowledge systems can also be seen as a point of reconciliation between these groups. Through the negotiation of repatriation issues, the political mediation of ideologies has apparently become a central preoccupation of academic anthropologists trying to unite otherwise divided camps. In addition, by mediating between Anglo-American and Native American politics, anthropologists who have worked in repatriation form a tertiary ideological arena that gives them a new base of power within the academy, creating a paradigmatic shift in ideology and influence.

In looking at interactions between Zuni and Anglo-American knowledge systems, we also become aware of how scholars and scientists largely deny the practice of secrecy in the academy. Whereas the Zuni system is represented as one dominated by secrecy, the Anglo-American system is most frequently characterized as open and objective. Bok argues in her study of Anglo-American approaches to secrecy that although the application of secrecy is commonplace, denial of this practice "is ritualistic in science" (1983:153). These invocations of openness occur "precisely because the conflict that secrecy creates for scientists is so strong," and "their declarations against it are in part efforts at conjuring away its power" (153). We also know that secrecy is used in scientific research for financial or political gains, either in environments where researchers compete to be the first to reach and disclose a discovery or in corporately funded research where private agendas determine that dissemination can happen only after a discovery has been patented. Unfortunately, this tradition of disclaiming secrecy has defused efforts to better understand opportunistic uses of powerful scientific knowledge. By denying the use of secrecy, the scientific community wishes to communicate that its research has the public's best interest in mind. To maintain this norm, however, the scholars within this community must practice active disinterestedness, or, as it is referred to within the scientific community, "objectivity."

Scientific knowledge and politics, however, cannot be compartmentalized or separated if we are to understand cross-cultural approaches to the control of knowledge. As Mithlo aptly points out, "both indigenous knowledge and Western knowledge systems can be interpreted as subjective enterprises with restricted codes" (2004:746). There should be no surprise that Puebloan peoples see academics as holding power gained through knowledge. Academics are, after all, paid outright or indirectly for their role in the transmission of knowledge. Although the norms require that knowledge gained through research should not achieve "property in its own right," as Bok points out, "those who discover it achieve new means to property" (1983:158). Academic books most commonly do not bring the author funds from publication, but they can be used for promotion and therefore for financial gain.

We can better understand these cross-cultural contexts, however, if Anglo-American and Pueblo approaches to knowledge are not oversimplified into frameworks that serve only to identify reduced categories such as "objective Western knowledge" and "subjective Native knowledge," because this simplification provides little comprehension of the cultural codes and strategies used by individuals or groups in all societies to advantage or restrict people's access to knowledges. In addition, if Anglo-American approaches to knowledge are more closely examined, not only from within their own constructs, such as the academy, but also through the eyes and minds of the communities that are actively aware of and critiquing different approaches to knowledge, such as Zuni, we can reach a more realistic and nuanced appreciation of the development of individual and/or collective methods used to navigate complex intercultural environments.

Contextually Controlled Knowledges

In concluding, I want to return to the principal topic of this study, the A:shiwi A:wan Museum, and to reflect on some of the broader issues that my ethnography has raised about this institution and its negotiation of different knowledge systems. In bringing together the history and current conceptualization of the museum, we can also see that the changes experienced by the museum mirror the political climate and shifts that have occurred in Zuni over the past thirty years. When the museum was first developed, it reflected the Lewis administration's economic development plans and the collaborative archaeological research projects being carried out in the Pueblo during the 1960s and 1970s. Yet over the past fifteen years, Zuni social and political institutions (i.e., the religious leadership and the tribal council) prioritized internal concerns that excluded non-Zunis from various activities and interactions. This priority is demonstrated not only by the ban preventing non-Zunis from attending the Sha'lak'o ceremonies, but also by the decision to close off archaeological sites to tourists. The museum board's interest in the eco-museum model also reflects this process of privileging a more intimate and inward-looking agenda. The process is also supported by the more recent informal move to name the museum the "A:shiwi Center" and to promote it as a community center. If the museum is, as Georgia Epaloose suggested, "part and parcel of the community," it will be integral to and affected by the political cycles that balance external and internal influences within the Pueblo.[7] Like most public institutions in Zuni, the museum and the community's response to it can be seen as a gauge that indicates the community's prevalent ideology and how it is negotiated.

The museum's trials in institutionalizing traditional knowledge reveal how public institutions are viewed in Zuni as a possible challenge to traditional authority—an authority that exists largely in compartmentalized and esoteric spheres of influence. In effect, the notion that these institutions cannot be controlled in the same way as families, clans, or religious societies causes them to be seen as problematic. The museum, from this perspective, gives insight into how other public institutions in Zuni, such as the schools, have faced problems when, for example, failing to separate out gender groups or when they have disregarded the way in which knowledge is traditionally transferred.

By studying an institution such as the A:shiwi A:wan Museum, we must also factor in the *current* diversity of the community because it reveals the immediate dynamics that are present. Acknowledging this diversity also prevents us from oversimplifying the dynamics when looking at the historical trajectory of public institutions over time. Through consideration of the principles that define mediation, we are able to establish the instrumental role Zunis play in these processes and to uncover the overlapping or contrasting perspectives within or between groups. Using this framework, we can elucidate the tension between knowledge that is contextually controlled and knowledge that is attributed significance by its circulation in new contexts, such as the museum. This framework also reveals the "discursive techniques" that aid or control the transmission of knowledge (Briggs 1988). The A:shiwi A:wan Museum—if we acknowledge this history of tensions—can also act as an indicator that reveals the ongoing processes that negotiate the changes taking place in Zuni and therefore shows the mediation of public history.

The museum was also designed specifically to counteract some of the pressures that had deepened the gap between younger and elder generations. This role politically places it both in a position of power and in a position of vulnerability with regard to the traditional teachers, who may feel threatened. During an interview, a non-Zuni teacher at Twin Buttes High School explained how he used the debates over teaching evolution as a way to educate Zuni students about conflicting systems of belief and issues concerning access to knowledge. The 1859 publication of Darwin's *On the Origin of Species* had been greeted with heated and prolonged arguments about its implications regarding preexisting philosophical and theological paradigms. In the United States, a still unresolved struggle exists between religious and scientific ideologies, most notably marked by the Scopes trial in Tennessee in 1925, but also by continuing power struggles in school boards across the country. The high school teacher in Zuni presented this trial to his students to spark discussions about conflicting belief systems:

> I used the Scopes trial and have used the old movie with Frederick Marks and Spencer Tracey. I use it entirely differently than I think it would be used in most classrooms in the United States. I get them to try and identify with the community in Tennessee and the reaction to someone who comes into a classroom and teaches something that is in violation of the community's mores, in violation of the community's religious beliefs—someone who is a threat because of their teaching and [their] guiding the children away from the religious

teachings of their own people, which is basically what happened in Tennessee. . . . This man is a danger—this man is teaching their children not to believe in what they believe in. . . . How would you feel if there was a teacher in Zuni who was teaching in opposition to Zuni religious teaching, who was trying to deviate from the religious beliefs of the Zuni people?[8]

His use of the film *Inherit the Wind* (1960) presents a remarkable and counterintuitive example of the questions raised by individuals within this inquiry concerning tensions between Zuni and Anglo-American knowledge systems and the recontextualization of traditional or privileged knowledge in public institutions. His self-awareness about his own role as a non-Zuni teaching in Zuni also created a dialogue in which his students became similarly reflective about their responses to Anglo-American ideology. In this manner, he constructed a forum in which Zuni students examined their assumptions about access to knowledge and the Anglo-American system of education in which they participated.

Yet not all participants in my research project were as conscious of the dynamics involved in the negotiation between different knowledge systems. I have highlighted the notion of vernacular knowledge in order to recognize the subversive or informal—and possibly unconscious—ways in which the transmission of knowledge may be played with or controlled. I have explained previously that Zuni knowledge is contextually controlled and that there are expectations about how specific knowledge associated with certain clans or medicine societies must operate within these contexts in order to guarantee that knowledge will be used responsibly. These contexts not only determine the interpretation of information but also indicate that knowledge cannot or should not be removed from the appropriate settings or used in external settings. Thus, in Zuni, knowledge is understood to be subjective, but, more important, subjectivity is a prerequisite for knowledge to be transmitted and used effectively.

In reflecting on the broader implications of this ethnography, I emphasize that the concept of contextually controlled knowledge has its foundation in vernacular approaches to power. The term *vernacular* implies that these approaches are also based on oral traditions, which is certainly true in Zuni. By recognizing the role of museum staff in everyday negotiations of different knowledge systems, we can distinguish between informal and formal influences over the transmission of knowledge. The concept of mediation has also highlighted our need to understand further the paradigm shifts only just now becoming visible in how both Anglo-American and other knowledge systems and institutions are interacting with each other. Although a conflict between contrasting knowledge systems is often imagined, institutions such as the A:shiwi A:wan Museum are developing strategies for reconciling these differences. In the process, new hierarchies of influence are being developed in which younger, previously marginalized generations are represented. As seen in the case of repatriation and in the introduction of values from Native American knowledge structures into the academy, anthropologists are also using new strategies to adjust relationships that previously privileged particular ideologies and hierarchies of power, resulting in the redistribution of the control of knowledges. We are thus entering into a notable period in which preexisting political influences are being tested and new conceptual frameworks are being forged from the reconciliation of the formerly separate paradigms of pluralist and comprehensive approaches to knowledge.

Appendix
Timeline

1965 Zuni governor Robert Lewis's survey "24 Months, 24 Projects" shows community interest in starting a museum.

1971–1974 Community Needs Assessment conducted during administration of Robert E. Lewis identifies a museum as one of the most desired community facilities.

1975 Zuni Conservation Team is founded. Tribal resolution supports the development of a museum. Castillo & Associates of Albuquerque do architectural plans for proposed museum.

1975–1978 Administration of Governor Edison Laselute further documents community need for a museum and engages the service of Mimbres & Associates as consultants for a feasibility study.

1978 The Zuni Conservation Team becomes the Zuni Archaeology Project.

1979 The Zuni Museum Study Committee is appointed by the administration of Governor Robert E. Lewis to work with Mimbres & Associates to clarify the goals and objectives for a tribal museum.

1980 Mimbres & Associates completes a feasibility study for a tribal museum funded by the National Endowment for the Arts (Grant R80-42-144).

1982 The Zuni Cultural Resources Enterprise and Zuni tribal council receive an Administration for Native Americans grant to build upon the preexisting Museum Study Committee, train board members, and develop the Zuni Museum Project.

1983–1990 Exhibits hosted by the Zuni Museum Project include Zuni Farming Villages and Zuni Then and Now (funded by the New Mexico Endowment of the Humanities) and Gifts of Mother Earth: Ceramics in the Zuni Tradition (in association with the Heard Museum and the Smithsonian Institution, funded by the National Endowment for the Arts).

1984–1988 Zuni Museum Project staff work at the Smithsonian on cataloging all Zuni photographs.

1988–1990 Rose Wyaco serves as the museum director.

1989 Nancy Fuller from the Smithsonian and the Ak-Chin delegates visit Zuni and introduce the ecomuseum concept. A community referendum is held that rejects the proposed Zuni-Cibola Historic Park, which was to be developed on Zuni lands.

1990–96   Nigel Holman serves as the museum director.

1992   The Zuni Museum Project becomes the A:shiwi A:wan Museum and Heritage Center.

1992–1995   Exhibits include The Pueblo of Zuni as Seen through the Eyes of Pioneer Photographers from 1879 to 1902; Zuni Pueblo: Then and Now; and Zuni Fetish Carvers.

1994   The Zuni Heritage and Historic Preservation Office is developed.

1996–2002   Tom Kennedy serves as the museum director.

2000   The A:shiwi A:wan Museum moves to the Hebadina Building.

2002   The Hawikku exhibit Echoes from Our Ancestors opens (in association with the National Museum of the American Indian and funded by the National Endowment for the Humanities).

2005–present   Jim Enote serves as the museum director.

Notes

Chapter 1. Introduction

1. I have chosen to use the term *Anglo-American* to refer to the cultures represented by Europeans, European colonizers, and the subsequent new cultures that were developed through independence from Europe and the founding of the United States of America. In the context of this research, I was also not comfortable with the excessive use of the term *Western cultures*. Although the term still holds currency, it is impossible to define what exactly is "Western" under present global politics and the realities of migration. When I do include the term *Western*, it is to highlight its continued use within certain theories. Native Americans often use the term *Anglo*, so it also seemed to best fit this particular cross-cultural framework.

2. In March 1997, I designed a series of questions on the museum and the control of knowledge, conducting interviews with staff and board members. Using the same series of questions, I then interviewed community members. Subsequently, I interviewed specific individuals in the Pueblo who were in departments (e.g., the ZHHPO) that encountered issues similar to those at the museum. I also chose to interview non-Zunis who had participated in the development of the museum but were no longer residing in Zuni (former museum director Nigel Holman and former ZHHPO director Roger Anyon). To gather material on similar tribal institutions in the Southwest, I interviewed curators and directors at three tribal museums in Arizona (the Ak-Chin Him-Dak Eco-Museum in Maricopa, the Ned Hatathli Center and Museum in Tsalie, and the Navajo Nation Museum in Window Rock).

3. Halona:wa Idiwana'a, or the Middle Place, is the symbolic center of the Zuni Pueblo and is also identified geographically as the "Middle Village." In the context of this inquiry, the term *Zuni Pueblo* refers to the larger urban agglomeration, and the *Middle Place* to the "heart" of the Pueblo.

4. The U.S. Census Bureau records for the Zuni Pueblo census in 2000 listed a total population of 6,204 American Indians and 195 non-Indians (155 "Whites," 9 "Blacks," 5 "Asians," and 26 of "other races").

5. Wilfred Eriacho, "Zuni Government," n.d., a preliminary study for a Zuni High School history course, Zuni Tribal Archives and Record Program (hereafter ZTARP), Pueblo of Zuni.

6. Ibid.

7. Pandey suggests that "the dominant role of religion in Zuni life prompted anthropologists and casual visitors alike to cite Zuni as an example of a theocracy ruled by a council of priests" (1967:75). Cushing (1979) records that the council of priests formed the highest governing body and that all members of the religious societies answered to them, so that Zuni, in this manner, did represent a theocracy. Pandey also argues that over time the division between secular and religious leadership changed according to the needs of the community (1967:75–78).

8. Eriacho, "Zuni Government."

9. In "A Brief History of the Zuni Nation," Richard Hart argues that "the Spaniards instituted a set of officers at the pueblo—governor, lieutenant governor, *tenientes* (deputies)—but all evidence indicates that although these men carried Spanish titles, they were appointed and directed by the *caciques*, or council of priests, at Zuni" (1983:21).

10. In a conversation I had with Roger Anyon, June 3, 2000, he pointed out that there was a U.S. government agent in Zuni prior to the establishment of the Blackrock Indian Agency.

11. Zuni Indian Agency Correspondence, 1911, ZTARP.

12. Robert Edward Lewis was governor in Zuni for four terms. He first became governor in 1965, and after the establishment of the Zuni Constitution, he was elected for three more terms, in 1979, 1986, and 1990.

13. The U.S. census in 2000 reported that government workers, including those employed through tribal programs, made up 43 percent of the workforce in the Pueblo of Zuni (U.S. Bureau of the Census 2000).

14. For a detailed survey of the development of cultural resource management in the Southwest, see Anyon and Ferguson 1995; Anyon, Ferguson, and Welch 2000.

Chapter 2. The Familial and the Privileged

1. The term *kachinas*, or *katcinas*, is often used to refer to the pantheon of Puebloan ancestral gods. It is a Hopi term, however, and Zunis continually correct its misapplication to Zuni gods, stating that *kokkos* is the correct term.

2. Jim Enote, interview by the author, Pueblo of Zuni, April 23, 1997.

3. Wilfred Eriacho updated and corrected Stevenson's spelling "A'wonawi'lona" to "A:wona:wil'ona" (personal correspondence, September 8, 2006).

4. During interviews, it became apparent that the term *role* was used to translate the Zuni concept of social responsibilities into the English language.

5. Rita Edaakie, interview by the author, Pueblo of Zuni, January 16, 1997.

6. It is worth noting that Malcolm Bowekaty went on to become the governor of Zuni from 1998 to 2002.

7. Malcolm Bowekaty, interview by Gwyneira Isaac and Wendy Fontenelle in Isaac, Fontenelle, and Kennedy 1997:42.

8. ZHHPO staff member, interview by the author, Pueblo of Zuni, November 10, 1997.

9. Zuni elder, interview by the author, Pueblo of Zuni, January 15, 1997.

10. Alex Seowtewa, interview by Gwyneira Isaac and Wendy Fontenelle in Isaac, Fontenelle, and Kennedy 1997:45–46.

11. Vernon Quam, interview by the author, Pueblo of Zuni, March 28, 1997.

12. Georgia Epaloose, interview by Gwyneira Isaac and Wendy Fontenelle in Isaac, Fontenelle, and Kennedy 1997:43–44.

13. Vernon Quam, interview by the author, Pueblo of Zuni, March 28, 1997.

14. Zuni elder, interview by the author, Pueblo of Zuni, November 10, 1997. A detailed discussion of the division of stories according to the calendar is given in Dennis Tedlock's *Finding the Center: Narrative Poetry of the Zuni Indians* (1972).

15. Zuni elder, interview by the author, Pueblo of Zuni, January 15, 1997.

16. Malcolm Bowekaty, interview by Gwyneira Isaac and Wendy Fontenelle in Isaac, Fontenelle, and Kennedy 1997:42.

17. Zuni High School teacher, interview by the author, Pueblo of Zuni, November 27, 1997.

18. Zuni museum board member, interview by the author, Pueblo of Zuni, April 22, 1997.

19. Zuni youth, interview by the author, Pueblo of Zuni, April 18, 1997.

20. Alex Seowtewa, interview by the author, Pueblo of Zuni, January 16, 1997.

21. Alex Seowtewa, interview by Gwyneira Isaac and Wendy Fontenelle in Isaac, Fontenelle, and Kennedy 1997:45.

22. Malcolm Bowekaty, interview by Gwyneira Isaac and Wendy Fontenelle in Isaac, Fontenelle, and Kennedy 1997:42.

23. Vernon Quam, interview by the author, Pueblo of Zuni, March 28, 1997.

24. Wilfred Eriacho updated and corrected Stevenson's spelling "Ko'mosona" to "Komos'ona" (personal correspondence, September 8, 2006).

25. Zuni High School student, interview by the author, Pueblo of Zuni, June 18, 1997.

26. Wendy Fontenelle, interview by the author, Pueblo of Zuni, March 27, 1997.

27. Lila Wallace Reader's Digest Community Folklife Program, application, 1993, A:shiwi A:wan Museum and Heritage Center, ZTARP.

28. Jim Enote, interview by the author, Pueblo of Zuni, April 23, 1997.

29. Zuni High School teacher, interview by the author, Pueblo of Zuni, November 7, 1997.

30. In "Factionalism in a Southwestern Pueblo," Pandey estimates the number of televisions in Zuni in the 1960s as four hundred, which would suggest that most families have had access to television for the past thirty years (1967:27).

31. Zuni High School teacher, interview by the author, Pueblo of Zuni, November 7, 1997.

32. Zuni elder, interview by the author, Pueblo of Zuni, January 15, 1997.

33. Zuni museum board member, interview by the author, Pueblo of Zuni, January 15, 1997.

34. Colleagues in Zuni have commented that the position of the Bekwinne has been vacant for several decades.

35. In some respects, this debate harkens back to disagreements between Protestants and Catholics and to tensions over whether the governor should be appointed or elected (Pandey 1967). Pandey notes, however, that the designations given to the factional groups did not wholly capture the essence of the underlying political processes. These arguments were less about the different sects of the Christian religion than they were about who was leading the Pueblo and how they came into power.

Chapter 3. Anthropology at Zuni

1. Bunzel emphasized the ceremonial aspects and argued that "all of Zuni life is oriented about religious observance, and ritual has become the formal expression of Zuni civilization" (1932a:480). Similarly, Benedict stated that "no field of activity competes with ritual for foremost place in their attention" (1934:59).

2. Nigel Holman, National Endowment for the Humanities proposal for an exhibit on Hawikku, 1995, A:shiwi A:wan Museum and Heritage Center, ZTARP.

3. Matilda Coxe Stevenson to Charles Walcott, November 17, 1908, Matilda Coxe Stevenson Letters, National Anthropological Archives (hereafter NAA).

4. This ethnography was published in 1904 as "The Zuni Indians: Their Mythology, Esoteric Fraternities, and Religious Ceremonies" in a BAE report. Stevenson's other publications that appeared in the BAE's reports were "The Religious Life of the Zuni Child" (1887) and "Ethnobotany of the Zuni Indians" (1915).

5. Matilda Coxe Stevenson to John Wesley Powell, May 23, 1900, NAA.

6. Matilda Coxe Stevenson to Walcott, November 17, 1908, NAA.

7. Matilda Coxe Stevenson to General Van Stone, June 15, 1914, NAA.

8. Nigel Holman, personal correspondence with the author, July 2006.

9. Knowles (2000) has written about the use of collections as academic collateral by anthropologists who are seeking support from colleagues around the world.

10. For the *Annual Report of the Bureau of American Ethnology*, Cushing published "Zuni Fetishes" (1883); "A Study of Pueblo Pottery as Illustrative of Zuni Culture Growth" (1886); and "Outlines of Zuni Creation Myths" (1896). He continued his interest in translating Zuni oral history in his publication *Zuni*

Folk Tales (1901). He initially published his personal account of his experiences in Zuni as "My Adventures in Zuni," which appeared in the *Century Illustrated Monthly Magazine*, a popular magazine with a readership wider than just those with ethnological interests. These stories were then reprinted as a book with the same title by the Peripatetic Press in 1941.

11. T. J. Ferguson told me that although the story of Cushing's death by choking is prevalent both within and beyond Zuni, the Brooklyn Museum has a letter written by Cushing several days after he supposedly choked on a fishbone, so the medical history of his death is more complicated than the anthropological myth that has grown up around it (personal correspondence, 2006).

12. Matilda Coxe Stevenson to S. P. Langley, March 2, 1904, NAA.

13. Matilda Coxe Stevenson to William Holmes, July 11, 1904, NAA.

14. Matilda Coxe Stevenson to Frederick Webb Hodge, July 15, 1914, NAA.

15. Matilda Coxe Stevenson to Holmes, April 7, 1906, NAA.

16. Hodge had been Cushing's secretary on the Hemenway Expedition 1886–88 and was also married to Cushing's wife's sister. Also note that "Hawikku" and "Kechiba:wa" also appear as "Hawikhu" and "Kechipawan" or "Kechipaun." See National Endowment for the Humanities grant application, "Hawikku and the Zuni People: Five Centuries of Resistance, Accommodation, and Survival," 1995, A:shiwi A:wan Museum and Heritage Center, ZTARP.

17. Following a request by the Pueblo of Zuni, the few human remains sent to the Museum of the American Indian have since been transferred to the NMNH after the former was nationalized.

18. Nigel Holman, planning grant application to the National Endowment for the Humanities, 1992, A:shiwi A:wan Museum and Heritage Center, 1992, ZTARP.

19. Owen Cattel finished the film on Sha'lak'o, and it is now in the library of the American Museum of Natural History in New York. Alongside accounts of the destruction of the films, we can be certain that some of the footage survived.

20. Whiteley (1997) has interpreted a similar approach to the control of anthropological research in Hopi. For the critique of tensions between anthropology and religion, see Deloria 1995 and Biolsi and Zimmerman 1997. The changes in the approaches to archaeological research have also been documented in Swidler et al. 1997.

Chapter 4. Negotiating Local Values

1. An account of the anthropologists who were hosted by Margaret Lewis can be found in Pandey's article "Anthropologists at Zuni," in which he writes that "A. L. Kroeber, Leslie Spier, and Franz Boas also visited Zuni. They lived with a Cherokee woman [Margaret Lewis] who had come to teach school at Zuni in 1899. She married a Zuni and settled down in the pueblo" (1972:329). It is also

worth noting that Kroeber's article "The Speech of a Zuni Child" (1916) recorded the first words spoken by the infant Robert Lewis.

2. Georgia Epaloose, interview by the author, Pueblo of Zuni, January 20, 1997.

3. Tribal Resolution M70-78-974, 1978, ZTARP.

4. Tribal Resolution M70-75-665, 1975, ZTARP: "WHEREAS, the Zuni Tribal Council recognises and is experiencing substantial reservation need for natural and cultural resource management of Zuni tribal land and artefacts [*sic*]; and WHEREAS, the Zuni Tribal Council fully supports the concept of a Zuni Tribal Research Museum to meet such needs."

5. Governor Edison Laselute to Susan Wagner, November 9, 1976, ZTARP.

6. Ibid.

7. The proposed park was authorized by Congress under Public Law No. 100-567. Journalists from the *Gallup Independent* covered the plan and referendum for the park in detail. See Del Valle 1988b, 1989; Schlanger 1989a, 1989b, 1990a, 1990b.

8. Lloyd Nielsen to Governor Laselute, September 24, 1976, ZTARP.

9. Minutes from the Museum Study Committee, November 13, 1979, ZTARP.

10. Ibid.

11. The Museum Study Committee held its first meeting on June 8, 1979, and was made up of community members Cal Seciwa (Zuni Economic Development Administration), Kirby Ghachu (Zuni School Redistricting Committee), Bill Tsikewa (public-relations director), Arlen Quetawki (Zuni Language Development Program), Andrew Neptcha (tribal historian), Shirley Bellson (Jewelry Co-op), Rose Wyaco (ZAP), Fern Peynetsa (ZAP). T. J. Ferguson, a non-Zuni tribal employee and project coordinator for ZAP, was also included as a committee member. It is also worth noting that participants in the study committee varied over time and on July 18, the following people were recorded as also present at a meeting: Ralph Casebolt, Anders Romancito, Standford Lalio, Alex Seowtewa, and Alonso Hustito (Museum Study Committee, minutes, July 18, 1979, ZTARP). Mimbres & Associates, Planners and Architects, was a Santa Fe–based professional organization that offered comprehensive services in urban and regional planning, project development, and architecture.

12. Museum Study Committee, minutes, June 29, 1979, ZTARP.

13. Ibid., emphasis in original.

14. Governor Laselute to Wagner, November 9, 1976, ZTARP.

15. Mimbres & Associates, Feasibility Study for the Zuni Museum, 1980, ZTARP.

16. From Museum Study Committee, "Zuni Museum Project Summary," n.d., ZTARP.

17. Museum Study Committee, minutes, June 8, 1979, ZTARP.

18. Michael Kakuska to Governor Robert Lewis, May 15, 1979, ZTARP.

19. Ibid.

20. Mimbres & Associates, Feasibility Study for the Zuni Museum, 1980, ZTARP.

21. Castillo & Associates, Architects of Albuquerque, report for the Pueblo of Zuni and Museum Committee, April 6, 1981, ZTARP.

22. T. J. Ferguson wrote to me that the park was to include four sites: Village of the Great Kivas, Hawikku, Yellowhouse, and Kyaki:ma, where there are active shrines (personal correspondence, July 2006). Issues dealing with the lack of tribal participation in planning were as controversial as the subject of tourist access to ancestral sites.

23. Roger Anyon, personal communication with the author, November 2000.

24. Zuni museum board member, interview by the author, Pueblo of Zuni, January 15, 1997.

25. Rose Wyaco was the founding Zuni director of the museum from 1988 to 1990. Nigel Holman served as the director from 1990 to 1995 and was followed by Tom Kennedy from 1996 to 2002. After Kennedy moved to the tribal offices to become the developer of a tourism program, Valerie Epaloose became interim director from 2002 to 2005. For a short period between 2002 and 2003, and overlapping with Epaloose, Carlton Jamon, from the museum board, also became interim director. In 2005, Jim Enote, who had also previously been on the board, was chosen to become the second permanent Zuni director of the museum.

26. Nigel Holman, interview by the author, Las Cruces, November 11, 1997.

27. Unknown author, "Working Paper: Zuni Museum Feasibility Report," n.d., ZTARP.

28. Ibid.

29. Nigel Holman, interview by the author, Las Cruces, November 11, 1997.

30. Malcolm Bowekaty, interview by Gwyneira Isaac and Wendy Fontenelle in Isaac, Fontenelle, and Kennedy 1997:42.

31. Vernon Quam, interview by the author, Pueblo of Zuni, March 28, 1997. A cultural heritage officer from the Navajo Nation Museum in Window Rock, Arizona, expressed similar ideas about how the concept of a museum is perceived by the community: "I think the term *museum* throws people off. People don't want to go in a museum . . . just [to see] old things or something . . . things that belong to dead people." The officer also suggested they would eventually think of dropping the term *museum* from the title and use *cultural center* instead (interview by the author, Window Rock, Arizona, 1997).

32. Pueblo of Zuni, application to Administration for Native Americans, 1990:25, ZTARP.

33. Pueblo of Zuni, report for the application to Administration for Native Americans grant, n.d., ZTARP.

34. Georgia Epaloose, interview by the author, Pueblo of Zuni, January 20, 1997.

35. Malcolm Bowekaty, interview by Gwyneira Isaac and Wendy Fontenelle in Isaac, Fontenelle, and Kennedy 1997:42.

36. Roger Anyon, Zuni museum papers, 1993, ZTARP.

37. Edith Cherry and James See, Architects' Architectural Program for the A:shiwi A:wan Museum, October 12, 1991, ZTARP.

38. Brochure for the A:shiwi A:wan Museum, 1993, A:shiwi A:wan Museum and Heritage Center, ZTARP.

39. Nigel Holman, "The Zuni Museum," *Highway 53 Express* (1991), Zuni Museum Project file, ZTARP.

40. T. J. Ferguson, personal correspondence with the author, July 2006.

41. Tom Kennedy, interview by the author, Pueblo of Zuni, March 21, 1997.

42. Ibid.

43. Zuni museum board member, interview by the author, Pueblo of Zuni, January 15, 1997.

44. Tom Kennedy, interview by the author, Pueblo of Zuni, March 21, 1997.

45. The process of self-discovery as a function of the ecomuseum is well documented in Nancy Fuller's report on the development of the Ak-Chin Eco-Museum, in which she states that this "model offers a new role for community museums: that of an instrument of self-knowledge and a place to learn and regularly practice the skills and attitudes needed for community problem solving" (1992:361).

46. Roger Anyon, personal communication, May 2000.

47. Wyaco was responsible for documenting Zuni collections at the Smithsonian and producing a catalog for the tribe. Wyaco, Dishta, and T. J. Ferguson also worked alongside consultants Keith Kintigh, Brenda Shears, Natasha Bonilla, Margaret Hardin, Barbara Mills, and Roger Anyon to create an exhibit on the Hawikku collections held at the Museum of the American Indian. This exhibit was eventually funded by the National Endowment for the Humanities and is currently on display at the A:shiwi A:wan Museum.

48. In the 1990s, ZAP became the Zuni Cultural Resources Enterprise and the ZHHPO.

49. The Mullarky Studio was based in Gallup, New Mexico, forty miles from Zuni. Although by the 1970s it no longer operated as a commercial studio, it still functioned as a photographic supply store and exhibited many of the images taken in the nineteenth century. By 2006, it was no longer in business.

50. Brochure for the exhibit The Pueblo of Zuni as Seen Through the Eyes of Pioneer Photographers, from 1879 to 1902, 1992, A:shiwi A:wan Museum and Heritage Center, ZTARP.

51. Ibid.

52. For further discussion on differential access, see Michael F. Brown, *Who Owns Native Culture?* (2004).

53. Otto Lucio, letter to ZCRAT, 1992, ZTARP.

Chapter 5. Finding the Middle Ground

1. Georgia Epaloose, interview by the author, Pueblo of Zuni, January 20, 1997.

2. Ibid.

3. Malcolm Bowekaty, interview by Gwyneira Isaac and Wendy Fontenelle in Isaac, Fontenelle, and Kennedy 1997:42.

4. Ibid.

5. Georgia Epaloose, interview by the author, Pueblo of Zuni, January 20, 1997.

6. Georgia Epaloose, interview by Gwyneira Isaac and Wendy Fontenelle in Isaac, Fontenelle, and Kennedy 1997:44.

7. Ibid.

8. Rita Edaakie, interview by Gwyneira Isaac and Wendy Fontenelle in Isaac, Fontenelle, and Kennedy 1997:44–45.

9. Ibid.

10. Georgia Epaloose, interview by the author, Pueblo of Zuni, January 20, 1997.

11. During the planning stages of the museum, Jim Ostler, the head of the Zuni Art and Crafts Center, also established the A:shiwi Publishing Company, which was designed to promote Zuni arts and culture. The publishing company was most active in the 1990s, publishing books on Zuni pottery, fetishes, silverwork, and food. By 2000, it no longer had an editor and has been inactive since.

12. Vernon Quam, interview by the author, Pueblo of Zuni, March 28, 1997.

13. Vernon Quam, interview by the author, Pueblo of Zuni, April 18, 1997.

14. Zuni High School student, interview by the author, Pueblo of Zuni, June 18, 1997.

15. Vernon Quam, interview by the author, Pueblo of Zuni, March 28, 1997.

16. Ibid.

17. Tom Kennedy, interview by the author, Pueblo of Zuni, March 21, 1997.

18. Vernon Quam, interview by the author, Pueblo of Zuni, March 28, 1997.

19. Georgia Epaloose, interview by the author, Pueblo of Zuni, January 20, 1997.

20. Tom Kennedy, interview by the author, Pueblo of Zuni, March 21, 1997.

21. Nigel Holman, interview by the author, Las Cruces, November 11, 1997.

22. The use of murals to depict creation stories occurs in a number of tribal museums. The Ned Hatathli Center and Museum in Tsalie, Arizona, has Navajo

sand paintings and dioramas that depict the creation myths (Simpson 1996). There are also creation story murals at the Mashantucket Pequot Museum in Connecticut.

23. Between 2002 and 2005, there were discussions in the Pueblo about whether these murals in the Spanish mission should be open to the public and, if so, who should control access. Conflicts arose once the title to the church was transferred from the Catholic diocese to the tribe, and subsequently there have been arguments over who has the rights to the paintings. During this time, the church has largely been closed to the public. By September 2006, it appeared that a resolution had been reached, and tourists can access the church through the tribe's visitor center and receive a guided tour from the Seowtewas.

24. It is worth noting that the earlier murals were largely geometric, whereas Seowtewa's are figurative.

Chapter 6. Living with Contradictions

1. In 2006, a larger museum opened that is adjacent to the Acoma casino complex. This museum now serves as the flagship visitor center for the Pueblo.

2. Nigel Holman, personal correspondence, July 2006.

3. Georgia Epaloose, interview by the author, Pueblo of Zuni, January 20, 1997.

4. Zuni museum board member, interview by the author, Pueblo of Zuni, January 15, 1997.

5. Wendy Fontenelle, interview by the author, Pueblo of Zuni, March 27, 1997.

6. Vernon Quam, interview by the author, Pueblo of Zuni, March 28, 1997.

7. Ibid.

8. Zuni museum administrator, interview by the author, Pueblo of Zuni, April 18, 1997.

9. Vernon Quam, interview by the author, Pueblo of Zuni, March 28, 1997.

10. Tom Kennedy, interview by the author, Pueblo of Zuni, April 11, 1997.

11. Ibid.

12. Tom Kennedy, interview by the author, Pueblo of Zuni, March 21, 1997.

13. Ibid.

14. Young Zuni woman, interview by the author, Pueblo of Zuni, April 18, 1997.

15. For a description of the teaching of social codes, see Gregory Cajete's (2000) discussion of the Tewa use of metaphors in education in Santa Clara Pueblo.

16. Briggs uses the Spanish term *viejitos de antes* to refer to the Cordovans' ancestors.

17. Zuni High School student, interview by the author, Pueblo of Zuni, June 27, 1997.

18. Zuni artist, interview by the author, Pueblo of Zuni, January 15, 1997.

19. Zuni High School student, interview by the author, Pueblo of Zuni, June 27, 1997.

20. Matilda Coxe Stevenson incorporated information received from traders into her ethnography "The Zuni Indians: Their Mythology, Esoteric Fraternities, and Religious Ceremonies" (1904); and Barbara Tedlock includes in *The Beautiful and the Dangerous* (1992) a conversation she had with Mormon settlers who lived near Zuni in the town of Ramah. However, neither ethnographer names these informants or discusses their views on their role as non-Zunis in the community.

21. Zuni High School teacher, interview by the author, Pueblo of Zuni, November 7, 1997.

22. Zuni High School teacher, interview by the author, Pueblo of Zuni, November 21, 1997.

23. Nigel Holman, interview by the author, Las Cruces, November 11, 1997. Holman added in personal correspondence (July 2006) that the museum had been flexible in its approach to programming and funding, and thus each director or consultant approached the concept of the museum in different ways, giving varying emphasis to external organizations or community agendas.

24. Nigel Holman, interview by the author, Las Cruces, November 11, 1997.

25. Ibid.

26. Ibid.

27. Ibid.

28. Tom Kennedy, interview by the author, Pueblo of Zuni, March 21, 1997.

29. Nigel Holman, interview by the author, Las Cruces, November 11, 1997.

30. Ibid.

31. Tom Kennedy, interview by the author, Pueblo of Zuni, March 21, 1997. *Melika* is the Zuni term used to refer to Anglo-Americans.

Chapter 7. Conclusions

1. In 2005, the new museum staff consisted of Jim Enote (director), Valerie Epaloose, and Curtis Quam. The board comprised Norman Cooeyate (Zuni Diabetes Prevention Program), Davis Peynetsa Jr. (contractor), Georgia Epaloose (Zuni Public Schools District), Edward Wemytewa (Zuni tribal council member), Barbara Gordon (Zuni Public Schools District), and Martin Link (University of New Mexico, Gallup).

2. Nigel Holman and Natasha Bonilla-Martinez, planning grant for the National Endowment for the Humanities, 1995, A:shiwi A:wan Museum and Heritage Center, ZTARP. The original team consisted of Joseph Dishta, Rose Wyaco, Keith Kintigh, Brenda Shears, Natasha Bonilla-Martinez, Margaret Hardin, Barbara Mills, Roger Anyon, and T. J. Ferguson. The authors of the grant were

Natasha Bonilla-Martinez and Nigel Holman. Holman had left the museum by the time the grant was awarded, and the exhibit was organized under Kennedy's directorship.

3. Ibid.

4. Although no labels explain this reading of the kiva outline, the current curator, Curtis Quam, who was responsible for tours of the exhibit in 2005, clarified it for me.

5. Jim Enote, in discussion with the author, August 25, 2006.

6. Ibid., my emphasis.

7. Georgia Epaloose, interview by the author, Pueblo of Zuni, January 20, 1997.

8. Zuni High School teacher, Pueblo of Zuni, November 21, 1997.

Bibliography

Archival Sources

National Anthropological Archives (NAA)
Zuni Tribal Archives and Record Program (ZTARP)

Interviews

Administrator, A:shiwi A:wan Museum and Heritage Center. Pueblo of Zuni, April 18, 1997.
Board members, A:shiwi A:wan Museum and Heritage Center. Pueblo of Zuni, January 15 and April 22, 1997.
Edaakie, Rita. Pueblo of Zuni, January 16, 1997.
Enote, Jim. Pueblo of Zuni, April 23, 1997.
Epaloose, Georgia. Pueblo of Zuni, January 20, 1997.
Fontenelle, Wendy. Pueblo of Zuni, March 27, 1997.
Holman, Nigel. Las Cruces, November 11, 1997.
Kennedy, Tom. Pueblo of Zuni, March 21 and April 11, 1997.
Quam, Vernon. Pueblo of Zuni, March 28 and April 18, 1997.
Seowtewa, Alex. Pueblo of Zuni, January 16, 1997.
Staff member, Zuni Heritage and Historic Preservation Office. Pueblo of Zuni, November 10, 1997.
Zuni artist. Pueblo of Zuni, January 15, 1997.
Zuni elders. Pueblo of Zuni, January 15 and November 10, 1997.
Zuni High School students. Pueblo of Zuni, June 18 and June 27, 1997.
Zuni High School teachers. Pueblo of Zuni, November 7, November 21, and November 27, 1997.
Zuni woman. Pueblo of Zuni, April 18, 1997.
Zuni youth. Pueblo of Zuni, April 18, 1997.

Secondary Sources

Ahlstrom, R. V. N., and Nancy Parezo. 1987. Matilda Coxe Stevenson's "Dress and Adornment of the Pueblo Indians." In *The Kiva: Journal of the Arizona Archaeological and Historical Society* 52 (4): 267–74.

Ames, Michael M. 1992. *Cannibal Tours and Glass Boxes: The Anthropology of Museums*. Vancouver: University of British Columbia Press.

Anyon, Roger, and T. J. Ferguson. 1995. Cultural Resources Management at the Pueblo of Zuni, New Mexico, USA. *Antiquity* 69: 913–30.

Anyon, Roger, T. J. Ferguson, and John R. Welch. 2000. Heritage Management by American Indian Tribes in the Southwestern United States. In *Cultural Resource Management in Contemporary Society: Perspectives on Managing and Preserving the Past*, edited by Francis P. McManamon and Alf Hatton, 121–41. London: Routledge.

Archambault, JoAllyn. 1994. American Indians and American Museums. *Zeitschrift für Ethnologie* 118: 7–22.

Bellah, Robert N. 1967. Religious Systems. In *People of Rimrock: A Study of Values in Five Cultures*, edited by Evon Z. Vogt and E. M. Albert, 227–64. Cambridge, Mass.: Harvard University Press.

Benedict, Ruth. 1934. *Patterns of Culture*. New York: Houghton Mifflin.

Berkhofer, Robert F. 1978. *The White Man's Indian: Images of the American Indian from Columbus to the Present*. New York: Knopf.

Bhabha, Homi K. 1993. *The Location of Culture*. London: Routledge.

Biolsi, Thomas, and Larry Zimmerman, editors. 1997. *Indians and Anthropologists: Vine Deloria Jr. and the Critique of Anthropology*. Tucson: University of Arizona Press.

Bloch, Maurice. 1993. The Uses of Schooling and Literacy in a Zafimaniry Village. In *Cross-Cultural Approaches to Literacy*, edited by Brian V. Street, 87–109. Cambridge: Cambridge University Press.

Boas, Franz. 1938. *Keresan Texts*. American Ethnological Society Publications, vol. 8 (2). New York: American Ethnological Society.

Bok, Sissela. 1983. *Secrets: On the Ethics of Concealment and Revelation*. New York: Pantheon Books.

Bolton, Lissant. 1997. A Place Containing Many Places: Museums and the Use of Objects to Represent Place in Melanesia. *Australian Journal of Anthropology* 8 (1): 18–34.

Brandes, R. S. 1965. Frank Hamilton Cushing: Pioneer Americanist. Ph.D. diss., University of Arizona.

Brandt, Elizabeth. 1980. On Secrecy and the Control of Knowledge: Taos Pueblo. In *Secrecy: A Cross Cultural Perspective*, edited by Stanton K. Tefft, 123–46. New York: Human Sciences Press.

——. 1981. Native American Attitudes towards Literacy and Recording in the Southwest. In *Native Languages of the Americas: Prospects of the 80s*, edited by A. Zaharlick. Special issue of *Journal of the Linguistic Association of the Southwest* 4 (2): 185–95.

——. 1985. Internal Stratification in Pueblo Communities. Paper presented at the meetings of the American Anthropological Association, December 4–5, Washington, D.C.

———. 1994. Egalitarianism, Hierarchy, and Centralization in the Pueblos. In *The Ancient Southwest Community: Models and Methods for the Study of the Prehistoric Social Organization*, edited by W. H. Wills and Robert D. Leonard, 9–23. Albuquerque: University of New Mexico Press.

Bray, Tamara. 2001. *The Future of the Past: Archaeologists, Native Americans, and Repatriation*. New York: Garland.

Brenner, Malcolm. 1995a. Sha'lak'o Ban Causing Lots of Confusion. *Gallup Independent*, November 29.

———. 1995b. Zunis Ban Non-Indians from Ceremonies. *Gallup Independent*, October 21.

Briggs, Charles L. 1988. *Competence in Performance: The Creativity of Tradition in Mexicano Verbal Art*. Philadelphia: University of Pennsylvania Press.

Brown, Michael F. 2004. *Who Owns Native Culture?* Cambridge, Mass.: Harvard University Press.

Bunzel, Ruth. 1932a. Introduction to Zuni Ceremonials. In *Forty-seventh Annual Report of the Bureau of American Ethnology for 1929–1930*, 467–835. Washington, D.C.: U.S. Government Printing Office.

———. 1932b. Zuni Katcinas: An Analytical Study. In *Forty-seventh Annual Report of the Bureau of American Ethnology for 1929–1930*, 837–1086. Washington, D.C.: U.S. Government Printing Office.

———. 1952. *Chichecastenango: A Guatemalan Village*. American Anthropological Society Publication no. 22. New York: J. J. Augustin.

———. 1992. *Zuni Ceremonialism: Three Studies by Ruth L. Bunzel*. Albuquerque: University of New Mexico Press.

Cajete, Gregory. 2000. Indigenous Knowledge: The Pueblo Metaphor of Indigenous Education. In *Reclaiming Indigenous Voice and Vision*, edited by Marie Battiste, 181–91. Vancouver: University of British Colombia Press.

Califano, Joseph A. 1991. *The Triumph and Tragedy of Lyndon Johnson: The White House Years*. New York: Simon and Schuster.

Castile, George Pierre. 1998. *To Show Heart: Native American Self-Determination and Federal Indian Policy, 1960–1975*. Tucson: University of Arizona Press.

Clements, Janice. 2000. The Integration of Traditional Indian Beliefs into the Museum at Warm Springs. In *The Changing Presentation of the American Indian: Museums and Native Culture*, 67–71. Washington, D.C.: National Museum of the American Indian; Seattle: University of Washington Press.

Clifford, James. 1991. Four North-West Coast Museums: Travel Reflections. In *Exhibiting Cultures: The Poetics and Politics of Museum Display*, edited by Ivan Karp and Steven D. Lavine, 212–54. Washington, D.C.: Smithsonian Institution Press.

———. 1997. *Routes: Travel and Translation in the Late Twentieth Century*. Cambridge, Mass.: Harvard University Press.

Crampton, Gregory. 1977. *The Zunis of Cibola*. Salt Lake City: University of Utah Press.

Cushing, Frank Hamilton. 1883. Zuni Fetishes. In *Second Annual Report of the Bureau of American Ethnology, 1880–1881*, 9–43. Washington, D.C.: U.S. Government Printing Office.

———. 1886. A Study of Pueblo Pottery as Illustrative of Zuni Culture Growth. In *Fourth Annual Report of the Bureau of American Ethnology, 1882–1883*, 473–521. Washington, D.C.: U.S. Government Printing Office.

———. 1896. Outlines of Zuni Creation Myths. In *Thirteenth Annual Report of the Bureau of American Ethnology, 1891–1892*, 325–447. Washington, D.C.: U.S. Government Printing Office.

———. 1901. *Zuni Folk Tales*. New York: G. P. Putnam's Sons; Knickerbocker Press.

———. 1941. *My Adventures in Zuni*. Santa Fe: Peripatetic Press.

———. 1979. *Selected Writings of Frank Hamilton Cushing*. Edited by Jesse Green. Lincoln: University of Nebraska Press.

Darwin, Charles. 1859. *On the Origin of Species*. London: Murray.

Davis, Peter. 1999. *Ecomuseums: A Sense of Place*. London: Leicester University Press.

Deloria, Vine, Jr. 1995. *Red Earth, White Lies: Native Americans and the Myth of Scientific Fact*. New York: Scribner.

Del Valle, Fernando. 1988a. Shalako Visitors Welcome. *Gallup Independent*, December 1.

———. 1988b. Zuni Park Bill OK'd by House. *Gallup Independent*, October 14.

———. 1989. Plans for Zuni Park to Begin. *Gallup Independent*, January 9.

Dilworth, Leah. 1996. *Imagining Indians in the Southwest: Persistent Visions of the Primitive Past*. Washington, D.C.: Smithsonian Institution Press.

Dockstader, Frederick J. 1985. *The Kachina and the White Man: The Influences of White Culture on the Hopi Kachina Cult*. Albuquerque: University of New Mexico Press.

Dozier, E. P. 1961. Rio Grande Pueblos. In *Perspectives in American Indian Culture Change*, edited by Edward H. Spicer, 94–186. Chicago: Chicago University Press.

Dubin, Margaret. 1990. Zuni Religious Events All Shut. *Gallup Independent*, June 15.

Dussart, Françoise. 1997. A Body Painting in Translation. In *Rethinking Visual Anthropology*, edited by Marcus Banks and Howard Morphy, 186–202. New Haven, Conn.: Yale University Press.

Edaakie, Rita. 1999. *Idonapshe: Let's Eat: Traditional Zuni Foods*. Zuni and Albuquerque: Zuni A:shiwi Publishing Ltd. and A:shiwi A:wan Museum and Heritage Center in association with University of New Mexico Press.

Eggan, Fred. 1950. *Social Organization of the Western Pueblos*. Chicago: University of Chicago Press.

———. 1979. Introduction. In *Selected Writings of Frank Hamilton Cushing*, edited by Jesse Green, 3–44. Lincoln: University of Nebraska Press.

Eriacho, Donald. 1995. Defending Religious Rights in Zuni. *Gallup Independent*, November 25.

Erikson, Patricia Pierce. 1994. "So My Children Can Stay in the Pueblo": Indigenous Community Museums and Self-determination in Oaxaca, Mexico. *Museum Anthropology* 20 (1): 37–46.

——. 2002. *Voices of a Thousand People: The Makah Cultural and Research Center*. Lincoln: University of Nebraska Press.

Fardon, Richard, editor. 1985. *Power and Knowledge: Anthropological and Sociological Approaches*. Proceedings of a conference held at the University of St. Andrews, December 1982. Edinburgh: Scottish Academic Press.

Ferguson, T. J., Roger Anyon, and Edmund Ladd. 2000. Repatriation at the Pueblo of Zuni: Diverse Solutions for Complex Problems. In *Repatriation Reader: Who Owns American Indian Remains?* edited by Devon A. Mihesuah, 239–65. Lincoln: University of Nebraska Press.

Ferguson, T. J., and E. Richard Hart. 1985. *A Zuni Atlas*. Norman: University of Oklahoma Press.

Ferguson, T. J., E. Richard Hart, and Cal Seciwa. 1988. Twentieth Century Zuni Political and Economic Development in Relation to Federal Indian Policy. In *Public Policy Impacts on American Indian Development*, edited by M. C. Snip, 113–44. Albuquerque: Institute of Native American Economic Development, University of New Mexico.

Fforde, Cressida. 2002. *The Dead and Their Possessions: Repatriation in Principle, Policy, and Practice*. One World Archaeology series. New York: Routledge.

Fine-Dare, Kathleen S. 2002. *Grave Injustice: The American Indian Repatriation Movement and NAGPRA*. Lincoln: University of Nebraska Press.

Foucault, Michel. 1970. *The Order of Things*. London: Tavistock.

Fowler, Don. 1989. *The Western Photographs of John K. Hillers*. Washington, D.C.: Smithsonian Institution Press.

Fox, Robin. 1967. *Kinship and Marriage: An Anthropological Perspective*. Harmondsworth, England: Penguin.

Fuller, Nancy J. 1992. The Museum as a Vehicle for Community Empowerment: The Ak Chin Indian Community Ecomuseum Project. In *Museums and Communities: The Politics of Public Culture*, edited by Ivan Karp, Christine Muller Kreamer, and Steven D. Lavine, 327–66. Washington, D.C.: Smithsonian Institution Press.

Fuller, Nancy J., and Susanne Fabricius. 1993. Native American Museums and Cultural Centers: Historical Overview and Current Issues. In *Zeitschrift für Ethnologie* 117: 223–37.

Garson, J. G., and Charles Hercules Read, editors. 1892. *Notes and Queries on Anthropology*. London: Royal Anthropological Institute of Great Britain and Ireland.

Gieryn, Thomas F. 1998. Balancing Acts: Science, *Enola Gay*, and History Wars at the Smithsonian. In *The Politics of Display: Museums, Science, and Culture*, edited by Sharon Macdonald, 197–228. London: Routledge.

Goody, Jack. 1987. *The Interface between the Written and the Oral*. Cambridge: Cambridge University Press.

Gruber, Jacob W. 1970. Ethnographic Salvage and the Shaping of Anthropology. *American Anthropologist* 72 (6): 1289–299.

Gulliford, Andrew. 2000. *Sacred Objects and Sacred Places: Preserving Tribal Traditions*. Boulder: University of Colorado Press.

Hart, E. Richard. 1983. A Brief History of the Zuni Nation. In *Zuni, El Morro: Past and Present*, 19–25. Exploration: Annual Bulletin of the School of American Research. Santa Fe: School of American Research.

——, editor. 1995. *Zuni and the Courts: A Struggle for Sovereign Land Rights*. Lawrence: University of Kansas.

Hart, E. Richard, and T. J. Ferguson. 1991. *Zuni History: Victories in the 1990s*. Seattle: Institute of the North American West.

Henderson, Amy, and Adrienne Kaeppler, editors. 1997. *Exhibiting Dilemmas: Issues of Representation at the Smithsonian*. Washington, D.C.: Smithsonian Institution Press.

Hinsley, Curtis M. 1981. *The Smithsonian and the American Indian: Making a Moral Anthropology in Victorian America*. Washington, D.C.: Smithsonian Institution Press.

——. 1983. Ethnographic Charisma and Scientific Routine: Cushing and Fewkes in the American Southwest, 1879–1893. In *Observers Observed*, edited by George Stocking Jr., 53–69. Madison: University of Wisconsin Press.

——. 1990. Zunis and Brahmins: Cultural Ambivalence in the Gilded Age. In *Romantic Motives: Essays on Anthropological Sensibility*, edited by George Stocking Jr., 169–207. Madison: University of Wisconsin Press.

——. 1992. Collecting Cultures and Cultures of Collecting: The Lure of the American Southwest, 1880–1915. *Museum Anthropology* 16 (1): 12–20.

Hinsley, Curtis M., and David R. Wilcox. 1996. *Frank Hamilton Cushing and the Hemenway Southwestern Archaeological Expedition: 1886–1889*. Tucson: University of Arizona Press.

Hobsbawm, Eric, and Terence Ranger, editors. 1983. *The Invention of Tradition*. Cambridge: Cambridge University Press.

Holman, Nigel. 1996a. Curating and Controlling Zuni Photographic Images. *Curator: The Museum Journal* 39 (2): 108–22.

——. 1996b. Photography as Social and Economic Exchange: Understanding the "Challenge" of Photographs of Zuni Religious Ceremonies. *American Indian Culture and Research Journal* 20 (3): 93–110.

Holman, Nigel, and Andrew Othole. 1993. Historic Photographs, Museums, and Contemporary Life in Zuni. Paper presented at Objects of Myth and Memory Exhibition. Second Culin Symposium, Heard Museum, Phoenix, January 30.

Hughte, Phil. 1994. *A Zuni Artist Looks at Frank Hamilton Cushing.* Zuni: Pueblo of Zuni Arts and Crafts, A:shiwi A:wan Museum and Heritage Center.

Impey, O., and A. MacGregor, editors. 1985. *The Origins of Museums: The Cabinet of Curiosities in Sixteenth and Seventeenth Century Europe.* Oxford: Clarendon Press.

Isaac, Gwyneira. 1995. Zuni: Selected Views: The Photographs of Matilda Coxe Stevenson, 1849–1915. M. Phil. thesis, Oxford University.

———. 2005a. Mediating Knowledges: Origins of a Zuni Museum. In *Museum Anthropology* 28 (1): 3–18.

———. 2005b. Re-observation and the Recognition of Change: The Photographs of Matilda Coxe Stevenson. *Journal of the Southwest* 47: 411–55.

Isaac, Gwyneira, Wendy Fontenelle, and Tom Kennedy. 1997. A:shiwi A:wan: "Belonging to the Zuni People": Interviews from the A:shiwi A:wan Museum and Heritage Center, Zuni, NM. *Cultural Survival Quarterly* 21 (1): 41–46.

Jaarsma, S. R. 2002. *Handle with Care: Ownership and Control of Ethnographic Materials.* Pittsburgh: University of Pittsburgh Press.

Kaeppler, Adrienne L. 1994. Paradise Regained: The Role of Pacific Museums in Forging National Identity. In *Museums and the Making of "Ourselves": The Role of Objects in National Identity*, edited by Flora E. S. Kaplan, 19–44. London: Leicester University Press.

Karp, Ivan, and Steven D. Lavine, editors. 1991. *Exhibiting Cultures: The Poetics and Politics of Museum Display.* Washington, D.C.: Smithsonian Institution Press.

Katriel, Tamar. 1997. *Performing the Past: A Study of Israeli Settlement Museums.* London: Lawrence Erlbaum Associates.

King, Richard C. 1998. *Colonial Discourses, Collective Memories, and the Exhibition of Native American Cultures and Histories in the Contemporary United States.* New York: Garland.

Knowles, Chantal. 2000. Ethnographic Collectors, Agents, and Agency in Melanesia 1870s–1930s. In *Hunting the Gatherers*, edited by Michael O'Hanlon and Robert L. Welsch, 251–71. New York: Berghahn Books.

Kroeber, Alfred L. 1916. The Speech of a Zuni Child. *American Anthropologist* 18 (4): 529–34.

———. 1917. Zuni Kin and Clan. *Anthropological Papers of the American Museum of Natural History* 18 (2): 39–204.

Ladd, Edmund. 1994. Cushing among the Zuni: A Zuni Perspective. *Gilcrease Journal* 2 (2): 20–35.

Lee, Molly. 1998. The Ugtarvik and the Yup'ik Piciryarait Museums: A Case Study in Comparative Anthropological Museology. *Museum Anthropology* 22 (1): 43–48.

Lyon, Luke. 1988. History of the Prohibition of Photography of Southwestern Indian Ceremonies. In *Reflections: Papers on Southwestern Cultural History in*

Honor of Charles H. Lange, 238–72. Published for the Archaeological Society of New Mexico. Santa Fe: Ancient City Press.

Mark, Joan. 1981. *Four Anthropologists: An American Science in Its Early Years.* New York: Science History Publications.

Matusow, Allen J. 1984. *The Unravelling of America: A History of Liberalism in the 1960s.* New York: Harper and Row.

Mauzé, Marie. 1997. On Concepts of Tradition: An Introduction. In *Present Is Past: Some Uses of Tradition in Native Societies*, edited by Marie Mauzé, 1–15. Lanham, Md.: University Press of America.

McFeely, Eliza. 2001. *Zuni and the American Imagination.* New York: Hill and Wang.

Merrill, William L., and Richard Ahlborn. 1997. Zuni Archangels and Ahayu:da: A Sculpted Chronicle of Power and Identity. In *Exhibiting Dilemmas: Issues of Representation at the Smithsonian*, edited by Amy Henderson and Adrienne Kaeppler, 176–205. Washington, D.C.: Smithsonian Institution Press.

Merrill, William L., Edmund J. Ladd, and T. J. Ferguson. 1993. The Return of the Ahayu:da: Lessons for Repatriation from Zuni Pueblo and the Smithsonian Institution. *Current Anthropology* 34 (5): 523–67.

Mihesuah, Devon A., editor. 2000. *Repatriation Reader: Who Owns American Indian Remains?* Lincoln: University of Nebraska Press.

Mithlo, Nancy Marie. 2004. "Red Man's Burden": The Politics of Inclusion in Museum Settings. *American Indian Quarterly* 28 (3–4): 743–63.

Morgan, Lewis Henry. 1877. *Ancient Society.* Cambridge, Mass.: Belknap Press of Harvard University Press.

Morphy, Howard. 1991. *Ancestral Connections: Art and an Aboriginal System of Knowledge.* Chicago: University of Chicago Press.

Ong, Walter J. 1982. *Orality and Literacy: The Technologizing of the Word.* London: Methuen.

Ortiz, Alfonso. 1969. *The Tewa World: Space, Time, Being, and Becoming in a Pueblo Society.* Chicago: University of Chicago Press.

——. 1986. Half a Century of Indian Administration: An Overview. In *American Indian Policy and Cultural Values: Conflict and Accommodation*, edited by Jennie R. Joe. Los Angeles: American Indian Studies Center, University of California at Los Angeles.

Oxendine, Linda Ellen. 1992. Tribally Operated Museums: A Reinterpretation of Indigenous Collections. Ph.D. diss., University of Minnesota.

Pandey, Triloki Nath. 1967. Factionalism in a Southwestern Pueblo. Ph.D. diss., University of Chicago.

——. 1972. Anthropologists at Zuni. *Proceedings of the American Philosophical Society* 116 (4): 321–37.

——. 1995. Zuni Oral Tradition and History. In *Zuni and the Courts: A Struggle for Sovereign Land Rights*, edited by E. Richard Hart, 15–20. Lawrence: University Press of Kansas.

Panteah, Loren. 1995a. The Threat to Zuni Religion. *Gallup Independent*, November 24.

———. 1995b. Time to Talk about the Zuni Religion. *Gallup Independent*, November 13.

Panteah, Martin. 1995. An Illegal Zuni Ban. *Gallup Independent*, November 15.

Parezo, Nancy. 1992. Ruth L. Bunzel at Zuni: The Search for the Middle Place. In *Zuni Ceremonialism: Three Studies by Ruth L. Bunzel*, by Ruth Bunzel, vii–xxxix. Albuquerque: University of New Mexico Press.

———, editor. 1993. *Hidden Scholars: Women Anthropologists and the Native American Southwest*. Albuquerque: University of New Mexico.

Parsons, Elsie Clews. 1939. *Pueblo Indian Religion*. Chicago: University of Chicago Press.

Peers, Laura. 2003. Strands Which Refuse to Be Braided: Hair Samples from Beatrice Blackwood's Ojibwe Collection at the Pitt Rivers Museum. *Journal of Material Culture* 8 (1): 75–96.

Plevin, Nancy. 1995. Zuni Pueblo Still at Odds over Non-Indian Loan. *Gallup Independent*, November 21.

Poulot, Dominique. 1994. Identity as Self-Discovery: The Ecomuseum in France. In *Museum Culture: Histories, Discourses, Spectacles*, edited by Daniel J. Sherman and Irit Rogoff, 66–84. Minneapolis: University of Minnesota Press.

Pratt, Mary Louise. 1992. *Imperial Eyes: Travel Writing and Transculturation*. London: Routledge.

Richards, Thomas. 1993. *The Imperial Archive: Knowledge and the Fantasy of Empire*. London: Verso.

Rivière, George Henri. 1985. The Ecomuseum—An Evolutive Definition. *Museum* 37 (4): 182–83.

Roscoe, Will. 1991. *The Zuni Man-Woman*. Albuquerque: University of New Mexico Press.

Rosoff, Nancy B. 1998. Integrating Native Views into Museum Procedures: Hope and Practice at the National Museum of the American Indian. *Museum Anthropology* 22 (1): 33–42.

Rushton, Ted. 1995. Turmoil in Zuni. *Gallup Independent*, November 27.

Sando, Joe S. 1998. *Pueblo Profiles: Cultural Identities through Centuries of Change*. Santa Fe: Clear Light Books.

Schlanger, Melissa. 1989a. Zuni Park Vote Due in 1990. *Gallup Independent*, September 20.

———. 1989b. Zunis Face Park Vote. *Gallup Independent*, December 28.

———. 1990a. Zuni Park Bill Still Survives. *Gallup Independent*, May 5.

———. 1990b. Zunis Reject Park: 87% Say No to Federal Project. *Gallup Independent*, February 1.

Schneider, William. 1995. Lessons from Alaska Natives about Oral Tradition and Recordings. In *When Our Worlds Return: Writing, Hearing, and Remembering Oral Tradition of Alaska and the Yukon*, edited by Phyllis Morrow and William Schneider, 184–204. Logan: Utah State University Press.

Simpson, Moira. 1996. *Making Representations: Museums in the Post-colonial Era*. London: Routledge.

Spicer, E. H. 1962. *Cycles of Conquest*. Tucson: University of Arizona Press.

Steiner, Christopher. 1995. Museums and the Politics of Nationalism. In *Museums and the Politics of Nationalism*. Special issue of *Museum Anthropology* 19 (2): 3–6.

Stevenson, Matilda Coxe. 1887. The Religious Life of the Zuni Child. In *Ninth Annual Report for the Bureau of American Ethnology, 1883–1884*, 533–55. Washington, D.C.: U.S. Government Printing Office.

———. 1904. The Zuni Indians: Their Mythology, Esoteric Fraternities, and Religious Ceremonies. In *Twenty-third Annual Report of the Bureau of American Ethnology, 1901–1902*, 1–608. Washington, D.C.: U.S. Government Printing Office.

———. 1915. Ethnobotany of the Zuni Indians. In *Thirtieth Annual Report of the Bureau of American Ethnology, 1908–1909*, 31–102. Washington, D.C.: U.S. Government Printing Office.

Swidler, Nina, Kurt Dongoske, Roger Anyon, and Alan S. Downer, editors. 1997. *Native Americans and Archaeologists: Stepping Stones to Common Ground*. Walnut Creek, Calif.: AltaMira Press.

Tedlock, Barbara. 1992. *The Beautiful and the Dangerous: Dialogues with the Zuni Indians*. New York: Penguin Books.

Tedlock, Dennis. 1972. *Finding the Center: Narrative Poetry of the Zuni Indians*. New York: Dial Press.

Thomas, Nicholas. 1994. *Colonialism's Culture: Anthropology, Travel, and Government*. Cambridge: Polity Press.

Turner, Trudy, editor. 2005. *Biological Anthropology and Ethics: From Repatriation to Genetic Identity*. Albany: State University of New York Press.

Tweedie, Ann M. 2002. *Drawing Back Culture: The Makah Struggle for Repatriation*. Seattle: University of Washington Press.

U.S. Bureau of the Census. 2000. *Census 2000*. Washington, D.C.: U.S. Government Printing Office.

Vogt, Evon Z., and E. M. Albert. 1967. *People of Rimrock: A Study of Values in Five Cultures*. Cambridge, Mass.: Harvard University Press.

Wedll, Joycelyn. 2002. Learn about Our Past to Understand Our Future: The Story of the Mille Lac Band of Ojibwe. In *The Changing Presentation of the American Indian: Museums and Native Culture*, 89–98. Washington, D.C., and Seattle: National Museum of the American Indian in association with University of Washington Press.

White, Richard. 1991. *The Middle Ground: Indians, Empires, and Republics in the Great Lakes Region, 1650–1815*. Cambridge: Cambridge University Press.

Whiteley, Peter. 1997. The End of Anthropology (at Hopi?). In *Indians and Anthropologists: Vine Deloria Jr. and the Critique of Anthropology*, edited by Thomas Biolsi and Larry Zimmerman, 177–207. Tucson: University of Arizona Press.

———. 1998. *Rethinking Hopi Ethnography*. Washington, D.C.: Smithsonian Institution Press.

Wyaco, Virgil. 1998. *A Zuni Life: A Pueblo Indian in Two Worlds*. Albuquerque: University of New Mexico Press.

Index

About the Author

Gwyneira Isaac is assistant professor and director of the Museum of Anthropology at the School of Human Evolution and Social Change, Arizona State University. She has worked as a curatorial assistant at the Pitt Rivers Museum at Oxford University and as a research assistant at the Peabody Museum at Harvard University. Her publications include essays in *Museum Anthropology, Cultural Survival, American Indian Quarterly, Journal of the Southwest,* and *History of Photography*. She has received awards and grants from the Royal Anthropological Institute (1995), the Economic and Social Research Council (1997), and the National Endowment for the Humanities (2006). Recent exhibits she has curated at Arizona State University include Time and Again: The Photographs of Allen Dutton (2004) and Visiones Sagradas: Sacred Sights: The Fifth Annual Dias de los Muertos Exhibit (2004). Her research focuses on the relationships people develop with their past through material culture, the history of anthropology and photography, the development of tribal museums in the Southwest, and the history of reproductive technologies such as photography and computers in museums.